Whatever you say, say nothing – Ulster adage

This is the first book to showcase second-generation Irish writers in Britain.

'Here the sons and daughters of mid-twentieth century immigrants to the UK speak for their parents – the blindingly heart-breaking and funny stories of that silent generation complemented by poems and several fine essays. Ground breaking and thought-provoking, *I Wouldn't Start From Here* is a vital contribution to the fascinating and complicated story of Anglo-Irish relations and a tremendous start for The Wild Geese Press.'

Martina Evans, Poet and Novelist

With fiction and poetry from Elizabeth Baines, Maude Casey, Ray French, Maria C. McCarthy, Moy McCrory, Kath Mckay and John O'Donoghue.

I Wouldn't Start From Here

The Second-Generation Irish in Britain

Ray French, Moy McCrory and Kath Mckay (eds)

the wild geese press

First published in 2019 by
The Wild Geese Press

the wild
geese
press

ISBN 978-1-9993753-1-7

Printed in Great Britain by Lightning Source UK Ltd

Contents

Introduction

This book of essays, fiction and poetry by second generation Irish writers in Britain attempts to capture for the first time the diverse experience of a group largely rendered invisible. Accusations of inauthenticity are also picked apart here in discussions which touch upon what is authentic, what is new, what evolves and what changes. The book offers a way of examining where these writers and thinkers stand in relation to a shared heritage and past, in a continuously changing present.

The contributors consider themselves as part of a diaspora. The term diaspora has several meanings, but is often used to mean 'involuntary migration'. Kenny states that while diaspora 'is not a neutral or passive term, it does allow people to make claims about their world'. Diaspora, he feels, informs the development of new cultural spaces which cut across boundaries with the 'connections migrants form abroad and the kinds of culture they produce'. (Kenny 2013:12). We embrace this reading of the word 'diaspora'.

If the word itself carries multiple meanings, its sense of never fully belonging has been a recurrent theme in the work of the contributors to this book. This introduction attempts first to define some of the characteristics of this group, made difficult by its lack of homogeneity and even the problems of describing what is meant by 'second generation'. For the purposes of this book we mean those who were the first to be born in Britain of Irish parents.

That anti-Irish prejudice has been a feature of their lives is acknowledged by many here, yet their whiteness and lack of accent has rendered them invisible. Many writers here recall the 1980s in England, the renewed hostility as the bombing campaign during The Troubles (another disputed term) began to affect England, with attacks in areas with large Irish populations – especially London – and the demonization of the Irish as a people driven with a blood-lust. When the *Daily Mail* depicted the IRA as cartoon murderers in a mock film poster, the use of racist tropes showed the Irish (who were here cast as synonymous with terrorists) as a race of people with knuckles dragging on the ground, heavy jowled and closer to beasts than to humans. This reworked earlier eighteenth century stereotypes of inferior races. (see Curtis 1984) What has been called a 'civilized England' (Arrowsmith 2006) now encountered this historic 'other' of monstrous grotesques.

From the twelfth century, when Gerald of Wales described the Irish as 'a filthy people, wallowing in vice', to the nineteenth century, when Thomas Carlyle called Ireland a 'human swinery', and well into the next, the Irish were viewed as an inferior race by the British. Declan Kiberd, in *Inventing Ireland: The Literature of The Modern Nation* argues that the English projected onto the Irish all the feelings and behaviour that they couldn't face in themselves, and that Ireland became England's subconscious. (Kiberd:1996)

The Irish who emigrated to America fitted neatly into a narrative that chimed with the American Dream, arriving dirt poor and oppressed, dragging themselves up by sheer hard work and determination. The Irish in Britain faced hostility, while their children found claiming an Irish identity in a British accent fraught with difficulty: the two identities, it seems, are mutually exclusive.

The work here reflects those tensions, those difficult times, the sense of not belonging and of never being taken seriously, but of ploughing on despite those who would reduce or render this area of identity into a 'nothingness' of little meaning. But lives lived have meaning, and if our parents made their homes among strangers, we inherited a sense of not fully belonging in the new country which was to become the only home we knew, as a return to their ways was impossible.

When Kenny notes the difference between anti-Irish prejudice and the racial subjugation inflicted on African Americans, he observes how the Irish could enter the United States freely and become citizens through naturalization. They could 'vote, serve on juries, testify in court, and take legal suits'. The Irish in Britain could also move freely between borders and be granted the same economic rights and privileges as British citizens. He claims that what the Irish experienced was largely bigotry and hostility. Because of this 'The global Irish are unlikely candidates ... for membership in some diasporic club of the racially oppressed'. However, he notes that the experience of the dispersal in the nineteenth century as a result of famine and poverty and the prejudice they faced in England 'clearly gave rise to a powerful and persistent sense of migration as exile'. (Kenny 2013:42)

This book looks at the contribution to culture by musicians and writers that have developed a sense of a past, and hopefully shows new emerging forms. They have the confidence to be seen and heard, which contrasts with the previous generation, their parents, concerned with maintaining a low profile. 'Whatever you say, say nothing,' an Ulster saying made famous by Seamus Heaney, echoes the situation of economic migrants who keep their heads down and do not draw attention to themselves in the new place.

The authors here write about how their backgrounds have informed their work, or reflect on the work of others. Elizabeth Baines writes about her father, who came to England at sixteen, hoping to leave his past behind and reinvent himself in a place where no-one knew him, but ended up 'caught between two stereotypes, the contemptible rough Irish peasant and the romantic Irish charmer, desperate to bury the one but unable to help playing up to the other'. An attractive figure in public, he wielded a fierce and frightening patriarchal power over his family, and their lives were dominated by the need for secrecy. This disconnect between what passed for reality outside and inside the home led to the author seeing fiction as a way of conveying truth. Ray French also writes about his father, who, in contrast, dreamed of returning to a simple life in rural Ireland, far from the factories, docks and noisy, crowded streets of an industrial town. His only problem was trying to persuade his Irish wife, who couldn't wait to leave 'the insular, feudal backwater of the late 1940s,' and had no intention of returning.

Maude Casey looks back at her experience of activism and of the increased hostility towards the Irish community in Britain in the 1980s. She speaks also for that most unconsidered section of the community, its young women, in her young-adult novel, which considers that difficult time of adolescence, made even harder by the issues of belonging and national identity her teenage protagonist experiences.

Considering the contribution made to popular culture in music by those of second generation background, Graham Caveney reveals the price paid by conflicted identity in his examination of the tortuous route of Shane MacGowan as he grows into front man and songwriter with the Pogues. If difficult political situations not only inscribe themselves in people's psyches but also into their health, Caveney explores how difficulties are reflected physically, and MacGowan's teeth become a metaphor for internal and external struggle. Sean Campbell examines the work of Kevin Rowland, singer/songwriter for Dexys Midnight Runners through the prism of his struggle to negotiate his second generation Irish identity via music, and enduring criticism and ridicule when speaking of his pride in his roots. While this reflects the experience of many second generation Irish who would claim authenticity of experience, Rowland's story is also part of the crucial and often neglected role that the Irish diaspora has played in British music.

The poet Ian Duhig expands on this theme with a personal essay about 'the road, and people who, from choice or necessity, find themselves upon it.' By tracing a line from his youth, from Kilburn High Road to the M1, he finds connections between traditional music and song and poetry, to Leeds, his adult home. His work recognises the 'tough lived life' of many, and the wit and creativity and what he calls 'dream songs' that feed into his work, soothing his 'blistering poetic feet'.

John O'Donoghue's contention is that poetry is 'an outward sign of an inward grace' and that all poets must find an 'inward place of asylum' where inspiration 'may blow in'. His early life split between East London and Monaghan 'bruised (him) into poetry' as a 'stay against grief' aged 14, the year his father died. His poetic education was interrupted as, 'clean cracked', he was sectioned into one of the old asylums. 'But if to be sane is to know who you are … then my Irishness and my sense of myself as a poet … kept me going'. Through recognising himself as 'a child of the Diaspora … [in] a city as big and as real and as dirty as London,' O'Donoghue has claimed his asylum.

Kath Mckay writes about an Irish city, Liverpool, her home-town, and the influence of this most un-English place on its population. While examining the history of the Irish and the famine exodus, she discovers between the myths and the stories of recent generations, a heritage as predictable as it was unexpected.

Moy McCrory reflects on a Catholic girlhood, populated by saints and miracles and examines how different experiences of reality can co-exist, giving rise to what she calls 'the knife-edge of Irish gothic', situated somewhere between magic-realism and dirty-realism. She explores hard lives lived in hope, and claims the possibility of a new way of considering what 'home' is for those whose home is no longer a physical place, but a site of memory and invention.

The need for archives, history and recognition of the Irish in Britain is reinforced in an interview with Tony Murray, Director of the Irish Writers' Summer School and Curator of the Irish in Britain Archive, where important evidence detailing the history of the Irish in Britain is stored, along with essential artefacts and documents from recent history.

Marc Scully's chapter focuses on the hybrid identities of the diverse communities that make up the Irish in Britain today, and how they sustain their Irish identities in different ways. His work combines interviews with research and stresses that integration does not mean assimilation, and focuses on the agency of the second generation, something too often ignored.

The collection of fictions that follow the essays show the delight, and sheer craic, the creativity and the hybrid nature of the second generation, who are finding voices to express themselves, and their own roads to walk.

The Editors
Ray French, Moy McCrory and Kath Mckay

Bibliography

Arrowsmith, Aidan (2006) *The Iirish Studies Review* **14(2)** Oxford, Taylor & Francis.

Curtis, Liz (1984) *Nothing But the Same Old Story: The Roots of Anti-Irish Racism*, London, Information on Ireland.

Hirsch, Marianne (2008) 'The Generation of Post Memory' in *Poetics Today* **29(1):**103–125.

Kenny, Kevin (2013) *Diaspora: A Very Short Introduction*, Oxford/New York, Oxford University Press.

Kiberd, Declan (1996) *Inventing Ireland: The Literature of the Modern Nation*, London, Vintage.

Music

Ian Duhig
The Road

I would say that knowing is a road – Anne Carson

I was the eighth child in my family, the first born in England, London to be precise, where three after me would complete the football team. My father Robert had a few years previously managed to get work here, saving and finding rented accommodation so the rest of his family could join him, which it did in due course. He had served in the Irish army where he was a "known shot", meaning rifles from the factory had their sights adjusted according to his performance, assumed to be perfect. At my Catholic school, after our headmaster once advised us "the difference between Catholicism and Communism is that Communism is wrong", my schoolmates and I got enormous wind-up mileage out of professing our admiration for the USSR and its achievements, asking if Catholics were allowed to join the League of the Militant Godless, swearing by Jesus, Mary and Joseph Stalin and so forth. But my father really might have been an Irish counterpart to the great sniper of Stalingrad, Vasily Zaitsev, had his young country that he was so well able to defend not been neutral in the Great Patriotic War. Zaitsev means "hare", an animal I always associated with my father who'd kept one as a pet in Ireland but was a creature of legend to me growing up in London and legendary his rural background to which he had been so attuned, so different from me in my urban one. I heard many stories of his exploits on my trips back: if no scholar, he was a notable soldier and horseman; once, at thirteen following a fox-hunt on a one-eyed Arab called 'Sightseer', he jumped a dangerous river bareback that the hunt baulked at only because Sightseer was too excited at the gallop and couldn't see the river. I like the scene: the fox, the boy and the half-blind horse turning to look back over the tumultuous waters at the gentry left behind.

Nevertheless, he could still find no work at home after he left the army so emigrated like many of his generation in the 1950s. As a consequence of his being in civilian life, I was the first child he knew from infancy and so he spoiled me rotten; he worked in the Cricklewood Express Dairy bottling plant, so I remember him in D.H. Lawrence's phrase, "the father of milk", powerful but gentle. I didn't inherit his physical strength, considerable even in his youth: he protected his older brothers from bullies of their age, but I took more after my bookish and sardonic mother, Margaret, who knew reams of poetry by heart and gave the impression she saw men as fundamentally absurd: balloons on legs as they were to Petronius. I'd witness how much he loved his wife unwaveringly over several decades, although she could be a little cool in return — a manual labourer and enthusiastic trade unionist, his sometimes stridently-expressed socialist analyses of TV news could annoy her, she taking a more philosophical view of a world's idiocies governed by men.

My parents' birthplaces were geographically close, although that county border seemed to matter a great deal when my mother's

Limerick beat Tipperary in one memorable All-Ireland Hurling Final. Tipperary dominated the game then, traditionally a part of the world that knew how to celebrate: the Bishop of Cashel and Emly in 1796 declared that if any behaviour other than religious devotion marked the celebrations of the patron saint's day in his diocese, that feast would be suppressed. I grew up in what seemed a very well-established London Irish community around Paddington and Kilburn, which also knew how to celebrate: Kilburn High Road marked the boundary between Brent and Camden, meaning that on one side pubs closed sometimes half an hour earlier than on the other, so there was frequently an undignified stampede for last orders across it into a hostelry opposite. When we were old enough, and often before, I would meet my friends in the Queens Arms on Kilburn Bridge because it was a Young's house, the best beer in the capital. Further up the road was Biddy Mulligan's, the only pub bombed by Northern Irish Protestant paramilitaries on the British mainland — Zadie Smith has written about being there when collections for the IRA were taken. Beyond that, there was the Lord Palmerston, but because he had been an absentee landlord in Ireland it was boycotted till it changed its name to The Roman Way. Further up still, near where my father worked in Cricklewood, was the Galtymore pub/club complex, a great barn of a place where Sligo flute player Roger Sherlock had been a regular performer in a semi-professional house band. Even so, Nuala O'Connor reports him saying, "It still wasn't enough to make a living out of, nothing like it." He also worked "six days a week with pick and shovel … mostly roads, you know, which was hard work." Near the Galtymore, the Crown was effectively a labour exchange for Irish construction workers where cheques could be cashed on pay nights. Driving north on this road it soon joins the M1 to Leeds but coming back down for now towards where we lived, you'd pass the huge Sacred Heart church in Quex Road where, on one occasion, the parish priest's housekeeper witnessed my friends carrying what seemed to her an inordinate amount of drink into a basement function room booked to celebrate the departure of one of our number returning to Ireland. She cast a cold eye on these proceedings in the House of God and declared them "a good away win for the Devil."

Also near Quex Road Church was the Banba dance hall and a hostel for homeless Irish people. We were aware of the extent of Irish homelessness in London as the Irish were disproportionately over-represented in mental health institutions and prison. In my generation, the Irish were the only immigrant ethnic minority whose children were statistically likely to die younger than their parents after they'd come to England: my own and my friends' families were no exceptions to that rule. We knew this, not least because some of us, including myself, were involved in one of the early research studies, which took particular note of our alcohol consumption. We just didn't talk about it. This is a problem with this pattern of emigration, an issue being raised in the Sikh community I worked with in Leeds recently, where again the building trade's male camaraderie can add to the dangers of the job. Many young Irishmen in London would lose contact with their families back home if they felt they had failed somehow. And some people did very well indeed: I'm thinking of a road haulage contractor in Manchester who was also one of the great pipers of his age, Felix Doran who played a set made of solid silver. Yet even his name means lucky and many with just as ferocious a work ethic as Felix had were not.

Attached to what our families called 'home' second-hand, my cohort developed brand new allegiances, including to perennial under-achievers Chelsea, not least because the number 28 bus ran from Kilburn High Road to Stamford Bridge. After evening matches, we'd drink at the White Hart nearby, of which O'Connor writes, "In MacColl's wake … Irish traditional musicians began to be considered [seriously] by folk enthusiasts who now frequented pubs like the White Hart in Fulham where 'pure' traditional music was played." I will return to the relationship between Irish and English traditional music later, but the aspect of its performance in pubs here I want to draw attention to now is that although people talked through musicians playing (in truth, more for each other anyway than any notion of an audience), a song always commanded silence. I envied that respect, one also shown to poetry in the Irish community: my mother had learned reams of it by heart at school, a feature of its teaching in those days, and she recited it often as she worked about the house, often singing too, although the same tune seemed to carry a wide range of lyrics for her. Very good Irish poets wrote words to be sung in a way that their English counterparts rarely did, in the last century anyway. I'm thinking here of Patrick Kavanagh's 'On Raglan Road' and of the beautiful 'She Moved Through The Fair', with all but the last verse written by Padraic Colum. Although I left school at 16, I soon got fed up with the world of unskilled work, took my 'A' levels at night school and ended up at Leeds University. My brother had moved to the city before me and told me was an easy place to live in on little money, still relatively accurate. It was certainly easy to get to: straight up Kilburn High Road to Staples Corner for the M1 and hitch from there, a direct line from the Roman way onto one just as true. Driving north, I'd remember from Tomás Ó Canainn's 'Traditional Music in Ireland' that in Kerry people shout "O Thuaidh!" ("Northwards!") to encourage sean-nós performers, something I didn't understand any more than the nature of the place I was going to live, off and on, for the rest of my life.

Loreto Todd taught at Leeds University when I was there and in her book 'The Language of Irish Literature' she describes Padraic Colum's 'The Fiddler's House' as "a play which deals with a recurrent theme in Irish literature: the road and people who, from choice or necessity, find themselves upon it." The modern course of Chapeltown Road was made by a blind man, Jack Metcalf, always striking me as highly appropriate for a centre of economic migration, where people came blindly to earn a living and make a new life on the strength of being able to do so. These people often knew little about the character and history of where they were arriving at, but proceeded to give it new character and history themselves. Leeds is disliked by natives of other northern cities for many reasons, and one of them is for this very immigration; now it has over 140 different ethnic communities represented within its boundaries and its old nicknames of 'the Holy City' and 'the

Jerusalem of the North' are antisemitic sneers originally dating from the waves fleeing Cossack pogroms, but I met families who later fled antisemitism in nominally-communist countries, corrupt regimes maintained by the tanks I'd fetishised as a child as symbols of rebellion. Chapeltown Road itself is a palimpsest of such often-forced immigration as each wave in turn settled, moved away when successful and had their traces overscored by new communities. Donald MacRaild has written "historians, like the Irish themselves, need to fan out from the classical centres ... to consider new areas of importance". He was thinking of less urban places than Leeds, but one migrant I want to write about came to Leeds from Connemara via London, fanning out as MacRaild describes, to pursue work and give his family a better life, as my father had done. Dudley Kane is better known as Darach Ó Catháin, the name given to him by Seán Ó Riada who considered him the finest sean-nós singer of his generation. Sean-nós singing's features include the glottal stop, alien to many European traditions but often found among those of the Indian sub-continent, whose broader connections to Irish music Seán Ó Riada spoke about many times. Indeed, Robert Welch while he was teaching at Leeds University described a meeting with Darach and Pearse Hutchinson in a different pub where, after Darach struck up, they were thrown out by the landlord who didn't want "any of that Pakistani singing." The landlord might have been a wiser racist than he knew.

The local Irish community was refreshed when many who worked on the M1 remained to capitalise on Leeds' determination to become 'the Motorway City'. Darach worked on the roads too, sometimes, and I'd get to hear him sing in the Roscoe on lower Chapeltown Road, a pub ironically knocked down later to make way for the Sheepscar Interchange, a ganglion of urban dual carriageways just north of the city centre. Named from County Roscommon, the Roscoe and other pubs in this area hosted regular sessions by traditional Irish musicians of a very high standard. One pub, The Regent, was where the Leeds branch of the Irish music organisation Comhaltas Ceoltóirí Éireann was first formed, growing to be the biggest in England, or so I was told. Interviewed for 'Folkworld' once, Karen Tweed remarked: "People in Ireland talk about a Leeds style that they play in Leeds and that you can tell is from Leeds, but it's Irish music"; similarly, cognoscenti here spoke of the late-lamented Paul Ruane's "Leeds/Sligo style" of fiddle-playing. Irish folk music's influence on that of its new environment too has been significant for a long time; Bert Lloyd's 'Folk Song in England' quotes Samuel Bayard characterisation of their different styles: "the English singer's leaning to relatively straightforward and simple melodic lines is counteracted in Irish tradition by love of ornament, of multiplying notes, of varying rhythmic patterns" giving the music a "wavering and unemphatic movement … impeding the course of the melody". I have drawn a parallel elsewhere (in 'The Irish Boomerang', an essay for Poetry Ireland Review) between this treatment of melody with that of narrative in writers from Sterne through Wilde and Flann O'Brien on to Paul Muldoon. But even in terms of social etiquette, in my parents' generation and background, a roundabout approach to conversation was considered politer than the blunt, up-front West Riding manner of speech. When they stayed with me in Hawksworth, our landlord, a farmer called Pickersgill, dropped in. My father, by way of an opening conversational gambit, said "the last man I knew called Pickersgill was a Master of Foxhounds in Tipperary." This was meant to elicit some sort of reply which would allow them to connect on the basis of their similarly-rural home areas, perhaps leading my father to share his observation that Yorkshire and Tipperary were coincidentally both divided into Ridings, something I hadn't noticed myself. At a more literary level, their developing conversation might explore the similarly coincidental revelation that Laurence Sterne's father had been a soldier in Tipperary where my father had served in the Irish army as perhaps Pickersgill had in the British. In fact, our landlord's response to my father was a hunted look, a grunted "T'weren't me" and a shuffling exit.

My father had been a wrenboy in his youth but when I mentioned this at a poetry reading once, I couldn't understand why afterwards people were coming up and congratulating me for my

brave revelation: eventually, one of them explained that they all
thought I'd said he was a "rent boy". In its own way, this mishearing
is indicative of the new world my family entered in London,
where the financial nexus dominated human relationships. More
immediately, when my family first moved over to London they
suffered exploitation at the hands of a profiteering private landlord
and where we lived was next to Rachman territory, whose surname
entered the dictionary for rack-rentism. Moving into Council
accommodation was definitely a step up into greater security of
tenure in a property responsibly maintained at a reasonable rent.
It provided the base from which I grew up in and was educated.
Although I left school after my O-levels for a more congenial
environment of work and A-levels at night school, maybe I was
also influenced by the talk of Ireland as "home" swirling around
me when I was young, but moving to Yorkshire began a process
of involvement in homelessness issues that continues to the
present. Initially, this was professional and I had several posts in
organisations serving the needs of homeless people with a variety
of related problems from those to do with mental ill-health to
substance abuse. Later, opening a York hostel for single homeless
people next to a well-known folk pub, when its landlord found out
what we were opening beside him, he barred us all immediately,
so on night shifts, I could listen to the folkies next door roaring
out 'I Am A Jolly Beggarman' knowing that if any of ours went
near the place they'd be nicked. I started setting the stories of
some of our residents to other tunes that were coming through
the wall, fiddling with other kinds of verses as well. I had always
maintained an interest in poetry from my mother's recitations up
to when I worked in Belfast in a hostel for young offenders during
the Troubles, I came in contact with the work of an astonishing
range of poets, too many for me to discuss here in detail, but
a gifted and innovative generation that influenced me deeply.
Seamus Heaney of course was one of them and he championed
Patrick Kavanagh, who wrote 'I dabbled in verse and it became
my life.' Something similar happened to me, verse becoming my
life after I was made redundant from a project in Bradford. Even

after my career change (if you can call them careers) I pursued connections between traditional music and poetry occasionally in my work, though this did not always go down well in England: Andrew Duncan, for example, wrote in his 'Handlist of Late 20th Century Poets' that my "admiration for folk styles … chased out literary interest almost altogether." Yet in the face of all charges of crudity, traditional music can be analysed with a subtlety completely absent from much contemporary poetry criticism. You could talk about Roscommon, Kerry or West Limerick bodhrán styles and aficionados would know exactly what you meant, while binary divisions as simplistic as Kilburn High Road's have been peddled in UK poetry for decades. This is being complicated by a younger generation of poets outside the traditional camps but the reflex here is to reach for adjectives like polarised when many people don't fit easily into boxes, or think outside them.

If Irish immigrants' children of my generation felt outsiders among the English, we were outsiders among the Irish too. Yet some of us were radicalised to a greater or lesser degree during what was so inadequately described as the Troubles, not unlike what has happened recently with second-generation Muslim youths. Tabloid demonization of Muslims echoes the 70s demonisation of Irish Catholics in Britain, when I felt compelled to write to the Guardian complaining about its coverage of the Birmingham Bombings. I admired how Northern Irish poets weighed very carefully their responses to complex and toxic problems of civil injustice woven into the very fabric of a society, dismissed by Iain Sinclair as "Bogs and bombs and blarney" in his 1996 poetry anthology 'Conductors of Chaos'. I remember noticing Rachman's old henchman Michael X in 'Children of Albion' and thinking about their victims; the Communist Party had been very active in organising private tenants and rent strikes around where I grew up and that left a lasting impression on me about the value of grassroots activism.

How poets negotiate what Lionel Trilling called "the bloody crossroads" of literature and politics became a very live issue during the time I was working on a project around Shandy Hall, the Sterne museum, now also a leading centre for conceptual writing, where

American lights such as Kenneth Goldsmith, Christian Bök and Craig Dworkin have held residencies. Goldsmith's appropriation of Michael Brown's autopsy report for a piece of conceptual writing was met with fury by writers and people of colour in the USA, many of whom were inflamed further by poet Ron Silliman's internet statements which included comparing black activists to Ferguson police and that "the police are not your enemy". The first job I had in Leeds was at Hepworth's in its cloth warehouse where the head of security was ex-PC Ken Kitching, gaoled for his part in the abuse leading to the death of David Oluwale, a homeless Empire migrant who came to Leeds seeking work. I now act as an advisor to the David Oluwale Memorial Association which had early contact with Black Lives Matter. One detail of David's story reflects on patterns of immigration and poverty in Leeds: the names on his mass paupers' grave are predominantly Irish. It was a young, second-generation Irish police recruit called Gary Galvin who exposed the scandal of David Oluwale's treatment, someone we should be proud of; if in the USA the Irish community has been used as a tool against others, here it often finds common ground with them, albeit shifting ground.

During 2018s Windrush scandal I edited a small poetry anthology from local immigrants' groups I have been working with in recent years called 'Any Change? Poetry in a Hostile Environment', poetry mainly from Caribbean, Bangladeshi, Jewish and Sikh communities but Leeds Irish Health and Homes were substantially represented with work from my parents' Fifties wave of Irish immigrants. Age takes its toll on their bodies if not their wits: one wrote in my workshop "I've had dementia for as long as I can remember…". However, if this generation is passing, their Ireland remains a constant, growing and changing but a vital place; for many of my own, our brave new world turned out to be fleeting, with no more permanent foundations than a navvy's shanty on a Yorkshire moor. After the navvies were given the choice to name their camp, they opted for 'Jericho Shanty', as they were always being told to "Go to Jericho!", an old idiom meaning more or less "Piss off!"

I'm trying not to conclude this with a second generation

version of Peig Sayers' mournful refrain, "Our kind will not be seen again", but when I visit Kilburn now I find a lively but strange place and in Fulham the White Hart (which had once been called 'The Beggars' Rest') is now 'Vintage', a cocktail bar. The working class my father belonged to, and I was born into, no longer exists in the vigorous and respected form it took in his day; in our situation of liquid modernity, to borrow Zygmunt Bauman's phrase, it's hard to stand together on shifting ground. In the end, the USSR folded as easily as the British Empire and Russian riches funded an unrecognisably-successful Chelsea. The Kilburn crew's particular hero was Paddy Mulligan, a stolid right back capable of buccaneering runs down his flank of such power it was sometimes difficult for him to stop: once, despite having lost the ball, his charge took him straight over a hapless opposition defender, "like a T-34 rolling over a Wehrmacht machine gun nest" as I described it at school, but Irish players seldom figure in modern Chelsea teams. At least we had Paddy Mulligan: Deirdre O'Byrne once asked in an email exchange where were the London Irish second generation writers' equivalents to 'The Buddha of Suburbia', 'White Teeth, 'Brick Lane', 'Small Island' and 'Anita and Me'. I would refine that further by asking why there are no London Irish second-generation literary equivalents to its visual artists like Sean Scully, its film makers like John Michael McDonagh and any number of its musicians. If I was to hazard guesses as to the reasons, they might include the extent to which particular genres in this country are dominated by particular social groups and that the London Irish of my generation were predominantly from working class backgrounds (as defined by their breadwinners' having unskilled manual jobs) and looked to arenas of cultural expression where they felt welcome.

Bringing it all back home, being second generation for me meant not only to be alienated from my parents' world but also from my wife and son's to some extent, although forty-odd years of marriage seems to have made me an acceptable part of the local scenery. Jane and Owen are both Yorkshire tykes who feel at home here in a way I never will, but that is a gift to the writer: she sees what others take for granted, uncovers memories of what has been forgotten, notices the overlooked. I labour this point because immigrants are routinely accused of obliterating local histories when we can also preserve it, connect with it and make it new, especially where it has been hidden from official chronicles which usually exclude or sanitise much of that of the working class. I tried to describe this complex relationship of communities within a hostile environment extended to the linguistic in a poem from my first book 'The Bradford Count':

Nothing Pie

When I told my Dad that the locals called
a dandelion an "Irish daisy",
I'd have to admit he looked disenthralled
and soon his farts were "Yorkshire nightingales",

a dandelion a "Yorkshire daisy",
a "Yorkshire screwdriver" banged in his nails,
Tipperary invented the "riding"
and "Nothing pie" meant my Yorkshire pudding.

Abide with me, Daddy. Be abiding.
Now Owen's asking what our garden grows,
"bud" and "good" full rhymes when he says "budding".
Mam will know. I call everything a rose.

My last book *The Blind Roadmaker* alludes to Jack Metcalf, mentioned earlier; I use his trade to follow love's blind roads, those of poets (Frost: 'I never started a poem yet whose end I knew') and migrants who chase work wherever it is to be found, enduring hostile environments to claim space for the next generation. Working with their descendants, I often quote Wallace Stevens' 'Adagia' on how we don't live in places, we live in descriptions of places, an idea I sometimes relate to dinnseanchas with Irish groups. Richard Murphy concluded his old interview with John Haffenden by saying "I feel now that my home is in the language", sentiments echoed more recently by Vahni Capildeo in 'Measures of Expatriation' where she wrote "Language is my home". I feel this is true of migrants as well as poets: think of Joseph Brodsky on the song of the nomad as opposed to the prose of the farmer.

'Carrickfergus Bernard' Davey was a refugee from Belfast, ultimately housed by Leeds Irish Health and Homes who'd earned his nickname from his signature performance of that song. It already had a Leeds connection in that Leeds-Irish Peter O'Toole claimed to have collected the song in Kerry, leading it to be known as 'The Kerry Boatman' in some quarters. It is taken worldwide to be a genuinely old Irish anthem and thundered in pubs rising to the line, "But I'm drunk today and I'm seldom sober…". In fact, the tune is modern, composed by Seán Ó Riada, who fitted it with words where that line is "I'm seldom drunk, though I'm never sober…". The Ballygrand of the song's legendary nights never existed, despite ingenious attempts to connect it to alternative real venues: it functions, as the name suggests, as an archetypal home of youthful buckleppery, the polar opposite of the navvies' Jericho. In the old joke, an Irish boomerang doesn't come back, it just sings about coming back; emigrants' songlines dream back to lost Edens but roads aren't only metaphors, and enduring their hardship called forth a hard Irish wit I love, particularly among the women: Loreto Todd in her book mentioned earlier quotes an exchange between two of them suffering down an unmade rough track. One woman tells her friend they send the stones of it off every year to have them re-sharpened — and they instantly lose some of their edge to laughter. My London Irish second-generation heritage included dream songs but also such cuts and blistering poetic feet; shifting ground prepared us for liquid modernity, the outside chance of the outsider, as the migrants' proverb has it, bíonn súil le muir ach ní bhíonn súil le tír, there's hope on the ocean but none from the grave. I want to finish with another poem, a group one from workshops I ran with Leeds Irish Health and Homes and published in the small anthology 'The Trojan Donkey' co-edited by Teresa O'Driscoll and myself. This workshop drew on the model of 'The Song of Amergin' to focus contributions from people mainly of my parents' generation, some of whom were doing well, others not so well. The poem is untitled and indeed many of its contributors remained anonymous but their signature is that marriage of poetry with the tough, lived life I have been describing; if that life and culture proved ephemeral, it wasn't worthless.

> I am the wind on the sea
> and in a horse's mane;
> I am the sound of the ocean
> and the engine of a plane;
>
> I am the tear of the sun
> and its loveliest flower;
> l am the hungry family
> in its emigrant hour.
>
> l know your streets
> aren't paved with gold
> because l laid them,
> come rain or cold,
>
> your M1s and your M62s,
> reading your B&B cards:
> No Blacks, No Irish,
> No Dogs, No Jews.
>
> I am the slighted Irish
> minding your sick,
> teaching your children.
> You called me thick.
>
> I worked like a donkey,
> a Trojan, a slave.
> I paid my way here;
> I earned my grave.

Bibliography

Bauman, Zygmunt (2000) *Liquid Modernity*, Cambridge, Polity Press.

Brodsky, Josef (1996) 'How to Read a Book', in *On Grief and Reason*, London, Hamish Hamilton.

Ò'Canainn, Tomás (1978) *Traditional Music in Ireland*, London, Routledge and Kegan Paul.

Duhig, Ian (ed.) (2018) *Any Change? Poetry in a Hostile Environment*, London, Forward.

Duhig, Ian (2016) *The Blind Roadmaker*, London, Picador.

Duhig, Ian (1991) *The Bradford Count*, Newcastle upon Tyne, Bloodaxe.

Duhig, Ian (2004) 'The Irish Boomerang' in *Poetry Ireland Review* No 78 (2004) ed., Sirr, Peter, Dublin, Poetry Ireland Review.

Duhig, Ian; O'Driscoll, Theresa, and Ian Duhig (eds) (2018) *The Trojan Donkey*, Leeds, Leeds Irish Health and Homes.

Horowitz, Michael (ed.) (1969) *Children of Albion*, London, Penguin.

Lloyd, A.L. (1967) *Folk Song in England*, London, Lawrence and Wishart.

MacRaild, Donald M (1998) *Culture Conflict and Migration: the Irish in Victorian Cumbria*, Liverpool, Liverpool University Press.

O'Connor, Nuala (1991) *Bringing It All Back Home: the Influence of Irish Music* London.

Sinclair, Iain (1996) *Conductors of Chaos*, London, Picador.

Smith, Zadie (2011) *Changing My Mind: Occasional Essays*, London, Penguin.

Squires, Michael (ed.) (2007) *D.H. Lawrence and Italy*, London, Penguin.

Sean Campbell
Dweller on the Threshold
Kevin Rowland, 'Irish–English' in-betweenness, and Dexys Midnight Runners' *Don't Stand Me Down*

In April 2016, Kevin Rowland took to the stage at the Royal Festival Hall in London as part of the 'Imagining Ireland' concert to mark the centennial of the Easter Rising (Denselow 2016). The event explored the musical elements of the Anglo-Irish interface, and – within this – stressed the role that the Irish diaspora had played in British popular music. In this context, Rowland served, at the event, as an embodiment of the second-generation Irish, and sang a song, 'Knowledge of Beauty' – taken from Dexys Midnight Runners' third and final album, *Don't Stand Me Down* (1985) – that invoked the dilemmas faced by this generation. This chapter explores the *Don't Stand Me Down* project as an important (and often overlooked) negotiation of second-generation Irish life in the sphere of popular song.

Following the commercial success (and international media attention) engendered by Dexys' second album, *Too-Rye-Ay* (1982), Rowland withdrew from public view, taking time to reflect on the strengths and weaknesses of this project (he had tired of the 'teeny fame' and 'wanted to make it serious') (Roberts 2002:76), before drafting ideas for Dexys' next phase. During this self-imposed hiatus, Rowland became – in his words – 'obsessed with Irish politics' (Roberts 2002:7). The early 1980s was an especially fraught moment in Anglo-Irish affairs, with the H-Block dirty protests and IRA hunger strikes being followed – during the years in which *Don't Stand Me Down* (henceforth *DSMD*) was written, conceived and recorded (1983–85) – by large-scale IRA attacks (including the bombing of Harrods and Brighton's Grand Hotel).[1] This context clearly informed Rowland's new (and more sombre) persona, which eschewed the sentimental folk Celticism of *Too-Rye-Ay* for a far more difficult and demanding address to Irish ethnicity and attendant issues. Rowland had begun to read books on Irish history, and became 'immersed' in this subject (Irwin 1985:32; Price 2002:15; Roberts 2002:76). His interests were not simply academic, however, for the singer's reading was augmented by more active pursuits. As well as visiting Irish social clubs and attending concerts by Irish republican musicians, such as The Wolfe Tones, the singer would travel to Northern Ireland in 1983. 'I wanted to find out what was going on', he recalls, citing the 'very difficult situation' at that time (Rowland 2007).[2] The singer would also participate in Irish political demonstrations in England. In this context, Rowland explains:

> 'I started going on marches in Birmingham, in 1983, '84. I
> contacted Troops Out, and started going to their meetings, going
> on marches. And there would be other people on these marches,
> there'd be Sinn Féin on the march, there'd be Troops Out,
> there'd be socialists, there'd be the Irish in Britain Representa-
> tion Group. And I got to know a few of those people, and one

1 For an account of this period, see Tim Pat Coogan, *The IRA* (London: HarperCollins, 2000, revised edn), pp. 514–16.

2 The Wolfe Tones' 'emotive accounts of the historical struggle for Irish freedom' have been 'very popular with the second generation Irish' (Ullah: 1990:179).

of the Sinn Féin guys contacted me and said "Do you want to
come and have a chat?", and he just said: "I heard you're going
on marches, but be careful: one extra person on a march isn't re-
ally going to make a massive difference, but your face … [could
make such a difference]'" (Rowland 2007).

After this discussion, Rowland was invited to Belfast with a
view to performing a concert for the Republican movement.

'[The Sinn Féin representative] just said: "The leadership are
wondering if you might do a gig for them", and he said: "Do
you want to go over to Belfast", and I said: "Yeah." So me and
a mate went over for a weekend, and we met with a guy, Richard
McCauley, who was the press guy for Gerry Adams, and also we
met with Danny Morrison, who was, like, head of communica-
tions at that point' (Rowland, 2007).

Plans were soon hatched for a Dexys concert in west Belfast (to
raise funds for an Irish-language school), and though this show did
not take place, Rowland's involvement with political activists would
undoubtedly play a role in the formation of *DSMD* (Rowland 2007).[3]
Invoking ideas of resistance, recovery and recuperation,
DSMD staged an introspective (and often oblique) excursion into
second-generation Irish life, alongside polemical commentary on
Anglo-Irish affairs. Its key tracks, 'Knowledge Of Beauty' and 'The
Waltz', enact a renewal of Irish ethnicity in the face of enforced as-
similation, while 'One Of Those Things' offers a critique of what
Rowland saw as the British left's silence on Irish affairs. The al-
bum's unusually serious tenor – and comparatively complex char-
acter – was not easily accommodated in the structural confines of
the traditional pop song, and Rowland sought appropriately chal-
lenging forms (theatrical dialogue, ornate arrangements, extended
tracks) in which to stage his address.[4] How might we make sense of
this album's invocation of Irish issues and sounds, and particularly
its endeavour to speak to second-generation Irish concerns?

---

3 The singer says that he felt 'very bad' that the planned concert did not take
place (Rowland 2007).

4 The singer's painstaking efforts in this regard meant that *DSMD* far exceeded
the album's original budget and scheduled release dates (White 2005:147–70).

Recovering Irish ethnicity on *Don't Stand Me Down*

If the 'Celtic' orientation of *Too-Rye-Ay* had been impelled by Rowland's wish to announce his ethnicity in the face of its socially negative status, then *DSMD* would be born of Rowland's 'urge' – in one critic's terms – 'to reconcile himself with his Irish roots' (the singer recalls that it emerged from 'a real yearning for Ireland' and a wish 'to do something for Ireland') (Easlea 2002:51; Hutcheon 2002:118; Roberts 2002:76). In contrast to the *Too-Rye-Ay* period, however (when Rowland had been somewhat coy about invoking Irish ethnicity), the singer was keen, in his new project, to assume an expressly Irish subject position. 'I'm Irish', he stressed unequivocally to British journalists, adding that he had an 'Irish upbringing', and visited Ireland often (McNeill 1985a:14; Cross 1985:55). The singer also made clear his concern for the Northern Ireland conflict, explaining that he was 'very interested in what's going on there' (McNeill 1985a:14). This newly resolute mode of ethnic self-ascription met with significant press criticism, with journalists inviting Rowland to partake in the often absurd forms of identity-contestation that have marked debates about second-generation life in England. Tackling a succession of questions about the frequency with which he visited Ireland, the number of close relatives that continued to reside there, whether he defined himself as British or Irish, and how his ethnic allegiance could be reconciled with his place of birth, the singer was insistent on his adherence to Irish ethnicity (McIlheney 1985:18–19, 45).

Such insistence provoked public ridicule, with the music press publishing satires of Rowland's identity politics (Anonymous 1985:39). The singer could not have been more serious, however, and he went on to assault a journalist that had questioned his claims to Irish ethnicity (Aizlewood 1996:135; Roberts 1988:30; Wilde 1999:5). The theme of contested identity was also invoked – via songs about ancestry and assimilation – on the new album. Before presenting my account of this material, another aspect of the *DSMD* project requires consideration. To announce the record's release in September 1985, the band adopted an entirely new set of stage attire, exchanging the 'gypsy' aesthetic of *Too-Rye-Ay* for pinstripe suits and ties. The new record's artwork was especially unusual, with the band adopting solemn facial expressions and excessively formal poses (legs crossed, hands clasped) in a self-consciously posed shot that seemed quasi-corporate. And while the singer would insist that this look was simply a reflection of the band's off-stage appearance (McNeill 1985b:28), there were a number of more likely explanations for this striking sartorial shift. Perhaps most obviously, the new outfits served to signal the band's wholesale eschewal of their nouveau-gypsy phase, whilst stressing the expressly 'serious' nature of their new songs. Rather ironically, their sharp-tailored suits and corporate body postures also evoked the harsh sartorial codes of Thatcherite Conservatism, and, consequently – despite Rowland's claims that this wardrobe offered a timeless 'Ivy League' aesthetic – many critics felt that it veered precariously close to the clothes of the contemporaneous 'yuppie' (Irwin 1985:32; McNeill 1985b:28; Rogan 2002:58).

The unusual attire may also have been conceived as an ocular adjunct to the new Dexys sound, with its highly decorous formality matching the meticulous production and refined performances of the new material. The band's conservative veneer was at odds, however, with Rowland's song lyrics, which staged a highly charged act of ethnic 'recovery'. In this sense, his apparel appeared to obfuscate his more oppositional lyrics, evoking ideas of decency and decorum – values that Rowland would extol in the *DSMD* period (Dexys Midnight Runners 1985).[5]

Perhaps with such propriety in mind, the more political aspects of the new Dexys album were somewhat less than upfront. Contemporaneous critics observed its 'obliquely political' themes, noting the 'buried clues' that Rowland's 'obtuse [*sic*] imagination' had 'scattered' across the album's 'obscure landscape' (Irwin 1985:32; O'Hagan 1985:31).

The record's often veiled address to Irish issues was an effect of the unease that the singer had felt towards its lyrical themes. In this context, he became anxious about the album's reception, and

---

5 For an account of the 'respectable' modes of Irishness that were evinced by the migrant Irish, see Maguire 1997:93.

chose to withdraw certain titles and words that engaged with Irish themes. 'I bottled out of some of the original Irish titles on the album', he later explained, 'and I cut out some lyrics about hunger strikes. I thought the press would crucify me' (Roberts 2002:76).

Elaborating on this withdrawn lyric about hunger strikes, Rowland recalls:

'I was afraid to say it. I was afraid of what people would say to me. I wasn't afraid of losing my career, of losing money or anything. That wasn't the fear. It was more that they'd go: "Who are you to fucking say that? You haven't got the right to say that. You're not even Irish. You were born here"' (Rowland 2007).

With such concerns in mind, a song that had been called 'Elizabeth Wimpole and Kathleen Ní Houlihan' was re-titled 'The Waltz', whilst 'My National Pride' became 'Knowledge Of Beauty'. Rowland explained that 'for most of its life during the recording', the latter song was called 'My National Pride': 'That is its true title, I just didn't have the courage to title it that when it came around to the artwork, because I didn't believe … that I had the right to be Irish' (Dexys Midnight Runners 1996).[6]

To compound this concern about claiming Irish ethnicity, Rowland also felt that such a frank invocation of patriotism was simply 'too strong' a gesture in the charged political climate of mid-1980s Britain (Easlea 2002:51). Apart from the intimation of far-right rhetoric contained in the title 'My National Pride', the singer's deployment of this term as an expressly *Irish* gesture was likely to have been viewed, in the context of the time, as support for political violence (Dooley 2004:17). With this in mind, one critic has explained that Rowland's 'urge to reconcile himself with his Irish roots' on *DSMD* was 'perceived in England as tantamount to wearing a balaclava and carrying a machine gun' (Hutcheon 2002:118). In light of this point, it was perhaps understandable that Rowland withdrew certain references that he had made to Irish affairs.

This caution was also evident in Rowland's press interviews. He sometimes refused to deal with questions about Irish issues,

---

6 Since this 1996 reissue, all pressings of the CD have listed the track as 'My National Pride'.

and asked that whatever remarks he had made be withdrawn from printed copy. During one interview, for example, the singer declined to elaborate on the record's Irish themes, refusing outright to answer a question on the topic of Northern Ireland. Only when he was faced with the charge of 'running away from the political situation in Ireland' did Rowland feel obliged to respond. 'I've said more about Ireland than any other musician, Irish or otherwise', he would claim (McIlheney 1985:19). Nevertheless, the singer refused to offer any extended commentary on the matter, and recanted any comments that he had made. In the immediate aftermath of another interview, Rowland made contact with the journalist to express his regret that he had 'let [his] own personal political views about Ireland be known', adding that such views 'don't matter', and advising the reporter to 'dilute' his remarks 'a bit' (Roberts 1985:9).

There is little doubt, then, that Rowland felt reticent about the ethnic orientation of this project. The caginess that he displayed about the record's reception was, moreover, not without foundation. It would be wrong to infer from this, though, that *DSMD* was wholly abstract in its address to Irish issues, for there were many overt signals in the song words, and these were drawn out by Rowland in interviews, videos and attendant media. An Irish theme was invoked, for example, in 'One Of Those Things', in which Rowland's spoken-sung dialogue assails the silence about Northern Ireland amongst Britain's political left (Sedgwick 1985:50). Rehearsing an imaginary exchange between the song's narrator and 'a couple of so called socialists', Rowland makes reference to 'Ireland' and 'Belfast', before inviting his addressees to elaborate on the elusive issue of Northern Ireland. The lyrics were drawn, it would seem, from the singer's personal experience. 'I'd be talking to supposed socialists', Rowland later recalled, 'and I'd say, "Do you know what's happening in Ireland?" and they'd say "What?" and I'd say, "It's being occupied, by the army of this country!"' Rowland's quarrel was that the conflict in Northern Ireland 'should have been top of their priorities', rather than 'way down there' (Price 2002:15). In the song, then, Rowland sought to 'make a very definite point', namely 'that it is very easy for most British socialists who pontificate about revolutions far away not to recognise the very obvious point that the most important problem facing them is what is going on in Ireland' (McIlheney 1985:19). Rather than viewing the Troubles as social turmoil, the left in Britain had, for Rowland, reduced the Irish to mere 'gangsters' (Roberts 1985:9).[7]

As well as addressing the disinterest in Irish affairs in British political life, 'One Of Those Things' introduced Irishness as one of *DSMD*'s central themes, setting up the fuller (if less overt) engagement on its two key tracks, 'Knowledge Of Beauty' and 'The Waltz'. In these companion pieces, the singer conveys an account of second-generation Irish life through the tropes of resistance, recovery and assimilation. If this marked a thematic departure from the lightweight lyrics of *Too-Rye-Ay*, then the languid pace and reflective tenor of these new songs deviated starkly from the buoyant mood of 'Celtic Soul Brothers' and 'Come On Eileen'. The words for 'Knowledge Of Beauty' had, as Rowland explained, sprung from a feeling of being 'misplaced', with the singer stressing – in interviews – its theme of 'roots' and 'parents': 'Ireland is obviously there', he made clear (McNeill 1985a:14).

The song enacts a symbolic resolution of exilic Irish angst, with its narrating first-person subject reverting – in the face of unfulfilled assimilation – to ethnic 'roots' and 'heritage' (White 2005:166). This 'magical recovery' of Irish ethnicity offers more than mere subjectivity though, for the singer's provenance also functions, in this scenario, as a recuperative well spring, supplying psychic rejuvenation in the face of emotional decline.[8] Like other second-generation Irish figures who have sourced their upbringing for its 'strength and sense of historical solidarity' (Maguire 1997:95), Rowland's narrating persona, in a quest for psychic 'strength' (to 'take bad on') elects to 'look back to where [he] came from', effecting a thematic closure that prompts the relief of the

---

7 'You mentioned Ireland and they fucking hated it', recalls Rowland of his conversations with left-wing activists (Rowland 2007). As Tom Hayden explains, 'the New Left … generally excluded Northern Ireland from its menu of progressive causes' (Hayden 2001:111).

8 This term 'magical recovery' is borrowed from early accounts of youth subcultures. See, for example, Cohen (1972) and Clarke (1976).

chorus. In this regard, the track bears a resemblance to other accounts of Irish ethnic 'recovery', not least John Ford's *The Quiet Man* (1952), in which the figure of Sean Thornton (John Wayne) forsakes the anguish of urban America for ancestral restitution in a curative Irish west.[9] The analogies between these (otherwise) disparate texts are realised in the video for 'Knowledge Of Beauty', which details Rowland's return to the parish of his Mayo-born parents.[10] There are profound differences, of course, between Ford's film and Rowland's song, with the sombre introspection of Rowland contrasting starkly with Ford's Hollywood whimsy. The slow-paced 'Knowledge Of Beauty' thus unfolds almost inaudibly, with a sparse piano supplying colour to a simple bass and gentle snare. While sliding steel guitars conjure a distinctly country and western style, a picked mandolin serves as a clue to the song's setting. In this mood of what one critic has called 'convivial warmth' (White 2005:166), Rowland emits a low, softly-controlled vocal, offering nostalgic gestures towards his speaker's homeland. This sets the scene for an address to Ireland's diaspora who 'these days' dwell in 'US and Britannia care'. Imparting an oblique critique of England, the speaker stages a sort of abdication, journeying west (beyond 'hollow words' and 'the "now" generation') to reconnect himself with the 'wisdom and warmth' of his 'past generations'.

It is in the song's final chorus, however, that the speaker unveils (in quietly mixed, spoken words) the track's resolution, which critics have viewed as 'an awakening' (White 2005:166). 'I've denied my beautiful heritage, gone away from my roots', Rowland narrates, stating a desire to 'come back home again'. If this 'home' was harmonically evoked by a 'Celtic'-sounding violin part, it was more conspicuously evinced in the aforementioned video, which literally relocates (the emotionally displaced) Rowland in the spatial terrain of Ireland's west coast, with shots of the singer voyaging

---

9 For an account of the film's significance for the Irish diaspora, see Gibbons (2002). As Martin McLoone explains, the Irish west has functioned, in popular culture, as 'a kind of ideal regenerative environment for the troubled and worried mind of modernity' (McLoone 2008:79).

10 The video, which was shot on 35mm film, is included on *Don't Stand Me Down: The Director's Cut* (2002).

through a series of Irish vistas in a physical manifestation of the song's symbolic passage. Shots of Rowland gazing at an ancient family tombstone in County Mayo and bowing at Catholic icons in a rural Irish church convey the quasi-religious aspects of the singer's ancestral voyage, whilst lingering views of archetypal Irish scenes (including a thatched cottage, stacked turf and the Cliffs of Moher) forge a sentimental portrait of Ireland. This is offset, though, by the video's slow pace and artfully unfocused images, which – like the visibly solemn Rowland and his song's reflective tenor – conjure melancholy more than schmaltz.

More problematic, perhaps, is the hook that Rowland intones in the stern lyrical coda. Here, as frantic brass figures and busy percussion conjure crescendo, the singer – who has hitherto been restrained – emits the abrasive words that gave the track its original title ('My national pride is a personal pride'), with Rowland asserting Irish ethnicity in what John Mulvey has called 'one of the most uncluttered outpourings of emotion ever recorded by a British singer' (2002:100).

By taking on the argot of Britain's far right, however, Rowland had effectively assailed *one* sort of nationalist enterprise (via his speaker's refusal to assimilate) by extolling another (through a reverence for 'roots' and 'heritage'). And though this gesture was intended, as critics have explained, to urge exilic Irish listeners to be 'proud of [their] roots' (Hutcheon 2002:118), it effectively effaced the motif of diaspora that was invoked at the start of the song, with its de-territorial impulse now displaced by an expressly nationalist outlook. This was at odds, moreover, with earlier aspects of Rowland's work, such as the critique of patriotism that he had expressed in certain songs (including 'There, There, My Dear' (1980) and 'Old' (1982)), as well as in interviews and ancillary media: 'one thing I detest is patriotism', he had told the Irish music paper *Hot Press* (Stokes 1980:18). In the course of 'Knowledge Of Beauty', though, Rowland had aligned himself with Irish nationalism and (what he called) 'nationalist music' (McIlheney 1985:19). The singer would later concede that he became 'very nationalistic' during this period: 'I did get into that thing then', he explains, 'of "everything Irish is great and everything English is shit".' He suggests that he 'retreated too much into that', viewing this position as a withdrawal from the actuality of his immediate (English) environment (Rowland 2007). As Malone and Dooley have explained, certain sections of the second generation have sought – in the absence of their own sense of 'home' – an idealised Irish elsewhere that was 'separate in time and place from the demands of everyday existence', and served 'to obviate the need to be thoroughly engaged in the "here and now"' (Malone and Dooley 2006:15–16, 22, 26). This is certainly how Rowland came to view the ethnic nationalism of his mid-1980s self: 'It's a way of disengaging … because you're here [in England]', he says. 'It's denying that you're *here* – something he sees as a 'really negative thing' (Rowland 2007).

The 'national pride' song lyric, then, suggests that Rowland's dislike of patriotism was less of an aversion to nationalism per se than a response to British nationalism from an outsider's (quasi-nationalistic) view. This view was occasionally evinced in Dexys' oeuvre, not least in their 1980 tour programme, which concluded with a refusal of patriotism and yet began with an endorsement of the IRA, a paradox also present in 'There, There, My Dear', which rebukes a 'dumb, dumb patriot' before issuing allusive succour to Irish nationalist actions (Dexys Midnight Runners 1980). Reflecting on this point, Rowland notes that he set out to find an identification that was distinct from that of Irish-born migrants and the Irish in Ireland. Seeing the second generation as 'a breed apart', he explains, 'We're so different from the first-generation Irish', laying special stress on the fact that 'we're much angrier than them'. Whether or not this helps to explain the IRA allusions outlined above, it evidently informed the singer's approach to Irish issues. 'I wanted to find out my *own* Irishness, not my dad's Irishness', he explains.

'I wasn't saying what my dad was saying about Ireland. I wasn't saying that the Irish flag is great. I wasn't saying that just because it's Irish it's good. I was saying "*This* is important." I was kind of finding my own way' (Rowland 2007).

This notion of 'finding your own way of being Irish' is one that appears in many accounts of second-generation Irish life (Free 2007:478, 481). In this context, John Lydon recalls that a lack of access to Irish culture in his early milieu left him feeling 'isolated and shallow inside', and prompted him to 'find out about [his] own Irishness' (1994:27).

This sort of symbolic journey – towards a second-generation Irish subjectivity – would be explored on *DSMD*'s final (and de facto title) track, 'The Waltz'. Tackling similar thematic terrain to 'Knowledge Of Beauty', it adheres to that song's pace, tenor and instrumentation. Rather than staging a recovery of Irish ethnicity, though, 'The Waltz' pursues the quandary of dual identity as a dysfunctional tryst between its subject and two mythical women, presented here as sisters. The song's original title had been 'Elizabeth Wimpole and Kathleen Ní Houlihan', and although concerns about its reception had led the singer to 'change the title and make some of the lyrics more vague', the latter figure is present in the revised song words (albeit in the truncated form of 'Kathleen') – an estranged 'sister' to the addressee (Rowland 1996). If Ní Houlihan acts as an embodiment of Ireland, then 'Elizabeth' serves, in the song, as an index of England (Rowland had heard someone refer to Elizabeth Windsor as 'Lizzie Wimpole' – hence the name in the song's original title) (Rowland 2007). It is 'Elizabeth', in any case, to whom the speaker projects, with Rowland recounting his regret at being tricked by her 'strategy' and for pursuing her 'course'. Evoking themes of assimilation, Rowland's speaker goes on – in the double-length third, and final, verse – to assail such English schemes, lamenting how he had 'swooned to the stories of Royal victories', before reproving England's dreaming ('your books of history were fairy tales'). The track thus acts as a critique of the 'imperial mentality' that, for Bhikhu Parekh, 'penetrated everyday life, popular culture and consciousness' in post-war Britain (2000:24).

The song also attacks, as White points out, 'all things monarchical', questioning the 'historical fallacies' of 'British myth' (White 2005:168). Amidst this admonition of England as Elizabeth, the singer cites Ireland – via the 'good sister', Kathleen – as an absent presence, a figure rendered invisible ('She's nowhere to be seen'), thus evoking the silence about Ireland in English textbooks (Hickman 1999:185). This seems to have resonated with Rowland's experience of school history lessons: 'There was no mention of Ireland', he recalls (Rowland 2007).

While 'The Waltz' registers the 'doubt' and 'confusion' of second-generation Irish life, there is no curative reversion, here, to the ancestor lore of 'Knowledge Of Beauty'. What the song offers instead is a lament for the silence on Irishness in the speaker's milieu ('They don't talk of Kathleen, things are not how they seem'). Rowland would explain that the track had been shaped by his 'strong feelings for Ireland and what was going on there' (Rowland 1996) However, the song's only discernible theme is that of English incorporation and Irish ethnicity, with the latter theme staged as a kind of return of the repressed: 'She won't wait anymore', the singer strains anxiously, prior to the heartfelt middle eight. Later on, in a gentle refrain that restores the song's tender prelude, the speaker declares his allegiance to the unseen figure of Kathleen ('Don't stand me down … for I'll never stop saying your name'), with Rowland reflecting in interviews that this lyric, which had supplied the album with its title, was an appeal from the diaspora to not be abandoned by 'home' (Warburton 1997).

Such gestures had, however, been rendered oblique by Rowland's wish, in the latter stages of production, to make the song lyrics 'more vague'. Nonetheless, the singer's final words – in the closing moments of what would become Dexys' last album – were unambiguous, distilling Rowland's long-term address to Irish issues. With his controlled delivery at the fore of the track's sparse mix – and with violin, guitar and slow-paced snare as accompaniment – the singer enunciates a simple vocal phrase, 'Here is a protest', dwelling on the contours of the latter word before the song's emphatic coda in which the brass section and Rowland's improvised singing supply a markedly upbeat mood. Like its companion piece, 'Knowledge Of Beauty', then, 'The Waltz' enacts a certain closure, renouncing assimilation whilst revering roots (and thus assuaging the ambivalence that is often associated with second-generation Irish experience).

In light of Rowland's concerns about the silence on Ireland in contemporary British life, it is somewhat ironic that *DSMD* was so veiled and oblique. The singer would defend this abstraction, explaining that the 'best' forms of 'nationalist music' had historically been 'the stuff in disguise when you don't know that it is actually about Ireland at all' (McIlheney 1985:19). As allusive as they no doubt were, the tracks on *DSMD* nevertheless comprised the most substantive engagement (to date) with second-generation Irish experience in the realm of popular song. With this in mind, it is worth noting that the album received a largely hostile response at the time of its release, with poor sales and mixed reviews leading to a low turn-out at the group's 1985 live shows (Elms 1985:101; Heath 1985:77; Irwin 1985:21; Morton 1985:20; O'Hagan 1985:31; Roberts 1985:31; Sedgwick 1985:50; White 2005:173). The album thus became, as critics explain, an 'object of derision' (Hutcheon 2002:118), a fate born of a range of factors (not least the band's unusual appearance and ornate songs, as well as the broader shifts in popular music since their last incarnation). However, the record's vexed address to Irishness arguably also played a part in its poor reception, which, in turn, as Mulvey explains, 'effectively destroyed' the group's career (2002:100). Rowland's forthright recovery of Irish ethnicity thus signalled (and perhaps helped to bring about) the end of the Dexys project. A quarter of a century later, however, Rowland would reform the band, under the truncated title of 'Dexys'. Significantly, the issue of Irish identity would inform the band's new songs, not least 'Nowhere is Home' (2012), on which the singer observed that he was 'born here of an Irish family', before concluding that 'national identity won't fulfil me'. At the same time, though, Rowland revived the *DSMD* songs explored in this chapter, including 'Knowledge of Beauty'/'My National Pride'. In this context, it is noteworthy that the latter song supplied the coda of Dexys' show at the Irish Embassy in London in June 2016 (as detailed in the *Irish Times*):

> 'I've denied my beautiful heritage … Gone away from my roots
> and come back home again. I gave away my individuality. And

listened to the "now" generation, when really I'm not one of those … My national pride is a personal pride' (cited in Sweeney 2016).

The second-generation Irish identity dilemma that the singer had staged on *DSMD* seems to remain, then, very much in process, with its invocation of an exilic (Irish–English) in-betweenness continuing to inform his work.

Bibliography

Aizlewood, John (1996) 'Bullish', *Q*, August, p.135.

Anonymous (1985) 'Desperately seeking attention', *Record Mirror*, 21 December, p.39.

Clarke, John (1976) 'The skinheads and the magical recovery of community', in Stuart Hall and Tony Jefferson (eds), *Resistance Through Rituals: Youth Subcultures in Post-war Britain*, London: Hutchinson, pp.99–102.

Cohen, Phil (1972) 'Subcultural conflict in a working class community', *Working Papers in Cultural Studies*, no. 2, University of Birmingham, pp.5–51.

Coogan, Tim Pat (2000) *The IRA*, London: HarperCollins.

Cross, Diane (1985) 'Status Quo? Great!', *Record Mirror*, 30 November, p.55.

Denselow, Robin (2016) 'Imagining Ireland review – remembering in song the rebels with a cause', *The Guardian*, 3 May

Dexys Midnight Runners (1980) *Intense Emotion Review* tour programme.

Dexys Midnight Runners (1985) *Coming to Town* tour programme.

Dexys Midnight Runners (1996) *Don't Stand Me Down* (Creation CD).

Dooley, Brian (2004) 'Your name could put you in jail', *New Statesman*, 4 October, p.17.

Easlea, Daryl (2002) 'Don't stand me down', *Record Collector*, April, p.51.

Elms, Robert (1985) 'Death to dull rock', *The Face*, November, p.101.

Free, Marcus (2007) 'Tales from the fifth green field: The psychodynamics of migration, masculinity and national identity amongst Republic of Ireland soccer supporters in England', *Sport in Society*, vol. 10, no. 3 (May), pp.476–94.

Gibbons, Luke (2002) *The Quiet Man*, Cork: Cork University Press.

Hayden, Tom (2001) *Irish on the Inside: In Search of the Soul of Irish America*, London: Verso.

Heath, Chris (1985) 'Albums', *Smash Hits*, 11–24 September, p.77.

Hickman, Mary J. (1999) 'The religio-ethnic identities of teenagers of Irish descent', in Michael P. Hornsby-Smith (ed.), *Catholics in England, 1950–2000: Historical and Sociological Perspectives*, London: Cassell, pp.182–98.

Hutcheon, David (2002) 'Rides up with wear', *Mojo*, May, p.118.

Irwin, Colin (1985), 'Stand and deliver', *Melody Maker*, 7 September, p.32.

Lydon, John (1994) *Rotten: No Irish, No Blacks, No Dogs*, London: Hodder & Stoughton.

Maguire, Meg (1997) 'Missing links: Working-class women of Irish descent', in

Pat Mahony and Christine Zmroczek (eds.), *Class Matters: 'Working-Class' Women's Perspectives On Social Class*, London: Taylor & Francis, pp.87–100.

Malone, Mary E. and John P. Dooley (2006) '"Dwelling in displacement": Meanings of "community" and sense of community for two generations of Irish people living in north-west London', *Community, Work and Family*, vol. 9, no. 1 (February), pp.11–28.

McIlheney, Barry (1985) 'Burning the midnight oil', *Melody Maker*, 2 November, pp.18–19, 45.

McLoone, Martin (2008) *Film, Media and Popular Culture in Ireland: Cityscapes, Landscapes, Soundscapes*, Dublin: Irish Academic Press.

McNeill, Phil (1985a) 'A man out of time', *The Hit*, 21 September, p.14.

McNeill, Phil (1985b) 'Let's get this straight from the start', *The Hit*, 28 September, p.28.

Morton, Tom (1985) 'Dexys Midnight Runners', *Melody Maker*, 9 November, p.20.

Mulvey, John (2002) 'The third coming', *Uncut*, May, p.100.

O'Hagan, Sean (1985) 'Tangled up in blue', *NME*, 7 September, p.31.

Parekh, Bhikhu (2000) *The Future of Multi-ethnic Britain*, London: Profile Books.

Price, Simon (2002) 'A dark knight of the soul', *The Independent*, 'Friday Review' section, 5 April, p.15.

Rogan, Johnny (2002) 'Don't Stand Me Down', *Record Collector*, April, p.58.

Roberts, Chris (1985) 'The Midnight's hour', *Sounds*, 12 October, p.9.

Roberts, Chris (1988) 'Stairway to Kevin', *Melody Maker*, 9 April, p.30.

Roberts, Chris (2002) 'Grand stand', *Uncut*, May, p.76.

Rowland, Kevin (1996) Liner notes, *Don't Stand Me Down* (Creation CD).

Rowland, Kevin (2007), interview with the author, 18 September.

Sedgwick, Harry (1985) 'Dexys Midnight Runners: *Don't Stand Me Down*', *Jamming!*, October, p.50.

Stokes, Dermot (1980) 'Dexys Midnight Runners', *Hot Press*, 14–28 August, p.18.

Sweeney, Eamon (2016) 'Dexys usher in their new Irish vision', *Irish Times*, 27 June.

Ullah, Philip (1990) 'Rhetoric and ideology in social identification: The case of second generation Irish youths', *Discourse and Society*, vol. 1, no. 2, pp.167–88.

Warburton, Neil (1997) 'It Was August 1997…', *Keep on Running*, no. 9 (October), no pagination.

White, Richard (2005) *Dexys Midnight Runners: Young Soul Rebels*, London: Omnibus Press.

Wilde, Jon (1999) 'My story: Kevin Rowland', *Dazed and Confused*, June, p.5.

Graham Caveney
The Scandalous Health of Shane MacGowan

We lost in that war of words. The syllables
Which sense all delight: mouth-exile.
Austin Clarke – *The Flock At Dawn*

I

The purpose of this essay is not to offer a biography or even an appraisal of the work of Shane MacGowan, but rather to offer a provocation, a cultural intervention (with all the more recent resonances of alcoholic 'treatments' which that term carries) into the ways in which his work has been appraised and his biography told. Written outside of the legitimising structures (and strictures) of academia, yet still indebted to it, my work hopes to reproduce some of the hybridity, marginality and liminality that it finds in the figure of MacGowan himself. As such this chapter does not move chronologically through or offer a linear story

39

st tenacious yet most reluctant of pop stars. Rather it
ocate him in some unexpected places, find a context for
which he is in dialogue with new voices and older traditions.
choosing to call this essay 'The Scandalous Health of Shane
cGowan', I hope to put in play the myriad of meanings which
that term carries. Although 'scandal' is currently used to denote an
outrage caused by moral or legal laxity, it has an earlier more barbed
etymology in which the word emerges as "obstacle or stumbling
block" or as "a trap or snare laid for an enemy" (OED)

The term thus conjures up both resistance and malicious
rumour, defiance as well as shame. I want to suggest that the
cultural outrage or scandal around MacGowan's drinking – the way
in which he seems to epitomise the figure of the drunken Paddy
– is also a stumbling block, an obstacle to thinking about him in
other -perhaps more political or performative ways.

In her 2007 novel, *The Gathering*, Anne Enright has her narrator
travel from Dublin to England to pick up the body of her brother
– a body that was found washed up, probably suicide. She reflects:
'Sitting on the Brighton train I am trying to put a timetable on my
brother's drinking. Drink was not his problem, but it did become
his problem, eventually, which was a relief to everyone concerned.
'I'm a bit worried about his drinking' – so, after a while, no-one
could hear a thing he said any more.'

She goes on: 'A drinker does not exist. Whatever they say, it is
just the drink talking.' (2007:54–55) Similarly, it is as though the
story of MacGowan's drinking – his drinking stories as it were – is
a way of not listening to his other stories, stories about folk and
literary history, stories of social and political dissent. The attention
given to his drinking has ensured that he does not exist, or exists
only through his drinking.

Strangely enough, it is also a way of disavowing any story he
might have to tell us about drinking itself – a subject about which
he knows a great deal. The insistence on him as an alcoholic means
that anything he may say about alcohol is heard through the prism
of his 'alcoholism'. It's as though the experience which gives him
the authority to speak also disqualifies from having anything to say.

40

In her book, *What's Wrong With Addiction*, Helen Keane explores precisely this double bind in which the alcoholic/addict finds her or himself. She discusses the ways in which drink or drug use discredit the credibility of the drinker or drug user, making them unreliable witnesses to their lives and experiences. She cites Eve Kosofsky Sedgwick who has argued how the figure of the addict is emptied of all subjectivity, denied any insight into her own condition by virtue of the very condition of addiction: 'From being the subject of her own perceptual manipulations she is installed as the proper object of compulsory institutional disciplines which ... presume to know her better than she can know herself.' (cited in Campbell:2011)

MacGowan, then, has nothing to tell us about drinking because he drinks. Furthermore, anything else he might want to tell us – be it his vegetarianism, his Catholicism, his republicanism – is subsumed by the totality of his identity as Drunk.

Rather than read him and his work as arising out of his so-called problematic relationship to drink and drugs, I want to place him in a context in which this relationship can be seen as part of a larger more politicised conversation between Ireland and England. In his classic study of Anglo-Irish rock music, *Irish Blood, English Heart*, Sean Campbell discusses the ways in which Irishness has been erased or refused in the discourses of popular music. He points out that popular music's last fifty years would be unimaginable without second generation Irish influence. From Lonnie Donegan to Lennon and McCartney, Dusty Springfield to Kate Bush, Boy George, to Elvis Costello, the history of British popular music is one which has been constituted by second generation Irish artists, yet one which has been reluctant to admit let alone embrace their ethnicity.

Campbell makes a compelling case for Anglo-Irishness as providing ways into musical explorations of exile, in-between-ness, fluidity. The book argues for what Josh Kun calls 'audiotopia', for music that celebrates a musical space in which 'contradictions and conflicts do not cancel each other out but co-exist and live through each other.' (2011:23)

Of course, as Campbell also points out, the experience of Irish immigration into England has almost always meant that the Irish contribution to this cross-cultural exchange is minimized, commodified or ignored. The most recent example of this was Britpop – an extraordinary display of jingoistic rhetoric and imagery which managed to bury or elide the ethnicity of most of its participants. Oasis consisted of five second generation Irishmen, Echobelly's Sonya Madan was from Dehli, yet these trivialities were swept aside in the rush to consensus between an aspiring-to-be-hip Blair government and a music press hungry for the next big thing.

The Smiths are probably *the* band who have been the most mis-read by this parochiality. The band's critical reception was one of staggering myopia, with critic after critic lining up to cheer Morrisey's 'essential Englishness' (*Melody Maker*), his 'singing for or of England … with a music that could only come from the urban heart of England' (*The Wire*) and whose 'qualities aspired to a myth of English purity' (*NME*). Morrisey's parents are from Dublin, Johnny Marr's – originally Maher – are from County Kildare and Mike Joyce's are from Galway. This was the band that the music press would regularly refer to as 'quintessentially English.' With this in mind it is perhaps worth re-considering the ironies and punk sensibilities involved in Morrisey draping himself in the Union Jack.

Needless to say, there is a long and ignoble history of such misreading. Indeed, students of English Literature were regularly introduced to writers such as Lawrence Sterne, Oliver Goldsmith, Richard Sheridan, Bram Stoker and Oscar Wilde without any mention of their complex ethnicity.

This invisibility and inaudibility is, of course, part of a wider pattern of non-recognition. As Campbell makes clear, the research done on second generation Irish immigration arrives at some curious conclusions. He cites one study done in the 1990s by the *British Medical Journal* which claims that 'the English-born offspring of Irish immigrants had experienced 'significantly higher mortality (rates)' than the host population 'for most major causes of death' and that – in the context of health provision – it is useful to conceive them as different from the host population.' (2011:5)

He then juxtaposes this with another study done on educational assimilation by the *British Journal of Sociology*: 'What they went on to discover, though, was that the second-generation Irish actually exceed(ed) the educational qualifications held by their English counterparts'. However, despite the fact that this evidence was at odds with their own criterion of assimilation, which required a 'substantial convergence' between the second-generation Irish and the English control sample, the authors nevertheless saw this educational success as evidence of second-generation Irish assimilation.' It is hard to resist Campbell's conclusion that: 'when the second generation exceed the educational achievements of the English group, they become invisible and are understood in terms of assimilation. Yet, when they exceed standard mortality rates, they become visible and are seen in terms of Irish difference.' (2011:6)

In fact the 'Irish in Britain' – however that is defined – were not even recognised as an ethnic minority by the Commission for Racial Equality until 1995. Not only then was there a problem, but there was a problem in not having a language with which to talk about it. Which was part of the problem.

Some facts: Shane MacGowan was born in Kent, England, on Christmas Day 1957, whilst his parents were on holiday there. He was raised in Tipperary on an extended family farm and then moved with his parents to London. He won a scholarship to Westminster public school but was expelled for minor drug possession. By seventeen he was suffering from acute panic disorder and was admitted to Bethlem hospital – to Bedlam – where he was prescribed tranquillizers (he recalls being given 100 mg of Valium per day).

This story is, unfortunately, all too common. It embodies many themes of that vast body of narrative known unhelpfully as The Immigrant Experience. It has all the tropes of aspiration and dislocation, educational over-achievement and social exclusion.

Terry Eagleton has pointed out that the power relations between

Britain and Ireland are often rendered in terms of the family drama – the mother country, our sister nation, brotherly affection and so on – and that the sheer proximity between the two places complicates the issue further: In *The Great Hunger* he argues: 'At once too near and too far, akin and estranged, both inside and outside each other's cognitive range, Britain and Ireland share in common the crisis of identity which each catalysed in each other; whereas if the Irish had been black, unintelligible and ensconced in another hemisphere, savages of the desert rather than the doorstep, their presence might have proved rather less unnerving.' (1996:128)

(There is, it needs to be said, the experience of the black and Irish immigrant to Britain. One such case was Phil Lynott, the lead singer of Thin Lizzy, a story deserving a chapter of its own.)

On the whole, however, the experience of Irish immigration to Britain was, in that troubling phrase, a colourless one. What becomes the issue is not colour but the voice; accent and inflection rather than skin pigmentation. The experience then is one which conflates invisibility with inaudibility, the speaking of words becoming the moment when the emigre announces her or his difference. In a re-working of the Victorian maxim about children, racialized difference is something that is heard and not seen.

This emphasis on the voice as signifier of difference is of vital importance within Ireland itself, particularly around the border. In his book, *Irish Times*, David Lloyd writes about his experiences of moving from the South to go to a boarding school in the North: 'They can tell, you were told, by the way you pronounce that 'h' sound; 'Spell Hell', aitch or haitch? Protestant or Catholic alphabets as telling as the mark of Abel ... I am still marked by that pedagogy of suspicion, always seeking out the shadows where my accent is hard to place. The dislocated voice is vulnerable, sheared from origin at the cost of belonging nowhere.' (2008:129)

What I want to ask is: If the voice becomes the site of identity – a declaration or a discovery – then what kind of investments does one have in the mouth? If the accent announces who we are, then what kinds of expectations do we have of the tongue, the throat, the teeth? On hearing himself banished from his country in Richard II Shakespeare gives the Duke of Norfolk the following lines:

> The language I have learned these forty years,
>
> My native English, now I must forgo,
>
> And now my tongue's use to me is no more
>
> Than an unstringed viol or a harp,
>
> Or like some cunning instrument, cased up,
>
> Or, being open, put into his hands
>
> That knows no touch to tune the harmony.
>
> Within my mouth you have engaoled my tongue,
>
> Doubly portcullised with my teeth and lips,
>
> And dull, unfeeling, barren ignorance
>
> Is made my gaoler to attend on me.
>
> (1 ii 160 – 169)

This issue then is not just about the words that are spoken, but it is also about the mouth that speaks them – a somatic as well as a linguistic concern. I will return to this later in discussing MacGowan's ruined and ruinous mouth.

II

MacGowan has always claimed that he found his salvation in punk. There is a clip of him dressed in a Union Jack shirt po-going at a Sex Pistols gig. I cannot look at this clip without seeing him as newly released from Bedlam, the flag a kind of strait-jacket, its symbolism being turned inside out. The song being sung by the Pistols is, of course, 'God Save The Queen'. I think there is a great little book to be written about Irishness in punk, the ways in which all that spitting and snarling was an attempt to avoid all those perilous accents. Johnny Rotten is of course from Irish ancestry, it is perhaps worth thinking about it as an Irish Rebel song.

Writing about the musical landscape that was left in the wake of punk and post-punk, the critic Simon Reynolds characterizes the early eighties musical scene as 'a camp comedy zone – an era characterized by clumsily pretentious stabs at video-as-artform, by English eyeliner-and synth fops with silly haircuts.' (2005:xv)

It was into this zone – 1983 – that The Pogues released their first album, 'Red Roses For Me'. Originally called Pogue Mahone – Irish for "Kiss My Arse" – the hastily re-named Pogues attempted to weld the energy of those early punk gigs to traditional Irish music, a kind of The Clancy Brothers meets The Clash. The sound was driven, abrasive, cacophonous; MacGowan's vocals tending to spit out or slur the lyrics.

Their look was also distinctive, what MacGowan called 'Paddy Chic' – plain black suits and tie-less white shirts, a look that was somewhere between appearing in front of the magistrates and having just returned from your grandfather's funeral. In his book, *Ways of Seeing*, John Berger has a superb essay on August Sander's photographs of a bunch of peasant-musicians and how their formal dress does not disguise their social class but underlines it. He writes: 'Their suits deform them. Wearing them, they look as though they were physically misshapen ... The musicians give the impression of being uncoordinated, bandy-legged, barrel-chested, low-arsed, twisted or scalene.' (1980:30)

Such was The Pogues' appeal.

The band seemed to revel in looking and sounding like a bunch of navvies on a night out. Their sets included bloodthirsty renditions of 'Poor Paddy' and 'Wax's Dargle', as well as ballads like 'Kitty' which were snarled out as though from the back of a prison cell.

Yet it is not all they were. MacGowan's lyrics showed a range and literacy that went far beyond the drinking song. The first album was named after a play by Sean O'Casey – 'Red Roses For Me' being a drama from the 1940s about the Dublin lockout of 1913. There were songs about Brendan Behan, references to Mai Lai in Vietnam, about Frank Ryan (an Irish Republican who went to fight against Franco during the Spanish Civil War). There were references to the battle of Cable St. On the very first song of the first album there is a repeated call to KMRIA (Kiss My Royal Irish Arse) a reference to James Joyce's *Ulysses*, a not unambitious way to set out your song-writing stall.

Their appeal was immediate and huge. It wasn't just to the Irish diaspora that the Pogues spoke – although they turned up to gigs in their thousands – but to a much wider community of émigrés and those who had been left stranded by punk's stolen promise. They had, in Elvis Costello's memorable phrase, 'saved folk from the folkies.' (cited in Cleary:2007) I think it is fair to add that they helped to reconfigure our notions of World Music – a term that was only just being coined – and that was in danger of disappearing into a vortex of tourism and piety.

Critically they were received with a certain anxiety right from the off, and this anxiety revolved around two things: where were they from and how much did they drink. What was interesting is how those two questions quickly became inseparable, as though the answer to one would provide the answer to the other.

Were they a London band who played Irish music: or an Irish band who lived in London? MacGowan was constantly asked about his birthright, his heritage, his passport, his education and of course his accent.

At the same time every interview took place in a bar, every journalist reported back on what he drank and how much. The record company were conflicted, eager to sell an image of Irish 'authenticity', yet wary of aligning themselves too much with the 'rebel' Irish which that seemed to entail.

The band themselves – Shane in particular – initially seemed to play up to the image. They used beer trays as instruments, would demand notoriously boozy riders for their gigs, were never photographed without a drink in their hand or a fag in their mouth.

By the second and third albums, however, this uneasy skirting with stereotype had become an obstacle to listening to the band as anything other than drunken Paddies. Their second album used a cover of them as survivors on Gericault's 'Raft of the Medusa' – quite literally stranded between the Republic and no-man's land. The third had them posed alongside a picture of James Joyce, but by this point Shane's relationship to Irish modernism was playing second fiddle to his much more publicised relationship to self-destructive excess.

Their reception in Ireland was even more contested around

questions of provenance and origins, accents and authenticity. The criticism was that they were not Irish enough, the term 'plastic paddy' being thrown around with the same disdain that 'drunken paddy' had in the UK. There was a (now infamous) appearance on an Irish radio show called *The BP Fallon Orchestra* in which people walked out in disgust, telling Shane and Cait O'Riordan to go back to London after hearing their accents. (First Broadcast, 21.09.1985) It seemed that The Pogues were an untimely reminder of everything that the new Ireland was trying to leave behind. Just as the Irish Republic was about to launch itself into a PR exercise proclaiming its modernity – the first stirrings of the Celtic Tiger, in fact – along comes this musical 'return of the repressed'.

There is not the space to go into the long journey by which MacGowan's reputation has been rehabilitated – sainted even – back in Ireland, but it is clearly linked to the success of The Pogues in America. Their 'Fairytale of New York' was perhaps the only song ever to accord counter-cultural heroism to the New York Police Department and, certainly after 9/11, the Pogues' music is regularly referenced as a kind of blue collar heroism. Think of the ways in which the Pogues are used as an unofficial soundtrack for the cop show, *The Wire*. (11)

III

I have already suggested how the mouth takes on a particular resonance in the experience of the Irish emigre, how it becomes a central mark of difference. Think of Samuel Beckett and his play 'Not I', in which a pitch black stage is illuminated by a single spotlight trained on the character's mouth. Think of the novels of Edna O'Brien. As Maureen O'Connor has so brilliantly pointed out, mouths are everywhere in O'Brien's novels: licking, yawning, swallowing, grimacing, biting, shrieking, chewing, singing: they are the site of her characters most profound emotional dramas, a way of testing or tasting the truth of their lives. (2013:5:2)

Think of Francis Bacon's Portraits of Screaming Popes – those famous triptychs about which Bacon said that he wanted to paint the mouth in the way that Monet painted a sunset. It is perhaps no mistake that after the Pogues split up, MacGowan's next band was called The Popes.

Before MacGowan, the most famous mouth in rock's history belonged to the Rolling Stones. The cover of their 1971 album 'Sticky Fingers' inscribed that now infamous pop-porn image of the red lips and tongue into a corporate copyrighted logo. MacGowan gave the mouth a new face.

There is not an article that I could find written about Shane MacGowan that does not mention his teeth. Whether it be with shock, disgust or derision – everyone feels moved to comment on it. At some point his mouth became a metonym for his drinking, a kind of testament to the decay of alcoholic addiction. It is as though he is a version of popular music's Dorian Gray, his mouth a portrait of the years of accumulated indulgence. Yet there is emphatically no shame on his part, no coy covering of the mouth or pursing of the lips. On the contrary, he seems to almost wield his mouth like a weapon, to flaunt his broken dentistry with a mixture of indifference and defiance.

The mouth, I would suggest, is central to our sense of selfhood. It is the chamber in which we enact the drama between Me and Other, between what is inside of us and what is outside, between language and the body.

If The Rolling Stones' mouth was a Warhol – kitsch, commercial, comic book, MacGowan's is a Francis Bacon – dissipated and monstrous, yet also triumphant and unrepentant. MacGowan's mouth, as it were, tells its own story.

Bibliography

Berger, John (1980) *Ways of Seeing*, London, Writers and Readers Publishing Cooperative.

Campbell, Sean (2011) *Irish Blood English Heart: Second Generation Irish Musicians in England*, Dublin, Cork University Press.

Eagleton, Terry (1996) *Heathcliff and The Great Hunger: Studies in Irish Culture*, London, Verso.

Enright, Anne (2007) *The Gathering*, London. Vintage.

Kun, Josh (2005) *Audiotopia: Music, Race and America*, Oakland, University of California Press.

Lloyd, David (2008) *Irish Times, Temporalities of Modernity*, Dublin, Field Day.

Meaney, Geraldine (2007) 'Not Irish Enough? Masculinity and Ethnicity in *The Wire* and *Rescue Me*' in Balzano, Mulhall and Sullivan (eds), *Irish Postmodernisms and Popular Culture*, London, Palgrave Macmillan (pp.3–14).

O'Connor, Maureen (2013) 'Animals and the Irish Mouth in Edna O'Brien's Fiction' in *Journal of Ecocriticism* 5(2) July. University of Northern British Columbia. Online at https://ojs.unbc.ca/index.php/joe/index

Reynolds, Simon (2005) *Rip It Up And Start Again: Post-Punk 1978–1984*, London, Faber.

Family

Elizabeth Baines
The Uncertainty of Reality

When I was submitting my first piece of fiction for publication, a short story, my immediate and very strong impulse was to do so under a pen name, the name I have used for publication ever since. People often ask me why I did, and I have never found it easy to answer. I have come up with reasons that have seemed true, and still seem so, but they somehow haven't got to the core of the matter. There was something obscure, so obscure to me that my first tentative, and jettisoned, draft for this essay didn't even include a mention of the fact that my writing name is not my real name; I didn't recognise at the outset, or perhaps I was simply suppressing, unable to face or handle, the fact that adopting a pen name was central to the issues involved for me in writing out of a second-generation immigrant background.

When I took on the pen name *Elizabeth Baines*, I didn't think, in any very conscious way, that I was protecting my family. I wasn't in those initial days writing about my family. 'I didn't want my mum to know I was writing about sex,' I have said to students and audiences at readings, which gets a good laugh, and is indeed quite true. Yet it feels fraudulent in its flippancy. There was something deeper: the mention of 'my mum' in that simple explanation for my pen name, and the thought of my family background that accompanied it, always conjured for me, in a half-conscious way, a sense of something larger and more amorphous that needed to be protected, beyond the mere matter of the sexual content of that story. At the time, however, the thing that was uppermost in my mind when I decided on a pen name was the thought of my story being rejected. I was afraid that it wasn't good enough, wouldn't be acceptable to the literary establishment (I was writing in isolation; there were no writing courses in those days, and no culture of writing groups that I knew of). If the story came back, I reasoned to myself, then I could drop the pen name, dissociate from the ignominy of failure and start again with a clean slate. Yet in retrospect it seems to me that that impulse alone – the fear of *not being good enough*, of not being *acceptable*, and the sense of the potential need for a clean slate – was a direct legacy of my family background.

My Irish father came to England at the age of sixteen in 1932. For us, his family, his Irishness loomed monumental, though in a negative and mysterious way. I grew up with the knowledge, given to me by my mother, that on arrival in England he set about putting his past behind him, intending to make of himself a clean slate, a reinvention. Blake Morrison's memoir about his mother, *Things My Mother Never Told Me* (2003) recounts a similar situation, a parent blanking her own Irish origins. However, unlike Morrison's mother, an educated and professional Irishwoman submitting to the culture of a dominant and conformist English husband, my father never managed to erase his Irishness, identifiably Irish to the end and retaining his Westmeath accent to his dying day. Equipped only with a garage mechanic's apprenticeship on his arrival in England, and acutely aware of the anti-Irish prejudice in which England was steeped at that time, he was seized by a fear of being seen as an Irish navvy, and when he couldn't avoid doing manual work – as for much of my early childhood he couldn't – he was miserable in a way that rebounded miserably on our family. I knew too from my mother that as a young man in the RAF during the war – a brief period that had seemed like a promise of escape from his background into education and conventional social status – he had worked on avoiding the threat of being called an Irish 'Mick' by getting people to call him by a different name from his real one, Michael. She would describe for me also the difficulties that she and my father had finding lodgings in London immediately after the war, and her own shock at the signs in the windows barring 'blacks, dogs and Irish'.

However, although my mother told me these things, as a child I was never properly aware of anti-Irish prejudice, since people in general were very attracted to my father: not only did he have exceptional (and classically Irish) good looks, but in the world beyond our household he played the other, romantic Irish stereotype, the talkative charmer. I was perhaps more aware of anti-Welsh prejudice: my father, who, like so many Irish fathers before and after, compensated for his immigrant sense of social inferiority by wielding a strong, even frightening patriarchal power in the home, could be privately contemptuous about what he considered the small-mindedness of the Welsh community in which he was enjoying such popularity. In addition, my Welsh mother, an inveterate teller of tales, would tell me in vivid detail how, when she worked at the Ministry of Food in London just after the war, she was sneered at by the other female office workers for her parochial Welshness. She did add that, relegated sneerily to a small side desk, she was relegated along with a young Irish woman, but the significance of that was obliterated by the fact that as I grew older it seemed to me that what Welsh and English people loved about my father was indeed his 'Irishness'.

Looking back from this distance it is easy to see that my father was conflicted, caught between two stereotypes, the contemptible rough Irish peasant and the romantic Irish charmer, desperate to bury the one but unable to help playing up to the other.

When we were adult my father did once tell my sister something of which there had been not a single whiff when we were young: that when he was a boy in Ireland he had joined the IRA along with the other village boys. The implication was that this wasn't serious, it was just something you did; and indeed my father as I knew him was never in any way politically rebellious – keep your head down was the family motto, and my own involvement in CND protest caused my parents dismay. After my father's death my mother found among his effects a well-thumbed novel she had never set eyes on before – if he read it frequently, he never let her see it. It's *I Am Alone* by the Irish writer Walter Macken (1949) and tells the story of a young Irishman coming to England just before the war, as my father did, and encountering just the same difficulties, the prejudice and the demeaning physical work, before managing with the help of his charm to become an insurance salesman just as my father precisely did at one time. Reading this novel gave me a new understanding of my father's fear of the judgement of the outside world. Like my father, its protagonist Patrick is non-political, but his life is disrupted when he comes across an old boyhood friend who turns out to be involved in the IRA bombings that were taking place in London just before the war (and which fuelled anti-Irish prejudice), and is being hunted by the police. For the first time in my life I fully grasped why my father would want to avoid some of the associations and assumptions that being Irish – and the details of his background – could bring.

His Irishness seemed nothing to do with us, his wife and three children: we felt shut out from it. It was for others that he turned on the charm – and I would feel envy and dismay that he shared that with others and not with us – and he talked little to us about his past. And yet in every detail of our daily existence then, and right through much of the rest of our lives, my father's conflict affected us all deeply. At home his frustrations and resentments found expression in a cut-off broodiness and bad temper, and there was an atmosphere of shame in the household, and of the need for secrecy and to present a different face to the outside world. We children spent a lot of the time in fear – in physical fear of him (another thing that made him seem alien) – and an even deeper fear of the situation in our home being revealed in the outside world.

To me as a child it was simply poverty, rather than its relationship with my father's Irishness, that seemed the main source of the shame. Although by the time I was a small child my father was silent about his background (irritably blocking us when we asked, or, if he were in a good mood, telling us clearly tall tales), when he first met my mother, during the war, he had told her snippets about its rural poverty-stricken nature. He was in the RAF then and I imagine he felt at that time that he could safely speak of it as something he had left behind and overcome – perhaps, even, as proof of his prowess and charisma in overcoming it – never envisaging that after he was demobbed he would hit rock bottom again. My mother, by contrast, was – and still is – a great spinner of stories, and in compensation for my father's silence she relayed to us these glimpses of his past in a way that gave them the romanticised air of lore. There was a one-room cottage with an earth floor, many children, the parents scrabbling a living from a field at the back and taking a donkey and cart to market, and the eldest son – my father – full of spirit, performing amazing physical feats and carrying out hilarious practical jokes, and fuelled with the ambition to escape and make something big of himself in the world. In the eighties, when I travelled to Ireland to receive a writing prize, I did see this house for myself, and it fitted the description, at that time still having a bare earth floor. (Interestingly, my mother has told me that she once met the daughter of one of my father's sisters, who had also grown up in England but with a different romanticisation: she had the impression that it had been something of a rich mansion.) Some local old people did confirm for me my father's madcap character as a young boy, and he seemed to be something of a legend.

By the time I was a small child, poverty had struck again. My father was a labourer, coming home covered in brick or coal dust and, I can see now, resentment and depression. Yet it was my mother's struggles, and her shame, of which I as a child was most acutely aware. She had been brought up in a stable middle-class family in a close-knit south Wales community to which she and my father had returned from London for the birth of their first child, me. But when I was five my father's desperate search for work took us away again. We made many moves in pursuit of work for him, first within Wales and then to several towns in England, although my father was still forced to spend a lot of time working away from home on contract labouring jobs. Isolated in strange towns with three children, my lonely young mother struggled, to pay the rent, to make the housekeeping stretch, and my memories of those times are filled with a swirling sense of loss, uncertainty and dread. Yet the biggest struggle was to keep up in the outside world an appearance of stability and respectability, and indeed happiness. My mother scrimped and saved to make us clothes out of remnants and cut-downs, outside the home we must keep up a respectable appearance and manner at all times; our father, when he was home, insisted with huge sternness (and imprecations and threats) on correct table manners – holding your knife wrongly could bring a clip round the ear. We must fit like chameleons into the English community, we must conquer it by being better than it was itself at its own rules (and we must never let anyone know about the uncouthness of those clips round the ear, and worse).

Yet as children we never felt we fitted. The sense that we were *different*, and the shame of it, felt like an almost physical burden on our backs. We longed *not* to be different, and we worked hard at not being: we became experts at picking up the local accents, idioms and cultural customs within a few weeks of arriving in any new place. (Though our father would get angry at that: although he himself was quite unable after all to rid himself of 'Irishisms', he saw our adoption of strong accents and ungrammatical idioms as betraying us as working class.) Yet we were always afraid of getting it wrong: of saying something that marked us out as strange or stupid. And we always found it excruciatingly difficult to account for ourselves: to explain why we had moved so many times (often we hid that fact), or why we didn't go to Sunday School like everyone else (there were huge tensions over religion between my once-Catholic father and my once-Wesleyan mother.) And there was great fear in the burden: after all, if anyone at school found out we were so poor and were beaten so often at home, we would be instantly castigated, we would be 'common' and rough, linked with the smelly kids who sat and made trouble at the back of the class and whom everyone despised and feared and avoided.

I was eleven years old when my father's past and Ireland, which by now floated misty and grey in my mind, seemed suddenly and briefly to become more concrete and more obviously relevant. We had been vaguely aware that he had five sisters scattered throughout England, and that when our parents lived in London after the war they had been briefly in touch with one or two of them. We knew too that another of them, much younger than my father, was a nun, though to us the notion was alien and, when we first heard about it, surprising. All we knew of religion was the Wesleyan Methodism that our non-church-going father held in contempt and which therefore our mother had basically given up (we had been to chapel in Wales with our Welsh grandmother, and now and then, in order to fit in with neighbouring kids, braving our father's contempt, we had begged permission to go to Sunday School with them). And we would wonder or laugh when our mother told us that our father – who with his violence and swearing seemed so heathen – had once been expected by his mother to go into the priesthood. This nun sister, it turned out, had been writing to my father yearly, though to us children she appeared as if out of the blue when, having decided to leave the convent, she came to stay with us for a month or so. There was something monumental about this to us: we were so used to our father's origins as an abstraction (and it was that abstraction that had been so oppressive), and here it was personified, made concrete. (And he became better-tempered while she was there: in fact, we were putting on a show for her too, but at the time it seemed briefly as though things were becoming resolved.) For the first time ever we became fully aware of the fact that we had close relatives in Ireland. Our mother had always told us that in spite of our parents' lack of money, whenever he could our father had always sent money to his parents back in Ireland – it was his Irish duty as the eldest son, she always said. But I had never really thought of those parents of his as our grandparents except in mere technical terms – they were as alien and vague as the rest of it. Now however, we were fired with a sense of our own relationship to them, and we wanted to claim them; my nine-year-old sister and I sat down and wrote to our grandmother in Ireland, introducing ourselves. When we received back a very belated and cold reply it took us some time to realise, even believe, that it was a rejection. At eleven and nine years old we had failed to understand the significance for us of two other facts our mother had told us (and their obvious role in the tension in our household over religion): that in her letters, our father's mother never referred to our mother by her first name, but as Mrs, and the fact that, having declined in spite of his mother's pleas to bring us children up in the Catholic faith, in his absence and without his knowledge, our father had been excommunicated from the Catholic Church, a fact that he found out only later from a third party.

Thus our father was squeezed from both sides, suffering a double prejudice: rejected and exiled from the background for which in England he could be ostracised, spurned for his espousal to a country that was all too likely to spurn him. This was the cloud under which he lived, and which in turn darkened the lives of the rest of us, his family.

I have to say that even now, all these years later, with my father long dead, I am not entirely comfortable writing this, here in this essay: it still feels like a betrayal. In the end he did make something of himself, obliterating his origins with the persona of a successful businessman in a small English town. I am sure that he would be heartbroken to have me lay out here for all to read the things he worked so hard to hide, and which he would not expect people to understand. And it's not just my father I feel I'm betraying: fierce privacy is the legacy he left for all the family.

And I am racked by the thought: who am I to say what my father felt and what motivated his life, especially when he was so taciturn about it all? Isn't it my right only to account for myself? Yet there is no way I can account for myself, unless I too dissemble, since an honest account of myself must include my experience of my parents, and my hunches and assumptions about them.

But then again, can I with any certainty account for my

own experience of being a child in that family? The way I have presented it above is how it has seemed to me as I have sat at my desk remembering and typing, but the trajectory of my theme has caused me to leave out those moments when it didn't seem so bad. Those were the times when my father was in a good mood; when he *did* share with us some of the persona he showed the outside world, when he joked, grinning wickedly, when he would take out his flute or his fiddle and play those Irish tunes, and his Irishness seemed a wonderful thing by which we were glad to warm ourselves. Those were the times which I believe ultimately caused my sister in adulthood to identify as Irish in a way we had previously not done. These are the things that others in the family remember, or would prefer to remember.

There were always different versions of us as a family, and as a child I would puzzle over which was the real one. Even as a small child I was very aware that we were *pretending* to the outside world, yet I would think: but were we? Wasn't the family we presented to others after all the real one? After all, we had come from a stable, happy environment in south Wales: that was the real us, and it was what we longed to be again. We were like caterpillars waiting to become the selves we really were. In my rebellious teens I was aware of my own power to expose my father, who was still beating us, but I could never wield it. At the very thought, I would suffer physical symptoms of panic – racing heart, dry mouth, sweating – panic at the thought of the social ruin of my family and frightened to lose that alternative reality. Those feelings have not entirely gone away.

This I think is why I have always been drawn to fiction, with its ability to accommodate alternative and multiple realities, and its lack of claim to be *fact*. And looking back, I think that this was perhaps a strong motive in adopting a pen name, although I didn't formulate it at the time. I'd never felt I had any authority over reality, but – if I wrote it well enough – I could have authority over the truth of a single piece of fiction (and in a different piece of fiction I could explore – with authority – an alternative truth). And I wanted to name that authoritative author who felt so separate from my doubting, uncertain identity as the daughter of my family. So I didn't, as other writers have done, adopt another family name with which I felt myself associated, or think one up out of my own fancies or pretensions. Instead, I asked my husband to put a pin twice on the Births and Deaths columns in the newspaper. This was highly symbolic; I wouldn't even do it myself; it needed to be that impersonal, that detached from my *self.* And then there they were, *Elizabeth* and *Baines*, two names that together could name my fiction, with no associations with my day-to-day self.

I suppose there was also to some extent the continuation of a more personal impulse of *escape* away from my real-life social existence, an impulse that had first started me writing fiction compulsively at a very early age. For me as a child fiction was a crucial haven from the uncertainties of our life. In fiction people were explained: people had backgrounds that were accounted for, events had clear causes, motives were clear, or if not, if there was a mystery, then that mystery was always solved in the end. By the age of six I was writing stories of my own. In many ways, of course, my background gave me the facility: the practice in alternative realities, as well as the fiction- and drama-writing skill of ventriloquism we learned in our constant moves throughout the country, adopting new accents and customs; our mother, actively making up for our father's silence, constantly told us tales about the past, and imbued us with the story-telling mode. Writing fiction of my own, fiction in which I could mimic the certainty and social norms I saw in the fiction I read, was a way of making a bridge with the outside world: teachers praised my writing. By the age of eight I was determined to be a writer when I grew up, and as I grew I saw writing quite clearly as my way of saving myself.

Eventually I came to see that fiction could be more than a salve and a way of *fitting* in; it could, on the contrary, be a way of seeking the truth and challenging the norms. I stopped making up stories I thought *acceptable* – as that first sent-off story most certainly was: in spite of my worries, it was accepted for publication straight away – and moved towards exploring in fiction my sense of the multiple, slippery nature of reality.

Although I haven't until now directly used the childhood I have described as material for fiction, my adult work was always about the issues it raised – issues of reality and perspective, of silencing and power, and the enabling power of storytelling versus its tyranny. One thing my background has taught me is that things can seem one thing and be quite another, or can reverberate at different times and in different lights with different, and contrasting, meanings. When I was very young – four, five years old – before I was aware of the religious tensions between my parents, the image of Christ was a comforting one, coming to me as it did via the Wesleyan Methodism of my mother and my comfortable Welsh grandmother. This was the 'gentle Jesus meek and mild' who turned the other cheek and healed the sick and suffered the little children to come unto Him. Later, when I saw that religion through my father's contemptuous (and, I see now, unhappy) eyes, and when I had been rejected by my Catholic Irish grandmother, and understood how the Catholic Church had rejected him in a way that seemed so cold and cruel, the connotations of that image became overlaid with others – feelings of anxiety and exclusion. The Catholic image of the bleeding heart seemed unbelievably violent and cruel, yet I was acutely aware that for others – my ex-nun aunt, for instance – it was not. Together for me in those images were the contradictory associations of succour and pain. In fact, for much of my childhood I saw the world through a kind of double exposure, through competing, often opposite connotations. As a result, I don't find entirely unproblematic the creative-writing mantra 'show don't tell' with its danger of assumption of consensus about the meanings of the appearance of things, and my early short stories specifically question this notion. Early stories such as 'Rat Trial' (1978) and 'Icing-Sugar Tree' (1979) are strongly imagistic, but operate by taking a central image – in the former, experimental rats in a cage; in the latter, a cherry tree in blossom – and investigating the possible various and even contradictory meanings of those images, for both the characters and the thematic concerns of the stories. My first novel, *The Birth Machine* (2010), is precisely about knowledge and power, and the language of power, and most especially about the dangers of certainty, explored here in the context of 'scientific' certainty. The novel continues a concern with the fluidity of imagery, conflating for instance the positive image of roses with the negative image of spilt blood, and the hypodermic needle with the magic spindle, and leans heavily on fairytale, that prime expression of paradox and transformation.

Fairytale was a huge aspect of my father's Irishness, and one of the ways in which he *was* attractive to us children, and creatively nourishing. When he did speak about Ireland, he did so in fairytale terms: they were so poor, he would tell us, that he and his sisters had to gather nettles to cook for tea. While we soon suspected these scraps of being tall tales, they were nevertheless imbued with a picturesque romance that could not but affect us. And he really did believe in fairies. He said he had seen them, and that in Ireland he had seen the Will o' the Wisp, and had heard the Banshee. While contributing to our sense of his difference – it made him seem gifted and in touch with special dimensions of the world – it gave us a precious, and indeed saving, sense of magic. (On the other hand, there was an aspect to this supernatural gift that frightened us: we understood he had an ability to put curses on people, and when he was angry with us, which was a lot of the time, we were terrified he would put a curse on us, his alien Welsh-English children.) From this distance, I can see that he too had a psychological need for the sense of some kind of magic power, and for the nourishment of fairytales with their promise of the possibility of transformation – the frog turning into a prince, the skivvy into a princess – and the sense of forces outside yourself to blame for your misfortune but with the potential to lift you out of it into fortune at any moment. I see it as significant that the first book my father bought me – just after I had learnt to read – was a beautifully illustrated Hansel and Gretel.

Fairytale was thus always a huge, and comforting, part of my mental landscape, but as I became adult I grew aware of its role in our family as a salve for painful truths. It seemed natural, therefore, to use the multiple and paradoxical implications of fairytale when I came to explore in my writing my sense of competing realities, and also to use those fairytale tropes of transformation, as others turned out to be doing, to expose the patriarchal structures under which I had grown up. *The Birth Machine* (2010) is a rewriting of the tale of Sleeping Beauty, in which the woman forced into supine passivity (on a hospital bed) is released not by the prince, whose contemporary equivalent turns out to have been collusive with the patriarchal structures that put her there, but by her own realisation of how those structures have bound her, both practically and psychologically. Interwoven in the novel is a Hansel and Gretel reference, in which children make the mistake of believing an old woman is a witch and that therefore she poses a supernatural danger to them, making them overlook the fact that an all too human danger comes from a human man, and thus rendering them more vulnerable to him. My novel, *Too Many Magpies* (2009), which specifically deals with the psychological need for a sense of magic, and again with the danger of magic thinking in so-called science, constantly recalls the magpie rhyming spell.

These stratagems have been instinctive; I didn't consciously or rationally choose them as indirect ways of tackling the subject of my background, but I can see now that that's what they are. When I first began publishing I was very aware of the middle-class ethos of the industry, that the more 'middle class' my characters or literary voice, the more likely I was to be published. I could make the choice whether or not to continue to conform to such literary norms, as I had in childhood, or to challenge them. It did not occur to me that my own literary techniques, which I saw as part of my challenge, were indeed another kind of veiling. Fairytale, allegory, myth and fantasy are of course time-honoured ways of writing indirectly about reality, of exploring socially or politically taboo subjects by removing them out of the societally particular into the universal. The more conscious I have become that this is what I have been doing, the more impatient I have become with the indirectness. Increasingly it has seemed to me to be a continuation of the imperative by which our family felt forced to live, a subsuming of our particularity into more generalised, accepted and recognised norms. I've come to accept that I've been labouring under the continuing sense that our particular family experience is so peculiar it is inexpressible, since no one would understand it or relate to it, however well I managed to express it. Conscious too of the fact that this is how certain cultural experiences come to be silenced and lost, I feel increasingly moved to challenge this and explore in my fiction the specific cultural situation of families like mine, and the issues arising from its particular ethos and textures.

Yet I am not exactly finding it easy, either emotionally or practically.

I have finally found myself, here in this essay, able to share frankly in writing my memories of my childhood, but the essay mode allows me to state outright that this is *my* version of our past, and that even I am uncertain of the reality of that version. Paradoxically, although fiction is where I have always felt that competing realities can be explored and accommodated, fiction now seems more dangerous in terms of exposing and damaging others. Firstly, since fiction operates dynamically on the emotions it can seem to offer the most searing and convincing truth. Secondly, once you start writing a piece of fiction, whatever real-life facts you begin with, imagination and the dynamics of story more often than not take over and lead you away from mere factual truth with exaggerations, distortions and indeed fabrications. And, as I was acutely aware all along, if a single fiction *does* lean on apparently factual truth, it most often provides only a snapshot, or one side, of a situation. Looking at Part 1 of my fiction piece here, 'Guidelines for a Daughter at her Irish Father's Funeral', I see that what it expresses most strongly is the anger that I did indeed, for much of my life, feel towards my father and our family situation. It draws on a time in my life when I did feel particularly angry, and in representing that, is emotionally authentic. But it is not the whole story. My anger would always alternate with love, and a sincere urge to stand up for my family against the world – and anger towards them is not something I ever feel now. Nowadays, from a longer perspective, I can see the situation more holistically.

I have thus come to realise that of my unconscious reasons for choosing a pen name to write fiction, protecting my family was after all crucial. However, that pen name can no longer provide this protection. Needless to say, it wasn't long after I started publishing that I had to appear in public as Elizabeth Baines, and not long after that, it was necessary to admit that *Elizabeth Baines* was a pen name. Nowadays many people who know me in life take Elizabeth Baines as my real name (since it's through my writing that they got to know me personally) and, like a nickname, it has become one of the names by which I, the real-life person, am known and with which, in personal life, I identify. It is easy to trace back from that pen name, via the real-life me, to my family origins, and one website, I discovered recently, has indeed done so.

Recently, feeling the need to ask permission, I discussed with two members of my family the possibility of publishing a novel based in our past, and was asked urgently to adopt a new pen name: that was the only circumstance under which one of them could feel happy with my doing so. But it's no longer possible for a writer to remain hidden behind the work. The moment a book is published there are author interviews and profiles and readings (you simply won't be published if you don't agree to this): writers' faces and the personalities they present to the world are attached to their writing. In these days when writers are expected to help out with marketing, and social media are the chief means of doing so, it's a tough job preventing your books from being overlaid with what people know, or think they know, of your personal life, and thus to prevent your books from being read as true personal history.

Add to this the fact that, with an increasing cultural insistence on 'reality' (which seems to me an unconscious reflex reaction to the fact that in our marketing culture we are constantly peddled and swallow fictions), there is an growing tendency to read fiction biographically in this way, and it is an irony that, of all the fiction categories, it is literary fiction that is most frequently sold on the looks and personal stories of its authors – presumably because it is the hardest of all fiction categories to sell – and thus the most liable to biographical readings, with publishers eager to flag the autobiographical nature of novels on their jackets whenever possible.

At the start of *Mantrapped* (2011), Fay Weldon's 'reality novel' as she calls it, written in direct response to this trend and alternating a fictional story with her confessed autobiography, she makes the following statement:

> Novels alone are not enough. Self-revelation is required. Readers these days demand to know the credentials of their writers, and so they should. (Weldon, Kindle Edition, 2011)

It's hard to know how serious the supremely ironical Weldon is being here, but her publishers are apparently in earnest, and here is the way they represent Weldon's argument on Amazon:

> ...in a world in which the writer can no longer hope to be anonymous, it is *devious, and indeed dishonourable*, to keep yourself out of your own books [my italics].[11]

It is a sentence that for me recreates the identity crisis that pervaded my childhood (and beyond), the oppressive sense of cultural pressure to account for oneself, and the impossibility of doing so, the panicked fear of misrepresentation, by others and by oneself, and the fear of breaking family taboos and damaging other people.

I posed a question on Twitter: is it at all possible nowadays, in any way, to write anonymously? The answer was a resounding silence. There was not a single response. It was as if people were embarrassed by the stupidity of the question (of course it's not possible!), or didn't even understand it, simply couldn't imagine such a thing. Or find it even interesting: why would you want to do such a thing? It's as if we all take for granted now that we should know a writer's 'credentials'.

Is it possible to find a mode for fiction that somehow challenges biographical readings?

A possible answer seemed to be to juxtapose a story based on the facts of my childhood as I remember them with a fictional family's contradictions. But are there other ways of steering readers away

---

11 Amazon page for *Mantrapped* by Fay Weldon. https://www.amazon.co.uk/
Mantrapped-Fay-Weldon-ebook/dp/B005806P3Y/ref=sr_1_1?ie=UTF8&
qid=1545387523&sr=8-1&keywords=Fay+Weldon+mantrapped.   Accessed
21.12.201

from reading a story as incontrovertible fact, and definitive? Part 1 of 'Family Story', 'Guidelines for a Daughter at her Irish Father's Funeral', was an attempt to look for some ways. I avoided the past tense because of its ring of historical certainty. The present tense seemed not much better: it seems to me that the immediacy and sense of felt experience that present tense can create can prompt readers, in the present climate, into literal biographical readings. First-person narration was out of the question: while on one hand it's technically a declaration of narrator bias, it is of course the accepted mode of confession. Yet it felt important not to disclaim or objectify via third person: that would be too much like the cultural dissociation that characterised my childhood and that the story was about. I wanted to draw readers *into* the experience.

So the story is cast in the second person and in a future tense, and in a guideline format. The guideline format, by separating 'You' from the narrator, is intended to discourage a reading of 'You' as a simple substitute first person. 'You' is at most a putative, conditional aspect of the narrator, and could indeed be read as someone else, or 'one', anyone in that situation. Furthermore, the story concerns not a definitive past, but an imagined future, or a past re-imagined as a future and thus made pliable, fluid, potential and conditional. And, as a set of guidelines, it encodes its own conditionality: suggestions, merely, that could be deviated from, and a course of events that could fail to happen.

But can I, in the current literary climate, expect readers to note and respect such subtleties? Would it ever be possible to publish Part 1 of 'Family Story' without Part 2, and have readers understand its contingency? Is the sister in Part 2 correct when she objects that nowadays 'No one reads fiction as fiction'? Are the complexities and uncertainties of my background therefore more inexpressible than ever?

Bibliography

Baines, Elizabeth (1978) 'Rat Trial' in *New Stories 4*, ed. Harwood and King, London, Hutchinson.

Baines, Elizabeth (1979) 'Icing-Sugar Tree' in *New Stories 5*, ed. Feinstein and Weldon, London, Hutchinson.

Baines, Elizabeth ([1983, 1996] 2010) *The Birth Machine*, Cambridge, Salt.

Baines, Elizabeth (2009) *Too Many Magpies*, London, Salt.

Macken, Walter (1949) *I Am Alone*, London, Macmillan.

Morrison, Blake ([2002] 2003) *Things My Mother Never Told Me*, London, Vintage.

Weldon, Fay ([2004] 2011) *Mantrapped*, London, Harper Perennial Kindle.

Ray French
Rage

This Ireland exists: but whoever goes there and fails to find it has no
claim on the author.
Irish Journal, Heinrich Böll 1957

My father believed that leaving Ireland was the biggest mis-
take he'd ever made. While my mother seemed perma-
nently scarred by her impoverished childhood, he trans-
formed his from base metal into gold. After a few years in Britain
he became convinced the life of a penniless Irishman in County
Wexford was far superior to that of an unskilled labourer in a pol-
lution-ridden industrial town. His second biggest mistake was to
get married and father a child and then, the final nail in the coffin,
saddle himself with a mortgage. Our man to man talks went like
this: 'Don't ever get married, boy. If you feel lonely get yourself a
dog, a dog is a great companion. A dog would never give you any
bother. Go on now, go out and play.'

Though my father didn't hear De Valera's famous St Patrick's

Day speech of 1943 since he was serving on a Royal Navy destroyer in the Atlantic, his view of Ireland was very close to the one imagined in that much lampooned broadcast: 'The ideal Ireland that we would have … would be the home of a people who valued material wealth only as a basis for right living, of a people who, satisfied with frugal comfort, devoted their leisure to the things of the spirit…'. (RTÉ Archives)

My father also fondly imagined Ireland as a rural haven, free from the corrupting influence of capitalism, its poverty a price worth paying for rejecting so-called progress in favour of the more spiritually fulfilling pleasures of the simple life.

He would outline to my mother and me how he planned to live once we returned to the auld country: 'A man wouldn't need a job in Ireland, he'd live off the land and the sea if he had his wits about him. You'd get yourself a field there for ten quid – Jayzus, you'd get 2 or 3 fields – and then build your own house on it, sure Ray would help me.' This was the uncle I was named after, quietly spoken, courteous and thoughtful, he was the kind of Irishman conspicuously missing from the popular imagination. Ray regarded my father as a hilarious cartoon who provided everyone with a good laugh every August with his mad schemes. Working with a wild-eyed dreamer like him, who rushed everything and frequently botched the simplest jobs would have driven a meticulous workman like my uncle to distraction.

My father's plan was that when we returned to the auld country we'd become completely self-sufficient, collecting driftwood and turf to burn on the fire (the fact that Wexford was an agricultural county with no bogs, that they dug and burnt turf in the west, didn't deter him, he'd figure something out). We'd cook on the fire too, like the old-timers my father took me to visit who hung a great blackened pot over the flames in their huge fireplace and made endless stews. They were in their late eighties and kept telling me I had the look of a French, no-one could mistake me for anything else. There was something about the way they looked at me when they said it which I found unsettling. Later it dawned on me that these visits were probably his attempt to bring me on board with his plan to return. They were a nice couple but their house was miles from anywhere, festooned with holy pictures and statues, but no telly or books and there was a pervasive smell of damp.

My father would also need a boat, and it took him several years to raise the money by stealing lead from the factory where he worked. He would tie the contraband around his waist with rope, button up his donkey jacket, then cycle out past the security man on the gates with a cheery, 'Good night now', only occasionally wobbling under the enormous weight. Every month a thin, seedy-looking man who bore a striking resemblance to Alan Burke, star of *Public Eye*, the grim but compelling private eye TV series, would arrive. Under cover of darkness the two of them would carry the lead from the shed into a van parked in the back lane, then the man would hand my father a wad of cash.

Once he had a boat my father's plan was complete, and he looked forward to catching cod and pollock every day and eating them with a big mound of floury Irish spuds grown in his garden, a different class of a thing altogether to the waxy auld things you'd get here. There'd be no gas or electric bills either, for in this simple cottage by the sea we'd rely on oil lamps – he believed the harsh glare emitted by electric light made people cantankerous. Exhibit A – my mother, who'd been so sweet natured when they were court-ing in Ireland, but whose personality changed after a few years of living in Britain, getting cranky on him whenever he brought up his plans to return home. The reason for this alarming change was clear. A naive Irish woman like her simply wasn't equipped to deal-ing with the prolonged exposure to electric light in Britain, and it had unhinged her.

There he'd be, turf burning on the fire, his foot tapping to the jigs and reels coming from RTÉ, as content as any Lord at home in his ancestral pile. And once my mother joined him and realized how much happier and relaxed she was sitting in the warm, soft light of an oil lamp she'd be won over, and finally realise just how lucky she was to have such a far-sighted husband.

'What a grand life it would be – and it wouldn't cost you a penny.'

This mantra was repeated on a daily basis, until it drove my mother crazy.

'Go on then, go back there, see if I bleddy care.'

'I bleddy will.'

The simple cottage by the sea became the Holy Grail that dominated my father's dreams for decades, but in the meantime he was stuck in Newport, south Wales, a place clotted with factories, docks and noisy, crowded streets. My father's hatred of urban life was visceral, and it frequently drove him into a rage.

'Breathing in petrol fumes, factories pumping muck into the air, tiring your feet out walking on concrete all day, there's no give in it at all, teenagers walking past with transistor radios stuck to their ears, listening to a shower of hairy gobshites screaming "Yeah, yeah, yeah". Oh god, you'd have to be a madman to go up town of a night, you'd be subjecting yourself to all kinds of indignity. Fellas roaring and shouting, staggering about mad with beer, you'd never know when one of them might go for you, or spew up all over your good clothes. The women are just as bad. Plastered in war paint, shrieking and swearing at the top of their voices, completely out of control, no bit of shame at all. Oh Christ, don't talk to me about towns. There's no bit of peace and contentment to be had in a town at all.'

Back in Ireland, he could walk out of the front door, stride along the cliffs and roam for hours without seeing another soul. Something he often did as a youth, to escape the constant bickering and fighting. 'Don't cross my bows', he'd mutter in disgust as another shopper cut across him, forcing him to slow down. His conversation was peppered with nautical terms. How he wished other people would keep a safe distance, just like ships at sea gave each other a wide berth.

My father may not have been a highly educated man, but he was the only adult who talked to me passionately about ideas when I was young, even if they were often a little on the extreme side. Once, on our way to the station to meet one of my uncles he grabbed my arm and stopped me in my tracks outside British Home Stores.

'Look.'

'What?'

'At the tide of screeching humanity all around us. Christ, they're like fecking rats.'

A documentary about rats had made a lasting impression on him. Apparently if you kept on cramming more and more rodents into a confined space, eventually they would be able to stand no more and begin attacking each other. A finding that made perfect, chilling sense to him. He thought that the documentary was a warning for humanity, that it was surely only a matter of time before Newport, London, New York or Peking erupted in an orgy of violence.

Years later I realized the documentary must have been based on the work of John Calhoun, an American ethologist who became world famous for his studies of population density and its potentially catastrophic effects on human behaviour. The findings seemed like a dark prophetic vision of the End-Time, overwrought and easily dismissed, but one you might, all the same, be foolish to ignore. So there we stood, the two us, while the impatient, puzzled folk of Newport squeezed past, absorbed in everyday mundane pursuits that they never stopped to question. My father was the only man who took the time to stop and reflect on the big questions: *Who are we, really? Is this the best we can do, isn't it worthwhile taking time out to consider if we've taken a wrong turn?* And I, his son, who would go on to be the first member of my family to attend University stood next to him, beginning to grasp that the unexamined life is not worth living and to surreptitiously scrutinize the good people of Newport for early signs of descent into rodent-like savagery.

'You see,' said my father, speaking out of the side of his mouth, like Bill Shankly channeling Elliot Ness, 'this is why we'd all be better off back in Ireland.'

This was the way his stories always ended. I remember how at his wake in Ireland my aunt said to me, 'That man should never have left Ireland', and I could only agree. But by the time he'd retired and was free to return, the Ireland he knew was already rapidly disappearing.

My mother, on the other hand, never regretted leaving the insular, feudal backwater of the late 1940s, a place firmly in the grip of the moneyed elite masquerading as proud nationalists. She drummed into me how lucky I was to be born in Wales, where I was guaranteed a good education and free healthcare and would never be forced to learn that awful Irish language, which she associated with a sharp blow to her opened palm with a wooden ruler every time she got a word wrong in school. In this country I would have the chance to ascend the ladder in a meritocracy and speak only English, as it wasn't until the 1980s that Welsh was taught as a second language in Newport, and many in south Wales still regarded the Welsh language with the same kind of distaste and suspicion as the English did. My mother would sometimes tune into the Welsh language channel by mistake and panic – my father would yell, 'Quick, get rid of that awful yakking, switch it to HTV West!' I pointed out that we were, to be fair, living in Wales, but realised that hearing the Welsh language reminded them of the humiliation they'd endured at the hands of the brutal teachers who'd taught them Irish. They only wanted to speak and hear English. Even in Wales.

My mother's simmering resentment about how she'd been treated in Ireland would always bubble over on St Patrick's Day: 'All those Irishmen crying into their stout about the auld country – they make me sick. If they love it so much why don't they go back there, the good for nothing lousers?' She held all rebel songs and stories about brave Irish martyrs in contempt. At her parents' house in Ireland a faded tea caddy celebrating the coronation of Queen Elizabeth II, perched in pride of place on the top shelf in the kitchen, was treated with the reverence usually accorded to the Pope or JFK. My mother, like her parents, believed Ireland had gone backwards since the English left, an opinion I was intrigued to hear recently echoed by Sinead O'Connor: "Frankly, I wish England had never left Ireland, I think we would be a lot better off. We were going to be colonised by someone, and as it happened the coloniser who took over was the church and that was disastrous. If the Brits hadn't left that wouldn't have happened."[12]

The Ireland she left in 1950 offered precious few opportunities for the poorly educated daughter of a farm labourer. Kevin O'Higgins, the Free State's first minister for justice and external affairs proclaimed: 'we were probably the most conservative-minded revolutionaries who ever put through a successful revolution.' (Lee 2012:105). John Banville recalled how in the 1950s and 60s, his history teachers 'never spoke of the 1916 'revolution' but exclusively of 'the Rising', as of a holy event, something akin to the Resurrection; no doubt the word 'revolution' smacked too much of Bolshevist anarchy and godlessness.' (Banville 2015:11–14) This successful revolution's goals never included improving social mobility. We might have been working class in Wales, but every August when we went back to Ireland my mother was able to measure how much worse off she'd have been had she stayed at home. Her parents' house lacked a flushing toilet and electric light until the mid-1970s. Most of the rooms were lit by oil lamps (which undoubtedly accounted for how generous and warm hearted my relatives were). My aunt often complained that when she was back in Ireland my mother swanned around with her nose in the air like a duchess, always immaculately turned out and never deigning to lift a finger. It was true. In Wales my mother was a tireless and very generous host, but back in Ireland she tended to let others wait on her. It's a familiar trope, the returning immigrant never able to forget their humiliating childhood, desperate to prove that it hasn't defined them. My mother, in turn, was scornful of her sister, who'd no idea how hard it had been to leave and try and make a new life for herself in another country, instead of settling for slow suffocation in rural Ireland.

Ireland, like America, likes to present itself as a classless society, a land where everyone, from merchant bankers to road sweepers, are rubbing shoulders in bars up and down the land every night, enjoying the egalitarian craic. Thirty years after my parents left Ireland the magazine *Magill*[13] produced a hard hitting issue on poverty,

12 'The Irish Rock Story: A Tale Of Two Cities' BBC4 13 March 2015.

13 *Magill* Vol 3, No. 7, April 1980 https://magill.ie/archive/magazine-archive

revealing that nearly a third of the population were living below the poverty line. Social inequality was the greatest in the EEC; the proportion of total income going to the poorest 30% was the smallest in Europe, while the richest 30% had a far higher proportion of the total income than the EEC average. Twenty three years later, post Celtic Tiger, an Oxfam Report showed that inequality in Ireland was four times the OECD average, so although I often recoiled from my mother's bitterness about Ireland, she had a point. Little has changed even now, according to the *Irish Times* 24 August, 2016: 'Despite recovery, Ireland remains a hugely unequal society' and 'children and women are worst hit by a society whose policies refuse to cherish all its people equally' (Irish Times Archive: 24.08.2016). 'Over the last three decades, the top 10 per cent have increased their proportion of net wealth from 42 per cent to 54 per cent, while the share of net wealth held by the bottom 50 per cent has halved (from 12 per cent to 5 per cent) … By nine, there is a strong negative correlation between children's self-image and their social class background, as children from more disadvantaged backgrounds are more anxious, less happy and report poorer behaviour. By 13, children have internalised their inequality by reducing their expectations.'

My mother was determined not to be a domestic at the beck and call of some farmer for the rest of her life. She already had friends who'd moved to Newport, and so she left. What my father never grasped was that she would never return, and certainly not to a ramshackle cottage by the sea with no electric light or proper heating, to subsist on a diet of spuds and fish.

The first job my mother got in Wales was working as a domestic for two doctors in Cardiff, the very thing she'd planned to avoid. They lived in a big house on the edge of Tiger Bay, or Bute Town as it's known to the locals. She was intimidated by their wealth and assurance, certain they paid her less than their previous employees because she was a desperate Irish woman straight off the boat, but lacked the confidence to ask for more. She only lasted a few weeks. One day the phone rang when she was in the house alone. Of course she'd seen people pick up a phone and answer it in films, but she'd never had to do it herself, or known anyone who owned one. She remained frozen to the spot as the ringing echoed through the house, terrified at the prospect of answering and hearing someone with a refined accent saying irritably, 'Hello, hello? Who am I speaking to?' She ran out of the room, slammed the door behind her and ran upstairs until it stopped.

A week later she got a job in a factory in Cardiff. On the bus from Newport she was immediately welcomed by the other women who worked there, and made to feel one of the gang. In what sounds like a parody of *How Green Was My Valley*, they sang all the way to work, all the way through and all the way back, look you. After a shaky start my mother was on her way – she had always wanted to be part of a gang. Finally she'd become upwardly mobile, leaving behind her feudal past and joining the working class – money in her pocket, her time her own as soon as she clocked off, and living and working in a place where no-one knew about her past unless she chose to tell them. She took the opportunity to drop the name she'd always hated – Anne, too dull for her liking – to Nancy, which she considered glamorous, and a little racy. Her face used to light up when she talked of those early years in Wales, and I sometimes think she was never happier.

I have a photo of her on my desk as I write this, taken during that first year in Newport – she has a shock of black curly hair and is wearing a black gabardine jacket with padded shoulders, the height of fashion – she always loved to treat herself to nice clothes. Although she's obviously very self-conscious, she is staring into the camera and smiling. It's a charming smile, her face betraying none of the worry that so often marked her later years, a classic immigrant photo of a young woman who's left the old world behind and is looking forward to an exciting future. It's my favourite photo of her, perfectly capturing the way my mother constantly struggled to overcome her shyness and insecurity, determined to present a confident and happy face to the world. You only need to look at that photo to see how Ireland was a place she had to leave if she was ever to become the person she wanted to be.

My parents were the first of their crowd to have a child and take out a mortgage, and were soon putting up a string of cousins and acquaintances from back home who had come to Newport to find work. I was surrounded all day by Irish voices telling stories about back home, and their plans to return. At night we'd be joined by others who still lived in digs, and impromptu sessions on the accordion, mouth organ and spoons went on into the early hours, with me in a pram in the corner of the room. My mother would often get up and dance a jig as they played. One year in Ireland she took to the floor with her sister after a few drinks, while my uncle played the accordion. She was a good dancer, fast and nimble – I was eleven or twelve – and the sight of my drunken mother, her face flushed and clearly enjoying herself enormously, the relatives whooping and cheering as she pranced around the living room, both impressed and embarrassed me.

We were also regularly treated to visits by the parish priests from some backwater in Ireland, who could sniff out an Irish household like a grizzly bear tracking down a deer. They would be offered a chair next to the fire and hold forth on the lamentable state of the world over tea and soda bread.

'That crowd of long-haired layabouts demonstrating in London and fighting with the police, begob if I was in charge I'd shave their heads first then treat them to the birch and after that send them all to fight in Vietnam, that would soon cure them.'

My father would turn to me and say, 'Do you hear that? Listen and learn, boy. The priest is a very clever man, he should be in the government.'

When I first went to school I was mocked for pronouncing 'three' as *tree*, 'I'll' as *oil* and 'mouth' as *mouwt*. At home everyone spoke like that, but, like most children, I didn't want to be the odd one out at school, and so I learnt how to say three, there, tea, and became the odd one out at home instead. I lost my Irish accent sometime in the 1960s, when it was something to be ashamed of. Now that it is imbued with cultural capital, and is regarded as a signifier of warmth and sincerity, I sound English, an accent often, and often unfairly, taken to signify the opposite of those things.

I am reminded of a late entry in John Cheever's diary, where he reflects on his immersion in conventional suburban existence, lamenting that he felt like a spy who'd insinuated himself among the enemy and then forgotten his mission. I still often switch to an Irish accent to express outrage – 'For feck's sake!', or astonishment, 'Ah, go on' – just to remind myself that the way I sound is not the way I always feel.

My mother however was delighted when I lost my accent. When I was eighteen she told me I was English.

'How could I be English? I was born in Wales, you and dad are Irish. Where's the English in that?'

'But you speak properly, not like me and your dad.'

Although my mother loved her Welsh friends and neighbours they were, in the end, too like the Irish, too brazenly proletarian, it was the English who had the class, the kind of gravitas that the Celts never would. When I got my British passport before going on holiday she was delighted – finally at least one of us owned one. My mother, born in the early years of the Free State, was an Irish citizen and envied my father who, born in 1919 and described as a British subject on his birth certificate, would have had the right to a British passport. For her this would have bestowed respectability, official proof that she had left her shameful origins behind. If anyone ever dared to look down their nose at her again she would say, 'How dare you speak to me like that, I'll have you know my husband is a British citizen. Paddy – show this man your passport.' But he had no interest in denying his Irish blood and pledging allegiance to the Queen. To her this was yet another indication of his sentimental clinging to mawkish sentimentality, just like that shower blubbering into their stout on St Patrick's Day.

It was a sensitive issue for my father. After returning home following the Second World War he'd been accused of fighting for Ireland's oppressor several times, arguments that led to at least one fistfight. Such accusations cut deeply.

When we embarked on our annual summer holiday to Ireland in the 1960s and 70s my parents were returning to two very different countries. My mother's scathing view of her homeland epitomized post-independence disillusionment, and she often claimed if it wasn't for her family she'd never set foot in the place again. My father wasn't on speaking terms with most of his family, but nevertheless saw Ireland as a lost paradise. Both managed to find ample evidence every year to support their views.

The preparations for our two week holiday in August would begin in June — every week my father would stuff some pound notes into an A3 envelope for my uncle and aunt, grandparents and cousins. My mother would scour the charity shops for clothes and shoes, while I rehearsed my favourite Dave Allen routines, the comic famously banned in Ireland for mocking the priesthood, so I could perform them for my cousins once my deeply religious grandmother had gone to bed. The growing excitement would be stoked by the letters that arrived from Ireland wrapped inside the latest copy of *The Wexford People*, the local paper of note, which my uncle rolled as tightly as layers of filo pastry before binding it tightly with string and topping with a blob of bright red sealing wax before posting to us every week. 'The lads are looking forward to seeing us,' my father would announce, reading the enclosed letter, in case we were worried they'd changed their minds and decided to go to Monaco that August for a change.

At Newport the boat train to Rosslare was always packed with other Irish families who'd got on at Paddington. Like us, they had brought bulging suitcases, holdalls and shopping bags crammed with hand me downs, cheap electrical appliances and food for impoverished relatives back home, the aisles blocked with luggage that wouldn't fit in the overhead racks. They stared at us in surprise as we entered the carriage, no idea the diaspora included such an obscure outpost on the edge of Wales. In turn, to the handful of locals who'd got on for the short journey to Cardiff, the train must have resembled a grass roots aid convoy, bringing relief to a country whose government had failed and whose plight the UN had ignored.

My mother saw the London Irish, making themselves at home and taking up all the room, as the kind of rough Paddies she thought herself a cut above. My father, in high spirits at the prospect of enjoying his two week experiment in living a pre-capitalist lifestyle outside the European social order[14] for two weeks, saw them as soul brothers and sisters. 'Isn't it great to be going back to the auld country?' he'd proclaim, to anyone foolish enough to catch his eye. 'Jayzus you'd miss it though, wouldn't you? Living in a dirty old town would bring you down.' He'd break into the song of the same name at the top of his voice. The other passengers turned away, appalled at the prospect of sharing a carriage with this wild-eyed evangelist for the next three and a half hours. My mother would hiss, 'Paddy, don't be bothering them, can't you see they're not interested?' He'd turn to her, furious, and yell 'Less of the jawing, you. Can't you let a fella speak?' I would bury my head in my comic and hunker down, hoping to remain anonymous.

It wasn't a family holiday as such, for once he reached Irish soil we rarely saw my father. He would be up and off on his travels before we were up in the morning, and rarely returned before nine or ten at night. He'd be flushed with excitement, eager to tell us of his latest discoveries: the glory of the sun setting behind the Saltee islands, if only he'd had a camera; a great old character he'd met in a bar in Colfers over in Carrig, eighty six years old, he lived on buttermilk, spuds and stout and was as strong and healthy as a twenty year old, a great advertisement for the simple life; the grand cockles he'd gathered on the strand at Bannow Bay and washed under a pump and eaten as he walked along. He was desperate to stock up on authentic experiences before returning to the rat race. He would also fit in 'doing a few jobs for the lads', such as painting the doors, clearing the guttering or laying a concrete path. If he wasn't yet in a position to build his own house, then at least he could be helping my mother's family with theirs.

14 'As Böll puts it in his own words, Ireland seemed to be 'outside the European social order', pXiii Hamilton, Hugo (Foreword) in Holfter, Gisela (2011) *Heinrich Böll and Ireland*, Cambridge Scholars Publishing. Hamilton also writes that *Irisches Tagebuch (Irish Journal)* 'pointed the way for many Germans to an idyllic place of rescue on the edge of Europe,' and that Mary Robinson 'suggested that Ireland should claim him as a national saint' (Pxi) My relatives began noticing the increase in German tourists coming to Ireland sometime in the late 1960s, and this in turn led to some buying houses in County Wexford, a development that intrigued and pleased them as the Germans were considered good mixers.

After he died, my Aunt told me how she'd once pleaded with him to stop rushing, have a lie in, put his feet up and relax – wasn't that what holidays were for? He'd turned to her, grim-faced and replied, 'I can't, Mary, A Stór, sure I've only got two weeks to live.'

As the time to leave again drew near my parents and relatives would become upset. I would too and on the day of departure it was painful to watch my aunt turn her head aside to hide her tears as the boat pulled away from the quay. Years later when I read Eva Hoffman's description of leaving communist Poland for Canada as a thirteen year old in *Lost In Translation*, it evoked that feeling perfectly.

> 'I desperately want time to stop, to hold the ship still with the force of my will. I am suffering my first, severe attack of nostalgia, or *tęsknota* – a word that adds to nostalgia the tonalities of sadness and longing ... it comes upon me like a visitation from a whole new geography of emotions, an annunciation of how much an absence can hurt.' (Hoffman 1991:4)

I was living in London by the 1980s, and whenever I came back to Newport for a weekend my parents and I would go for a drink. Two crucial factors always needed to be taken into consideration when deciding on a suitable venue. The pub needed to serve a decent pint of Guinness, and in the 1980s in Newport it wasn't so easy to find a pint that wasn't bitter, thin stuff, a sort of ersatz stout. The second crucial factor was the danger of encountering the wrong kind of Irish people. My father began to worry about this as soon as an outing was mooted: 'You wouldn't want to get stuck in a pub with a crowd of fecking rough Paddies.' He meant the kind who peppered their conversations with coarse language, laughed too loudly, or might break into song or offer strident opinions on the situation in Northern Ireland. On the one occasion some rough-looking types entered (from Mayo he was sure – well what could you expect?), my parents sat quietly in the corner, studiously avoiding eye contact, speaking in hushed voices in case one of these roughnecks might hear their accents and attempt to include them in their conversation, *as if they had something in common*. Then all the nicely behaved Welsh people who'd made my parents feel so welcome and who never looked down their noses at them in the way that the snooty English did, would turn to each other and mutter, 'See that – they're taking over. This used to be a decent pub, now look at it.' In an instant thirty years of unstinting effort to fit unobtrusively into the host society would be undone in an instant.

So, once a suitable looking venue had been identified, it was my job to go inside and do a recce, then report back any sightings of the wrong kind of Irish people. I was the obvious candidate, as I no longer sounded Irish. The three of us had a mixture of accents that must have struck people as odd. My mother sounded Welsh, only lapsing back into her native accent when she lost her temper or returned to Ireland in the summer. My father sounded as if he'd just stepped off the boat, his accent had never altered, because in his head, where it mattered, he still lived in the auld country, and I sounded English.

Before entering our chosen pub my father would meet my gaze and hold it: 'Good man – you'd know them straight away.' To be absolutely sure the coast was clear I would hover, pretending to take an interest in what beer was on tap, or pretend to peruse the songs on the jukebox, or look as though I was searching for a friend, in case someone began talking and I would be able to identify their accent. Once I was satisfied the coast was clear I would step back outside and find my parents waiting, as still and silent as rocks, anxiously awaiting my report. If the coast was clear my father would rub his hands and say, 'Come on, let's get in there quick and grab a pint' and there'd be the usual tussle over who'd buy the first round. All would be fine for a while. But, gradually, imperceptibly the initial relief began to wear off and my parents would start to look up nervously every time a new customer came through the door. Would a shower of rough Paddies burst in just when you were settled? Oh god, wouldn't that be just typical? Once the dreaded prospect entered their minds they couldn't banish it and it became impossible to relax and enjoy their evening out: 'Oh god you may as well drink up and get out of there. Come on, let's go before we get caught, and then we'll never be able to show our faces here again.' Of course the other problem was that the two crucial factors to be taken into consideration when deciding a venue conflicted with each other, for where else would you be most likely to come across other Irish people than in a pub which served a decent pint of Guinness? So often, unable to contain my father's anxiety, we would eventually settle for grim establishments which served a rotten pint of Guinness, sparsely populated by a smattering of middle aged couples who hadn't said a word to each other in a decade, an elderly man with a decrepit dog lying at his feet and a seedy-looking bloke pumping coins into a fruit machine.

From the middle of the 1990s until the late 2000s Ireland was transformed from a sleepy backwater into one of the few western countries whose economy rivalled the performance of countries like Honk Kong and Singapore. As my parents grew older they had struggled to cope with the rapid, bewildering changes back home. My mother found this reversal of fortunes particularly hard, as it robbed her of her raison d'etre for leaving. Now she ceased to be the benefactor, the one who took pride in wearing her new clothes and handing out gifts – everyone had caught up. Her family now lavished hospitality, eager to repay *her* for the years she'd helped them out. It was painful to witness her wounded dignity.

In 2006 with the Irish economy still riding high I was one of four male writers, along with James Nash, Tom Palmer and John Siddique, who wrote memoirs of our fathers, and accounts of our own attempts at parenting in a book called *Four Fathers*. Over the next two years we did over forty readings. I approached these readings worried that I might be accused of perpetuating Irish stereotypes. But I was also angry that the Irish who'd come to Britain between the 1940s and 1970s were now being airbrushed out of history. This group were something the newly affluent Ireland would rather forget. By the height of the boom in 2007, the property supplement of the *Irish Times* was so big it had to be published in two sections. The Irish didn't want to be reminded of past failures.

However I was moved by the amount of people who told me, either in person or by email, that my story about my father had rekindled memories of their own. Several said, 'What a shame your father and mine never met, they would have got on so well.' It felt like a taboo had been broken. Clearly there was still an enormous amount of affection for that generation on this side of the Irish Sea.

Then, about a year after our last reading, came the crash. My father had stopped going to Ireland several years before, when it was still booming. He no longer felt comfortable there. His worst nightmare had come true – Ireland had lost its unique qualities, and was becoming more like other countries. While my mother went to Ireland in those final few years of his life I would visit him in Newport and keep an eye on him.

There he sits in the gathering darkness, reluctant to turn on the light and waste electricity, shaking his head in bewilderment at what kind of a place the auld country has become, as strange and unwelcoming as Newport ever was.

Bibliography

Banville, John (2015) 'Moral Lepers', review of *The Revolutionary Generation in Ireland, 1890–1923*, R.F. Foster in *London Review of Books* (Vol. **37**:14, 06.07. 2015).

Böll, Heinrich (1984) *Irish Journal*, London, Sphere Books.

French, Ray; Nash, James; Palmer, Tom; and Siddique, John (2006) *Four Fathers*, Pontefract (Route).

Hoffman, Eva (1991) *Lost In Translation*, London, Minerva.

Irish Times Archive https://www.irishtimes.com/opinion/despite-recovery-ireland-remains-a-hugely-unequal-society-1.2766053.

Lee, Joseph (1990) *Ireland, 1912–1985: Politics and Society*, Cambridge, Cambridge University Press.

Llewellyn, Richard (1939) *How Green Was My Valley*, Penguin Classics; new ed (28 Jun. 2001).

Magill Vol 3, No. 7, April 1980 https://magill.ie/archive/magazine-archive

RTÉ Archives: The Ireland That We Dreamed Of https://www.rte.ie/archives/exhibitions/eamon-de-valera/719124-address-by-mr-de-valera/

Weighing the Past

Remembering the Past, Looking to the Future, and Celebrating Writing

Kath Mckay interviews Tony Murray about the Archive of the Irish in Britain, and the Irish Writers' Summer School

Those who cannot remember the past are condemned to repeat it.[15]

The present and the future are built on the past; documentary heritage is crucial to our knowledge and understanding of the past, and to informing our identity and our future.

Anne Barrett, archivist at Imperial College[16]

---

15 https://archive.org/details/lifeofreasonorph1917sant/page/284

16 https://www.imperial.ac.uk/news/188268/imperial-hosts-event-mark-artfe-facts-joining/

I

The Archive

In 2016, the Irish Studies Centre, London Metropolitan University, celebrated its thirtieth anniversary. The centre was the first of its kind in Britain, with its main purpose to promote Irish Studies as an academic area. Professor Bronwen Walter (Anglia Ruskin University) has said that one of the most important things it has done has been 'to put the Irish in Britain on the map'.[17]

Researchers at the Irish Studies Centre have always considered themselves to be at the 'coalface' of research, with their work springing from people's lived experiences, and feeding back into active change. For instance, a ground-breaking conference (Northern Ireland: What Next?) in 1995, attended by the DUP and Sinn Fein three years before the Good Friday agreement, helped seed the peace process.

Under its umbrella, two of the centre's main areas of work are The Archive of the Irish in Britain (AIB) and an annual Irish Writers in London Summer School

Dr Tony Murray, Director of the Irish Studies Centre 2012–17, now Curator of the Archive and Director of the Summer School, believes that that the Archive is an important and invaluable resource about aspects of Irish life in Britain.

It began informally in the 1980s, as part of a community project in Brent. The Irish in Britain History Group had been set up to collect documentation and oral interviews on the Irish in Britain, as nothing of its kind was being done.

The Archive now comprises a collection of documents, audio and video recordings, books, photos and ephemera that catalogue the history of the Irish in Britain from the late nineteenth century to the present day. Students, researchers, academics and journalists from Britain, Ireland, and all over the world consult the archives.

Tony, who ran an Irish community bookshop (Green Ink), and

---

17 https://student.londonmet.ac.uk/library/using-the-library/special-collections/the-archive-of-the-irish-in-britain

a literary festival before studying and subsequently teaching Irish Studies (and English Literature), says that when he worked in the bookshop in the nineteen nineties 'I found a great constituency of lay Irish custodians, with an enormous knowledge of Irish history. Gradually people brought along stories about migration, and arte-facts and mementos, documents and objects. It was not planned, but it was the nucleus of a collection.'

He points out that the mid-80s were a time of dramatic change, with a new wave of migration from Ireland to London and the South-East. When the Irish Studies Centre was set up in 1986, a year after the Anglo-Irish agreement, Tony began to take an interest in Irish Studies. Like many other students who studied under the tutorage of Professor Mary Hickman and others on the degree programme of the Irish Studies Centre, he wanted to explore the Irish side of his London Irish heritage. Irish Studies included archaeology, literature and sociology.

Tony returned from living abroad, to work at the Irish Studies Centre in 1995. Based for many years in the Holloway Road branch of the university, close to a sizeable Irish community, the Archive is now housed in a larger space in Aldgate, with professional archivists from Special Collections taking specific responsibility for it.

The Archive received support from the Irish government in 1999, which enabled them to obtain subsequent funding from the Smurfit Foundation and others in the following decade.

'With funding, we expanded, put on exhibitions, made a documentary film (*I Only Came Over for a Couple of Years*, available on the open access AIB website), interspersing the 2003 St Patrick's Day parade with interviews with Irish elders,' says Tony.

'The Irish Embassy has been supportive. The Irish President, with family in Manchester, has taken a special interest, and been enormously supportive.'

Michael D. Higgins visited in 2016, for the thirtieth anniversary celebrations of the Centre.

'There are gaps in the Archive,' Tony admits. With no resources for searching out material 'We are dependent on people coming to us.'

Because of this, the Archive has more on London than other areas. But when able to expand a little, they did a touring exhibition *When Did You Come Over?* (2000–2003) that went to Birmingham and Leeds and other cities with Irish communities:

'We understood then that various Irish communities were unaware of each other's work, and this was a way of reaching out. Now we see the Archive more as a hub.'

In 2003 article *Holding up a Mirror to the Irish in Britain*, on the AIB website,[18] Tony Murray wrote of the launch of a scheme 'to preserve, catalogue, expand and disseminate a unique collection of documents, photos, books and audio visual materials relating to the Irish in Britain'. As part of the launch, items from the Archive were exhibited in public for the first time.

He continued 'My abiding memory from the time is watching the way in which people saw their own experience of migration and life in Britain reflected back to them in a way that is still relatively rare for our own community … the fact that so many visitors to the exhibition wanted to contribute to the development project … convinced me of the importance of ensuring that such a venture had to at least attempt to be as inclusive and representative as possible.'

The thinking has always been to preserve, expand and disseminate the Archive. To this end, funded by the Irish government's Emigrant Support Programme, and timed to fit in with their move to Aldgate, in 2018 the Archive has just completed a major digitization project of some of their collections. Materials digitized include the St Patrick's Day Programme Collections, papers of the late nineteenth century London Irish writer, Winifred M Patton, historical records of the London Irish Centre and the Irish County Associations and ephemera of the Gaelic League of London.

'Since digitization, people are much more aware of us, and now we are inundated with offers,' says Tony. This wider accessibility is part of their long-term plan to make the collections available to all,

18 https://student.londonmet.ac.uk/library/using-the-library/special-collections/the-archive-of-the-irish-in-britain

unhampered by geographical distance or lack of mobility.

The main purpose of the digitisation project is to 'ensure that the historical and contemporary records of the Irish in Britain are preserved for posterity and disseminated ... for the benefit of current and future generations of Irish people at home and aboard ... protecting, sharing and celebrating the heritage of the Irish in Britain ... will raise awareness and deepen understanding of the Irish diaspora ... this project will nurture a sense of pride in Ireland and Irish identity abroad and help to contribute to the strengthening of Irish-British relations now and in years to come'.[19]

The archive is a fascinating place, the type of place where you go to look up one topic and get interested in many others. The contents range from community newsletters, through to articles, photos, posters, oral history recordings and donated items such as step dance medals, rosettes, sashes and banners.

Amongst their holdings are a copy of the first ever book length history of the Irish in Britain by John Denvir published in 1892, a collection of St Patrick's Day programmes produced for events in London dating back to 1922, oral history recordings of individuals' experience of migration to Britain in the 1930s, photos of Irish community events in the 1950s, political posters from the 1980s, material on a 2000 Irish Studies Centre conference on The Irish Diaspora; the prison letters of Paul Hill, and files on the Maguire Seven miscarriage of justice trial.

I asked Tony which collections in the Archive he is particularly fond of:

- 'The Winifred M. Patton collection because I have a done quite a lot of biographical research on her, so much so that I almost feel like I knew her. I think she was a remarkable woman for her time who with relatively modest means achieved so much and yet never got the recognition she deserved, partly because she sadly died of TB when she was still only in her thirties and partly because she was a woman at a time when their work was

---

19 https://student.londonmet.ac.uk/library/using-the-library/special-collections/the-archive-of-the-irish-in-britain

not considered as important as men's.'

- 'The Paul Hill Prison Letters. I remember collecting them one wet winter's night from his aunt and uncle and carrying them in two supermarket carrier bags down the Holloway Road to the university. They are heart-breaking to read and probably the most historically significant single collection in the Archive.'

- 'The St Patrick's Day Programme collection – simply because it is so visually interesting to look at, especially the early twentieth century ones produced by the Gaelic League of London – they are beautiful artefacts and also contain some fascinating adverts in them for Irish businesses in London such as tailors in the city which tell their own history.'

- 'I also like the photograph of the 'No Irish, No Blacks, No Dogs' notice in the B&B window, because it has generated so much debate about the history of immigration and racism in Britain more generally. I was involved in one such discussion in the letters pages of the Guardian about three years ago.'

And amongst users of the Archive, Tony says 'We've had visitors from all over the world, including one of our earliest visitors, a Japanese professor who was doing comparative research on Irish migration to Britain and Korean migration to Japan; the historian Tim Pat Coogan for his book on Irish migration entitled 'Wherever Green is Worn'; researchers from TV programmes such as 'Who Do You Think You Are?', and Channel Four News; curators of the 2015 Changing Britain Festival at the South Bank Centre and the current 'Room to Breathe' exhibition at the Migration Museum.'

Archives are not composed of dead words, they bring history alive. And through bringing history alive, we may understand better how to map the future.

Coming back to Tony's 2003 article, one passage is as pertinent today:

"The Archive will be seen as a process as much as an end product, which all sectors of the community can feel they have a stake in. There is still a massive shortfall amongst large sectors of British society in awareness and recognition of the contributions, needs and achievements of the Irish in Britain as compared to other ethnic groups. The Archive of the Irish in Britain is one means of attempting to put this right. To that extent, I hope this particular Archive is as much about the future as the past.'

Considering the future, Tony has also run the Irish Writers in London Summer School since 1996.

II

The Irish Writers in London Summer School

KM: How did it start?

TM: Almost by accident. The university Short Course unit asked did we have any ideas for a two nights a week short course for 6 or 7 weeks. A friend of mine said 'You know a lot of Irish writers.' When it started in the mid-nineties, there were not many writer events. The idea was to break down some of the mythology around literature and get the library out onto the streets.

The summer school runs for two nights a week for five and a half weeks, with a different writer each week. Every Tuesday evening a set text is discussed in class with a tutor, and the following Thursday, the author reads and speaks about it to students. It's a very popular course, as popular with the writers as the students:

(Bridget Whelan, writer) 'The Summer School is unique. Its gentle, inclusive atmosphere encourages real debate. Being invited is both an accolade and a very good night out.'

Over three decades they have hosted over 80 writers.

KM: How does it work?

TM: We used to have up to fifty students at one point, but we'd end up having three groups and a plenary that was more like a public lecture rather than a discussion with the writer. Now we have a limit of 25, and mostly have 15–20. The format works really well – they read the work and discuss it with their peers and the tutor, so when it comes to meeting the writer they are familiar with the questions raised by the text and they ask very good questions, and the writer loves it.

Moy McCrory, who has appeared at the summer school in 1996 and 2012, vouches for this: when I asked how it differed from working at other writing events her answer pinpointed its essence:

(The difference) 'was that largely the audience was drawn from an Irish identified group, who were keen to discuss both similarities and differences, and to whom I didn't have to explain my own identity as 'outsider status' or indeed any 'status', but with whom I felt there was a ready rapport and a common willingness to understand. There was a remarkable openness, with people coming from a range of work backgrounds and experiences, far wider than usually experienced at readings etc. and which went beyond the academic and the literary. There was a genuine life interest in the group I met, with people all having things to contribute, equally valid. I also remember they were great fun.'

The summer school covers all varieties and genres of writing, with non-fiction as well as fiction. They have had bloggers, journalists, and writers of radio and stage plays, comics, songwriters, historians, biographers and writers of memoirs. In 2018 they had novelist Jess Kidd, alongside Judy O'Kane, talking about her memoir/travelogue, playwright Martin McNamara, short story writer Deirdre Shanahan and poet Róisín Tierney.

The main criteria for choosing the writers are those of an Irish background who live in Britain.

The first session in 1996 had seven writers, including Matthew Sweeney, Michael Donaghey and Moy McCrory.

Guests over the years have included Edna O'Brien, Blake Morrison, Emma Donoghue, Julia O'Faolain, Roy Foster, Maurice Leitch, Colette Bryce, and Catherine O'Flynn.

Unlike some literary festivals, writers are invited back – some, such as Martina Evans, writer and poet, have appeared several times: 'My involvement with the Summer School has hugely contributed to my life as a writer', she has said.

KM: Some writing festivals don't invite writers back. The summer school seems different in that respect. And do your students return?

TM: It's great to have writers back again, at earlier and later stages in their career.

Being in a university can put people off. But I have noticed students coming back. They don't come for a few years, and then they come back. There's a regeneration effect, with the old and the new students mixing.

KM : It's an eclectic list, looking at who's appeared. Could you take me through some writers?

TM: John Bird, founder of the *Big Issue* (who calls himself 'a working-class Tory') talked about his book (*Some Luck*) about growing up in London. Edna O'Brien was open and frank, and value for money. I have memories of the great poet Michael Donaghy playing a flute and reading his poems. He learnt from O'Neill's Jigs and Reels 1892, compiled when O'Neill was a Chicago police officer.

KM: And what about your own research?

TM: My own research on migration grew out of the summer school. A student asked why there was no set text. 'Why don't you write it?' they said. So my PhD, writing on migration in a deeper way, became a book. My aim with the book was to do two things. Firstly, to open up the wealth of under-researched prose literature written about the Irish in London since the Second World War. People who have read it often tell me they use it as an introduction to works they would never have otherwise heard about. Secondly, I wanted to explore how narrative is employed in these texts to mediate the complex experiences and identities of the subjects they portray. I find now that the issues I pursued with the book inform my teaching on the Summer School, but equally that the year-on-year contributions of the writers and students on the Summer School enrich my continuing research in this field.[20]

KM: Which writers struck you as illustrating particularly interesting angles of second generation experience?

TM: Apart from Moy, and Ray, who were great, there was Joe

---

20 Murray, Tony (2012) *London Irish Fictions: Narrative, Diaspora and Identity,* Liverpool, Liverpool University Press

Horgan (journalist and poet) on how going to live in Ireland had influenced his reflections on his 2G upbringing in Birmingham: Gerry McKee for his outstanding radio play *My Sky Blue Trades* about growing up of Irish parentage in rural Hertfordshire after the Second World War; and the late, great Bridget O'Connor for her quirky humour and inventiveness.

KM: And writers coming from mixed ethnic or cultural backgrounds?

TM: We had Gabriel Gbadamosi talking about his novel *Vauxhall*, and growing up in 1950s Vauxhall of Irish and Nigerian parents; Lana Citron on her Irish/Jewish upbringing; Michael Donaghy on a displaced American sense of 2G identity; Christina Reid, Cherry Smyth and Lucy Caldwell with reflections on Protestant Irish identity.

KM: Any work that might be classed as 'experimental'?

TM: A poet called Patricia Scanlan who came to talk in 1997 about her commitment to avant-garde poetry, which she workshopped with us – it was one of the strangest but most memorable sessions of the Summer School; also Sarah Strong's short impressionistic film *I Hear Fish Drowning*, about exile, psychoanalysis and feminism; Seaneen Molloy's blog *The Secret Life of a Manic Depressive*.

(Tony had mentioned earlier that Seaneen said she never edited her blog, wanting it to keep the sense of spontaneity, but as she did more and more blogging, she got better able to get down what she wanted to say. He agreed this provoked some interesting discussion.)

TM: The late Pete McCarthy brought the skills of stand-up comedy to his perfectly pitched reading and sense of timing. And Eimear McBride is coming in 2019 to discuss *The Lesser Bohemians*.

Ray French, who worked at the Summer School in 2014, reiterates how rewarding it is to teach on:

> 'I've done a lot of readings and met a number of readers' groups over the years, but what made the Irish Summer School a unique experience was knowing that the people there understood both what was said and what was left unsaid in your work. Most of

them also had a second generation upbringing, and although they may have come from a different generation or part of Britain, and we were able to explore those differences, we always found certain things in common. It was also nice to be able to continue the conversation afterwards in the local Irish pub.'

Students showcased on the Summer School website certainly seem enthusiastic:

'It is obvious why the Summer School is now going into its third decade. Where else would you get a chance to meet such a range of contemporary Irish Writers to discuss their work? As well as being interesting and stimulating, it's always relaxed and a lot of fun. I'll be back!' – Peter Hammond, student.

'...the Summer School is a fantastic model. The range and depth of discussions, between students, tutor and authors is truly impressive and rewarding to be part of. My reading and thinking have been challenged, stretched and stimulated.' – Carolyn Morris, student.

KM: To sum up, what is the essence of the Summer School?

TM: I like to think of the Summer School as a welcoming and supportive environment where Irish writers and their readers can explore at length their mutual experiences of migration and literature in a way which doesn't often happen in the run of the mill world of literary events.

Marc Scully
Negotiating Irishness
Ray French interviews Marc Scully about his research into hybrid identities

n the interview that follows Marc Scully refers to a draft of a 2009 paper with the working title, 'Second Generation Research Dialogues: Comparative Perspectives on children of immigrants', research which he is still developing. Marc's work explores the ways in which the second generation Irish in Britain have claimed legitimacy despite scornful comments from not only British people, but also the more recent wave of highly educated Irish migrants, as well as those who never left Ireland. He points out that as Irish migration to Britain has been taking place for hundreds of years and the sense of Irishness is often handed down over the generations, one would expect those who see themselves as second generation Irish to be a very diverse group. Marc interviewed a number of second generation Irish from London and Birmingham about how they have sustained their Irish identity.

Below are some short extracts from the interviews (all the names have been changed to preserve the interviewees' anonymity), and the paper's conclusion, followed by an interview with Marc about his work in which Ray French (RF) interviews Marc Scully (MS).

> 'The first extract comes from an interview with one of my
> London participants: Kate, a woman in her forties. Kate's 'Lon-
> don–Irish identity' was very much situated in her involvement in
> the London–Irish music scene of the early 1980s, spearheaded
> by The Pogues. Campbell (1999) has written of the significance
> "of the Pogues' post-punk reconfiguration of Irish 'folk' music,
> which articulated a peculiarly Diasporic (London) Irish experi-
> ence at a time when it was neither popular nor fashionable to be
> Irish in Britain", something of particular relevance to the second
> generation.'

Kate: that whole scene … was very much about saying we're Irish but we're not paddies, we're London–Irish, and it was a very different identity to being first generation … I've got a bit of a collection of kind of Irish hybrid music, you know, ska bands playing traditional Irish tunes but reggae style … there was a lot of cross fertilisation going on which was really exciting … I think with The Pogues singing it was very much 'we're Irish and proud of it better believe it, but we're not the same as the Irish, the first generation Irish.'

MS: And in what kind of ways do you think that distinction was drawn?

Kate: Erm, (we) weren't going to take any crap you know, I think that was a clear message … 'we're here, we're here to stay' (pp. 6–7).

MS: I mean now you would describe yourself as London–Irish?

Sinéad: I don't think I ever *wanted* to differentiate myself as London–Irish but a few things that were said and done, a few things that have happened to London–Irish people, it makes you feel, 'okay well we need to … fight your corner a bit more', so I don't think I ever wanted to be a London–Irish person but somehow it's evolved (p9).

The people Marc interviewed from Birmingham, 'all worked in a community organisation which specifically described itself as being 'Birmingham–Irish', so the hyphenated identity was one that was readily available.' (p9)

MS: But it is kind of, the Birmingham–Irish term is one that you use as that kind of hyphenated term

Eileen: Yes, and I think … to include maybe, to make people feel included like my son, … who are of value to the community and who, you know … proud of their Irish roots but are not a hundred percent Irish then if you put the term 'Birmingham–Irish', then it's a lot more inclusive isn't it? (p.10)

Becky: Birmingham is a multi-cultural city which is an attraction for some and not for others … I think the Chinese Quarter, I think it's brilliant. You know, you walk round it, it's great. You know where you are, there's no question about it. Nobody resents it; why should they? It's well done, it's well kept, its clean and its tidy and it adds something to the city, and that's exactly what we want to achieve here; something that adds something to the city … Soho Road, the street furniture has been painted in, say Pakistan's colours. The street furniture has been adapted to reflect different cultures, I think; it's down the road, but why not do that here? (pp. 13–14)

The paper concludes: 'As previously stated, I believe that the implications of this research for second-generation integration theory lie in the need to place more emphasis on the agency of second generation individuals in constructing their own identities and determining their own level of integration. I would suggest that it may be of more benefit to examine integration at a local, city-based level, rather than a national one, and agree with Thomson & Crul (2007) on the need for a nuanced approach that takes into account the 'dynamic interplay between structure, culture and personal agency'. Finally, I would emphasise the need not to conflate integration with assimilation; as I have demonstrated, in the diaspora spaces that many cities have now become, the second generation are as likely to negotiate identity in relation to the other minority groups in the city as they are to do so in relation to the majority culture.'

RF: How has the Irish border question and the attitude to the Republic during the Brexit negotiations affected second generation opinion about their relationship with England?

MS: Over the last few years, I've become interested in the widely-reported phenomenon of people of Irish descent in Britain applying for Irish passports in the context of Brexit. This is generally reported, both in Ireland and Britain, as being in order to maintain free movement, or avoiding queueing at the airport, but my suspicion is that there's far more complex identity work going on here. So, I wrote an article for *Irish Times Abroad* about it[21] and invited people in that situation to contact me. The response has far exceeded my expectations, with over 90 people contacting me to date – many of whom seemed eager to have an opportunity to expand on their decision to apply for a passport, and how Brexit had impacted on their sense of identification with both countries. So, this is an ongoing project – I held a focus group in London on the topic last July (2018), and I'm hoping to expand with a series of interviews, allowing for time and funding constraints.

Based on what I've heard so far (and I do want to stress that it's far too early in the process to consider these as findings), there does seem to be something of a re-evaluation of their relationship with Britishness happening among my participants: and it does tend to be Britishness rather than Englishness, presumably because people are discussing citizenship. This obviously varies from person to person, but as an example, one of the women in the focus group spoke about not identifying as British when growing up in the seventies, due to experiencing anti-Irish prejudice, then coming to like what Britain was becoming as seen from multicultural London: one that incorporated a general positivity towards

---

21 Are Irish passport applicants in Britain becoming 'more Irish'? *The Irish Times* May 4, 2018.

Irish people. Brexit has disrupted this.

Interestingly, some of my participants who continue to primarily identify as British are nonetheless distancing themselves from a specific kind of Britishness – one that has limited or inaccurate knowledge about Ireland, specifically Ireland's position as an independent, separate country. So there's an interesting form of hybridised identity positioning happening here – in order to have some kind of rhetorical claim on Irishness, they aren't fully disavowing Britishness, but they are trying to present themselves as the kind of British people who actually know something about Ireland, as opposed to those who don't. It's also striking that a number of this cohort explicitly talk about putting in the work in order to inform themselves about Ireland, as a kind of responsibility associated with their new found citizenship. It'll be interesting to see how this develops: effectively this cohort is not just a new population of citizens for Ireland, but also a new population of self-identifying second-generation Irish in England, as they may not have seen themselves that way previously.

It's also important to note, though, that this is work drawn from a self-selecting sample: out of the over 90 people who have contacted me, only 2 were self-identified Leave voters, which is a proportion unlikely to be representative of the population of second-generation Irish in Britain.

RF: Referring to your paper 'Second Generation Research Dialogues: Comparative Perspectives on children of immigrants', you say on page 5: 'I argue that many second-generation Irish people feel constrained in 'officially' identifying themselves as Irish due to the variety of cultural understandings of what 'Irishness' constitutes.' So are you here talking about the second generation Irish being caught between different interpretations of Irishness by both the British and the Irish in Ireland, or something else?

MS: Predominantly, yes, but I'd also draw a distinction between 'public' and 'private' Irishness, 'official' and 'unofficial' Irishness etc.

RF: Also on page 5 you say: 'There is some evidence of a 'second wave' of second-generation Irish emerging i.e. the children of the 1980s wave of Irish migrants. However, as pointed out by Walter (2008a), the high level of return migration among the 1980s cohort of migrants has resulted in this 'second wave' being numerically smaller than might have been expected – how much of a cultural impact they will have remains to be seen.' Could you say more about this?

MS: A lot of those Irish people who migrated to Britain in the 1980s, subsequently returned to Ireland in the 1990s and 2000s. Their reasons for doing so have been explored in detail by researchers such as Mary Corcoran and Caitríona Ní Laoire – largely, it's 'pull' factors, rather than 'push' factors. Family networks are important: Ní Laoire (2008, 2011) highlights how the wish to raise one's children in Ireland appears to have been a major motivation for return for many migrants, as well as caring responsibilities for elderly parents. The strong Irish economy at the time also created the material opportunities to return – Corcoran (2002) points out that many of those who did return had the cultural capital to do so.

The quite strong narrative that 'you return home to ensure a better upbringing for your kids' that Ní Laoire highlights is, presumably, somewhat challenging for those who choose to stay in Britain, and I do wonder what the second-generation Irish make of it. I know at least one second-generation participant in my own research found the idea quite offensive! (Scully, 2010, p.311) Interestingly enough though, the concept of 'return migration' has been expanded recently to include those of Irish descent who have moved 'back' to Ireland (Hannafin, 2016). We may see more of this phenomenon in years to come. (On a personal note, my wife and I returned to Ireland shortly after our son's first birthday. Being aware of the socially constructed nature of the "innocent Irish childhood" narrative doesn't make you immune from it!).

In terms of the cultural impact of the 'second wave' of second-generation Irish, I do wonder whether the passports issue is an indication of this particular cohort finding its collective voice.

RF: It's difficult to overestimate the importance of The Pogues in giving a voice to the second generation Irish in Britain. On their first visit to Ireland, in 1985, the traditional Irish musician Noel Hill famously called The Pogues 'a terrible abortion of Irish music'. It does suggest quite a gap in attitudes and experiences between native born Irish and second generation Irish. Any thoughts about that?

MS: I tend to defer to Sean Campbell when it comes to the cultural significance of the Pogues! I think they've been viewed as mainstream in Ireland for quite some time now — arguably at the expense of recognition of their London-ness.

I am idly curious about the line that could be drawn from the Pogues through the Gallagher brothers to Ed Sheeran in terms of high-profile musicians of Irish descent who actively work with that hybridity. I suspect that because Sheeran is a less transgressive figure, he'll attract less academic attention, but at the same time, there might be something interesting going on in how his claiming Irishness in an English accent is so readily accepted in Ireland. I don't quite have the analytical tools to do this myself, but somebody should!

This seems as good a place as any to refer to the work of Brendan O'Sullivan (2017), who has taken a lot of the analysis around second-generation Irishness in music and applied that to comedy.

RF: Coming back to your paper, On p13 you say: 'However, given that Irish migration to London is a constant phenomenon, albeit in greater or lesser waves, it is more likely that London–Irishness will continue to be reinvented, both in reaction to new arrivals and to the multicultural milieu within London itself — integration in this context ought not to be seen as having an obvious end-point.' Have you noticed any new trends or developments in this reinvention of London–Irishness since your paper was published?

MS: Yes. It's a personal viewpoint, but I think London–Irishness as a public identity within the last decade has become a lot more self-consciously diverse. I think, at least partly, that this has been the result of what you might call the main/official London–Irish organisations realising that they needed to reach beyond what had been their core constituency. But it's also the legacy of groups like the London Irish Women's Centre, and its successor organisation, Mind Yourself (of which I was on the board of trustees for a few years), which actively aimed to reach out beyond those traditional Irish networks. And particularly, it's been about organisations representing previously marginalised people of an Irish background becoming an integral part of the Irish community – so, for instance, I think the London Irish LGBT Network having its launch event at the Irish Embassy was a significant symbolic moment. I also think the work Rosemary Adaser and the Association of Mixed Race Irish have been doing is incredibly important. And I suspect that the wave of activism around the London–Irish Abortion Rights Campaign in the context of the recent referendum on the 8th Amendment might indicate further transnational and transgenerational orientations in London–Irishness more generally. And, of course, all of these developments haven't necessarily supplanted the previous forms of London–Irishness that existed. It's a mosaic, and will continue to be so.

RF: On p15 of your paper, you say: 'I have argued that for the second-generation Irish, it is important that Irishness becomes a prominent aspect of the multicultural city, both for the sake of articulating their own sense of identity, and for what Irishness can contribute to the city. However, it is likely that this process may involve contestation as well as collaboration with other ethnic groups.' How do you feel this has developed since your paper was published, and have you any thoughts about how it will be post-Brexit?

MS: Yes, I think this sentence has been overtaken by events somewhat! I didn't anticipate the extent to which the multicultural city as aspiration would fall out of fashion, at the level of national politics at least. A lot of my thinking at the time about the Irish in the multicultural city came from looking at Birmingham, and in particular the attempts to redevelop the Digbeth area of the city and rebrand it 'The Irish Quarter'. As far as I know, those plans were shelved by austerity, although Irish groups in Birmingham do still use the term 'The Irish Quarter' occasionally.

In terms of contestation and collaboration, well … As I've already discussed, I think that there's been a greater recognition that being Irish and being a member of another ethnic group are not necessarily mutually exclusive. I think it's fair to say that the top-down pressures to assimilate within Britishness are stronger than they were 10 years ago, so that may have reduced the ability to establish the city as a mutual point of identification for ethnic minorities … Beyond that, I'm speculating, although I do wonder to what extent Brexit may prompt some people of Irish descent to lean into what Hickman et al (2005) have termed as the 'incorporating' nature of Englishness/Britishness towards white English speakers, and so distance themselves from other ethnic groups. It'd be interesting to know how many people of Irish descent voted for Brexit, and how many of those who did so were motivated by immigration – if the letters pages of the Irish Post are any indication, it's a not insignificant cohort.

RF: You draw attention to how Mary Hickman identified the Plastic Paddy slur as originating in the wave of highly educated Irish who arrived in the 1980s. To me this seems to raise questions about class. When my parents joined the industrial working class it was a rise in status, affording them jobs where their time was their own once they'd finished their eight hours, allowing them a level of freedom and dignity they'd never experienced at home. Has this class element perhaps been underestimated?

MS: That's an interesting perspective. I do think that there's been an increasing tendency with the passage of time to pathologise the experience of the post-war working class migrant. The hardships experienced by that cohort have become the dominant lens through which we understand them. However, if you look at oral histories or first-hand accounts, the positive aspects of the experience are also emphasised: and it's particularly that sense of opportunity, whether through an improved social life, or the 'freedom and dignity' that you describe above that comes with regular work that comes through in such accounts. I wrote an article a few years ago for the Irish Journal of Sociology about the role that the collective memory of '1950s emigration' plays in narratives around contemporary Irish migration particularly in terms of comparisons by class (Scully, 2015). Briefly, in order to portray recent migrants as having the agency to migrate as a lifestyle choice (and not due to government action/inaction), you need a group to compare them to, who *didn't* have a choice. Within contemporary Ireland, the 1950s cohort fulfil that role: by comparing them unfavourably to today's migrants in terms of class and education, their agency, and the complexity of their experience is diminished. I think a similar dynamic is at play regarding the "from the building site to the boardroom" trope that you regularly get around descriptions of Irish people being successful in middle-class occupations in London. While it's fine to celebrate success, I'm not sure why this is so regularly rhetorically accomplished at the expense of a more working-class version of Irishness in Britain. I think the work of people like Ultan Cowley (2001) stands as a necessary corrective to this, and Clair Wills' (2015) *The Best Are Leaving*, which also looks at these issues, is on my 'to read' list!

RF: Although the London/Manchester/Birmingham Irish identity is a very interesting development, you don't mention the clannishness that can arise when people cling to their county identities. Is this a phenomenon you've come across?

MS: Yes, absolutely! I think the persistence of county identity is something that's been completely overlooked in Irish diaspora studies – as far as I know, it's only myself and Miriam Nyhan Grey who have looked at this in any kind of detail (Scully, 2013; Nyhan, 2015), at least in an academic sense: oddly enough, Dara O Briain's book *Tickling the English* has a section on it. The county seems to be the major rubric through which Irish diasporic life is organised – you only need to attend one St Patrick's Day parade in England to be aware of that. And, yes, that can result in the kind of clannishness you allude to above. Going back to Birmingham's Irish Quarter, one of the examples my participants brought up was the inability of the Irish community in Birmingham to agree on a piece of public art because everyone wanted something that represented their 'home' county! (Incidentally, this kind of clannishness isn't unique to the Irish diaspora – Winston James (1993) refers to a similar impulse among Carribbean migrants in Britain as 'island chauvinism'). I think there's more going on here than just clannishness though – one of my arguments around county identity is that it's a way of articulating the specificity of one's Irish identity at times when Irishness itself seems overly broad: so on St Patrick's Day, when *everyone's* performing Irishness, it adds an extra layer to publicly identify with Waterford, or Wexford or Kilkenny. Similarly, it seems to be a way through which second-generation Irish people can attempt to assert their 'authenticity' in claiming Irishness.

RF: Do you think that your findings connect in any way with Aidan Arrowsmith's theory of a three stage negotiation of identity ('Plastic Paddy: Negotiating Identity in Second-generation 'Irish–English' Writing', Irish Studies Review, July 2010)? Stage one being the rejection of parental heritage, along with a desire to conform to English norms and expectations; stage two, a reassessment of cultural roots that typically produces a nostalgic desire for 'authentic' Irishness; stage three, 'the person questions the very possibility of discovering any 'authentic' memory. Any thoughts?

MS: It's an interesting lens through which to look at the second-generation experience: I think I've seen a lot more of the conflict between stage two and three than I have of stage one. But then, it's self-selection again: people at stage one aren't necessarily going to show up on my radar, so to speak.

Bibliography

Corcoran, M. P. (2002) The process of migration and the reinvention of self: the experiences of returning Irish emigrants. *Éire-Ireland* **37(1):**175–191.

Cowley, U. (2001) *The men who built Britain: a history of the Irish navvy*, Wolfhound Press.

Hannafin, S. (2016) Place and belonging: The experience of return migration for the second generation Irish from Britain. *Irish Geography* **49(1):**29–46.

Hickman, M. J., Morgan, S., Walter, B., & Bradley, J. (2005) The limitations of whiteness and the boundaries of Englishness: second-generation Irish identifications and positionings in multiethnic Britain. *Ethnicities* **5(2):**160–182.

James, W. (1993) Migration, racism and identity formation: the Caribbean experience in Britain. *Inside Babylon: The Caribbean Diaspora in Britain*, 231–287.

Ní Laoire, C. (2008) 'Settling back'? A biographical and life-course perspective on Ireland's recent return migration. *Irish Geography* **41(2):**195–210.

Ní Laoire, C. (2011) Narratives of 'innocent Irish childhoods': return migration and intergenerational family dynamics. *Journal of Ethnic and Migration Studies* **37(8):**1253–1271.

Nyhan, Miriam (2015) Oral History: County Societies in Irish New York. *American Journal of Irish Studies* **12:**159–169.

O'Sullivan, B. M. (2017) John Bull's Other Ireland: Manchester–Irish Identities and a Generation of Performance.

Scully, M. (2010) *Discourses of authenticity and national identity among the Irish diaspora in England* (Doctoral dissertation, The Open University).

Scully, M. (2013) BIFFOs, jackeens and Dagenham Yanks: county identity, 'authenticity' and the Irish diaspora. *Irish Studies Review* **21(2):**143–163.

Scully, M. (2015) 'Emigrants in the Traditional Sense?' – Irishness in England, Contemporary Migration and Collective Memory of the 1950s. *Irish Journal of Sociology* **23(2):**133–148.

Wills, C. (2015) *The Best Are Leaving: Emigration and Post-War Irish Culture*. Cambridge: Cambridge University Press.

Maude Casey
An Untold Story:
Writing as Resistance
Moy McCrory interviews Maude Casey

n the following interview Maude Casey, a second generation Irish author, answers questions put to her by Moy McCrory, about the writing of her young adult novel *Over the Water* which looks at a young girl's route to self-identity through her life in England with Irish parents during one particular summer, on the annual return home to visit relatives. Maude considers her own experience and reflects on the time when she was writing her book in the 1980s.

In the following pages Maude Casey is noted as MC, Moy McCrory as MM and the questions set in bold, to indicate the speaker and the answers.

MM: You mentioned in your chapter 'Writing as Survival' in *The Northern Ireland Troubles in Britain* **that living in Brighton after the IRA bombed the Grand Hotel, became increasingly difficult as people were able to vent their hostility (Dawson,**

Dover Hopkins, eds., 2017:213–226). How did this impact on you personally, as someone who is white and sounds English?

MC: I wrote *Over the Water* in 1986–1987. It came into being because of the ripple effect of a number of events: the emerging facts around the imprisonment of the Guildford 4 and the Birmingham 6 during the late 1970s and early 1980s; the hunger strikes in the Maze; the IRA bombing of the Grand Hotel in Brighton in October 1984. In 1986, it was the experience of walking with my baby into a post office in Brighton, that gave me my first taste of naked racism, in the viciousness directed at me by the man behind the counter, when he jeered at my Irish names on the child benefit book I'd handed to him.

He called out to enlist the collusion of all the people in that post office, and, in a flash of fear, I experienced how easily the mood of a group of people can flip into hatred and aggression.

I'm white, so how can I ever know what racism does to the person of those subjected to it on a daily basis? But racism isn't just about casual violence: it's also about silencing; about not being seen; about not being heard – and about the self-censorship that can come about as a result of all of these.

That incident was a small taste of racism. But when an entire community is made suspect by the state, this gives carte blanche to an everyday, xenophobic hostility, which can easily tip over into lethal violence. We see this in the simmering anti-Muslim, anti-immigrant racism behind so many murderous attacks, even on children, today.

I guess it's difficult for people to realize, these days, just how tense it was, in the 1970s and 1980s, when every Irish person in England was a person of interest to the security services. Irish accents were there to be disparaged, mimicked or ridiculed – and the state was ready to stop, search and detain you if you resisted, even if this resistance was as mild as the shrug of a shoulder. My mother often kept her head down while we were shopping. I reference this right at the start of *Over the Water:*

> Mammy knows no-one in our road. She is so afraid of scornful

> glances at her Irish voice that she opens her mouth to no-one.
> She says that we should do the same. 'Keep your business to
> yourself, she says. 'Don't get involved with anyone,' she says. We
> have something to hide. (Casey: 1987:2)

It's perhaps this silencing that has the most damaging effect on
people. It's an untold story. In those days, with your personhood
diminished, whether by a stage-Oirish diphthong, or as the butt of
one of the relentless 'Irish jokes' which you heard as soon as you
put on the radio, and which were backed by the full force of state
violence and a cosh or a gun, it was exhausting to be able to just be
yourself. Indeed, it was hard to have any sense of who you were;
where you came from; where you fitted.

For our Irish parents, it was hard enough being immigrants.
They'd left their native place behind, in a flight from colonial
underdevelopment, or military occupation, and they'd gone to
where the work was. But once there, they were othered. And,
for Irish people, this othering took place in the context of the
conflict consequent upon the nailing-down of the border between
the twenty-six counties of the Irish Republic, or Eire, and the six
counties claimed by the United Kingdom of Great Britain and
Northern Ireland. As a white Irish-born person, it was from the
moment that you opened your mouth that you were othered. In
those days, as a second generation Irish person, it was an othering
which had an element of the schizophrenic about it: of the cracked;
of something being broken. We felt it in our bodies; we knew it
was happening. However, Irish-born friends in England said, "Get
away! You don't have a clue what it feels like! You're English!" Our
accents were jarring; we weren't Irish enough.

As fourteen year old Mary says, in Chapter Fifteen, when she's
in Eire:

> All they ever do here is talk. Talking, talking: morning noon and
> night, they are always talking. And I am silent. When I do say
> something, my voice is flat and awkward with the dead vowels of
> London, and it sounds so weird among the rising falling song of
> the way they talk here. (1987:70)

MM: How did the bombing campaign impact on you as

someone who had such action carried out in your name?

MC: I never thought that such actions were carried out in my name. It never occurred to me. I was in England; the war was in Ireland. I'm the daughter of a father who'd come here as a child migrant in the early 1930s. He'd read James Connolly and passed on to me a message of international socialism. He'd stood with his Irish and Jewish neighbours in Cable Street and physically resisted the police-backed lines of Oswald Mosley. He'd gone to Accra and been taken by his Ewe friends to see the slave forts along the Gold Coast. Two years before I was born, he'd watched in horror as the Palestinian Nakba unfolded. He instilled in me a sense of the connectedness of these events. For him, pirates were not jolly swashbucklers, but genocidal slave traders, rapists and pillagers. Both my parents did all they could to keep toy guns out of the house. I can't even remember when I first heard the word 'colonialism' because it was a word I learnt early from my father, as a young child. His second-to-last words were "Don't forget Palestine."

According to my father, empires operate using maximum and barbaric force. They employ theft in all its guises: theft of time, space, bodies, souls, hope, earth, sea, sky, past and future. Opposing this is the resistance of people standing together. Non-violent ways are best, but frequently result in everyone ending up dead. As a child, during the Rising and its aftermath, and then during the Civil War in the 1920s, my father was engaged in the physical resistance of his whole community in County Clare: digging trenches for the armoured vehicles of the Black-and-Tans to topple into when crossing the bog in the silence of the night; making explosive devices out of cocoa tins to throw into the trenches after them; watching the bodies of the resultant dead sinking into the dark waters of the bog; running messages from house to house. All his life he lived with the trauma of these events. The military occupation of his country of birth, and its resultant underdevelopment, gave him a thirst for education and travel, and led to him leaving the place he'd called 'home'. I accepted his interpretations of Panama, Suez, the wars in Laos and Vietnam, and the struggles in the Six Counties. If people defended themselves, it was because they were oppressed beyond all endurance. If the powers-that-be took no notice and carried on oppressing, desperation led to the fight being taken into their public spaces.

My father was a railwayman in a London terminal, among a staff of mainly Irish and Jamaican workers, beneath a management structure of white, English freemasons. During times of intensity in the Anglo-Irish conflict, when the bombing campaign brought the effects of military occupation home to England, it was he whom his bosses ordered to go down and search any bags left abandoned on the station concourse. We hoped for peace; my parents devoutly prayed for peace. We wished there was not violence, although we understood why it was there, and knew it would only end when there was justice.

MM: What were the chief attitudes towards the Irish when you were growing up in the 50s and 60s in England before the Troubles? Can you also discuss why you question that term (The Troubles) as a description?

MC: I was in Luton in the 50s and north London in the 60s. Our neighbours were Jamaican, African, Italian, Polish: migrants from trouble, like us. In my school, the playground had a line down the middle: during playtime boys had to stay on one side, girls on the other. The son of our Polish neighbours was my friend. We held hands and skipped along the line, one on each side of it. Then we turned around and skipped back, each on the wrong side. We were six. It makes me happy that even at that age I found borders ridiculous.

When we went to Eire, we entered a different world, which we loved for its sense of freedom and the open air; its horses and dogs and conviviality. For my parents, it was definitely a complicated time of 'going home'. This was something Irish people could do relatively easily, unlike people from the Caribbean or Africa. Sometimes, on the journey there, we had five or six watches strapped to our arms, under our jumpers, with orders to remain silent when we passed through Customs; on the way back, same story, only this time with butter, tea, a slab of ham and a dead chicken, wrapped in sacking, stuffed under our clothes in the suitcases. It was all a mystery, but one which did not trouble us.

As for "The Troubles": accepted wisdom defines these as an ethno-nationalist conflict in Northern Ireland during the late twentieth century, which began on 5 October 1968 with the Civil Rights marches in Derry, and ended with the Good Friday Agreement on 10th April 1998.

In Volume IV Se-Z of the 1986 edition of the *Supplement to the Oxford English Dictionary*, its meaning, in this English context, is given as:

Any of various rebellions, civil war and unrest in Ireland, *spec* in 1919–23, and in Northern Ireland since the 1970s.

1880 W.H. Patterson *Glossary of Words Antrim and Down*, 109 *Troubles, the,* the Irish rebellion of 1641. 1922, JOYCE *Ulysses* … 613: He vividly recollected when the events alluded to took place … in the days of the land troubles … early in the (eighteen) eighties … 1942 E.WAUGH *Put Out More Flags* iii 235 The ruins of a police barrack, built to command the road through the valley, burnt in the troubles … were one green with the grass." (Burchfield: 1986:996)

As a descriptor of what was going on in Ireland during the 1970s and 1980s, I find these words 'the Troubles' troubling in themselves, and physically difficult to say. They feel like a convenient but disgraceful euphemism, demanding collusion, gliding over the brutal realities of war and concealing the behaviour of the British state from those whom it claims to represent. Some would say there was only one 'Trouble' for Irish people, and that was the presence of the British state: booted, suited and messing with the intimate details of people's lives. In the 1980s, on returning from West Belfast, I'd wish that I could lift up all the people I knew here in England and beam them down there, so they could experience for themselves the visceral effects of being in those streets, in that mixture of fear and defiance, subject to 24/7 violence and abuse. Even inside their homes the people were surveilled from watchtowers and helicopters. There was a roaring trade in Venetian blinds and mass prescription of Valium.

I recall that from an international perspective, in European news programmes for example, the events between 1968 and 1998 were known as the Northern Ireland conflict, and the Conflict in Ireland. They were also sometimes described as a 'guerrilla war' or a 'low-level war'.

The powerful validate themselves by reference to those who have no power, whom they dismiss as morally wrong, thereby justifying their own behaviour. In this context, the term 'the Troubles' is a fiction, created by those with power, to diminish and silence the experience of millions of people. I couldn't believe that supposedly enlightened people here in England, could possibly allow that state of affairs to continue, while the population of part of the UK was trying to live out every second of its days in a police state. It was clear to me that if these techniques of population control were being used in the Six Counties, sooner or later they would be used in England itself: the experience; the hardware; the techniques are all there, in the wings, biding their time.

MM: You have stated that, in England, the left's response to the situation in Ireland was invisible – you note they worked for the end of apartheid for example, a sort of competitive cause politics. Can you expand on this?

MC: My activism at that time was all around CND, women's liberation, gay liberation, anti-racism, Greenham Common, anti-apartheid and the miners' strike. I felt exasperated by the blank-eyed response I got when suggesting solidarity with the struggles of people in the Six Counties, or similarities between what was happening in the Six Counties and in Palestine and South Africa. It felt like I had the wrong words. As a young woman, I was frequently batted down by male leftists, and I'm not proud to say that I found it easiest to just stop talking.

In addition, there was a distinctly strange response whenever we first and second generation Irish people suggested that being held and interrogated under the PTA didn't automatically make you a member of the IRA. This often had people who prided themselves on referring to the police as pigs, or filth, gazing at us uneasily – something about no smoke without fire.

My experience was that for those who identified as belonging to 'the Left', apartheid in South Africa existed; the brutal policing of the miners' strike existed, but the divisions being viciously maintained in a part of Britain, by a paramilitary police force, armed by Westminster, with the full might of the British army and of covert surveillance behind them, didn't appear to exist. These were 'the Troubles': an inchoate state of affairs, erupting out of the mist like geysers: Irish, mystifying, uncontrollable, violent: other – and seemingly endless and insoluble.

Eventually, we Irish people ourselves began to develop the confidence to self-organise, in the campaigns around the Birmingham 6 and the Guildford 4, in the pages of the *Irish Post* newspaper, and in groups such as the Irish in Britain Representation Group (IBRG) and Troops Out, both of which I joined at the time. As for the wider Left, I recall the Labour Left in London and the Greater London Council expressing solidarity, as part of their commitment to anti-racism. They funded the Irish Women's Centre and grassroots Irish women's groups which formed to support women. In Brighton there was a strong Labour Women and Ireland group, which organized delegations to West Belfast.

MM: Can I draw you out about the writing of your book *Over the Water*. Was it a creative urge or a political one?

MC: For me there's little distinction. The personal is political; the creative is an expression of both: all are one. From the Greek, the idea of the political comes from a sense of the life lived in public. We are all public creatures, sustained by the contexts into which we were born. To say: I'm not interested in politics, is to deny this beautiful intertwining of the public and the personal. It's also quite a terrifying statement, because it gives powerful elites an open field to do what they like to the people, who are, if you like, sleepwalking into tyranny. So really, we're all implicated: silence or inaction is itself a kind of collusion. As humans, I think we know this, if we let ourselves feel and think. I think we are all connected with one another and with the ancestors whose DNA has brought us here.

If we ignore this, we can feel it in our spirits and in our bodies: we enter a culture of depression, tamping down our sensitivity, our connectedness, and running the risk of becoming inhumane ourselves. Because, as humans, I feel that we do share a sense that the opposite of 'good' is indifference.

Of course, we want to turn away from things which are 'too big' and which we find overwhelming. Each day on our planet, millions of people continue to endure trauma on an unimaginable scale. What of those? What of the people who are running along the margins of what Mohsin Hamid has called 'the age of perma-war' (*The Guardian*, 22nd August 2015) in which wars are created so that missiles are traded? And what of climate change?

The impulse to turn away is understandable, particularly when mainstream media, acting in the interests of those who pay them, blare a non-stop barrage of terrifying dystopian narratives in which we have no power, beyond that of shopping and consuming. But, in fact, we have considerable power. Even the smallest personal change, from a position of thoughtful responsibility, has considerable political effects, within the continuum of resistance. Many have died, in order to claim the human rights we have today. These rights can be stripped away in an instant, unless we are alert. We owe it to those who have died, and who continue to die, to be vigilant ourselves.

I've written elsewhere about how it was a personal/political/ creative urge, walking home after the incident in the post office, which got me writing *Over the Water:*

> I was frightened, but I walked out with my head up, talking to my baby to shield her from the abuse directed at us. I clearly felt the presence of my grandmother, and women like her, who had survived dispossession, famine, slaughter and hardship, to produce my daughter and me. In this experience was the seed of the ancestor story I later began to write, a story in which a teenage girl grapples with ideas of identity in her grandmother's kitchen in rural Ireland, and which I wrote to show my daughter that her history was one of courage rather than abjection. (Casey, 2017:214)

The story I wrote that day was that of a fourteen year-old girl connecting with a grandmother. It later became woven into Chapter Fourteen of *Over the Water*. The story of how this became a book is part of the story of the 1980s, and of the creation of women's publishing houses which championed works by marginalised women. I wonder whether *Over the Water* would have been published, had it not been for The Women's Press in London.

MM: You spoke about how, as a young woman, the normal reading of first-person literature for you at school had been to assume male identity for the protagonist, and the realization of the first-person being female was a later startling realization. This was common for our generation. Today girls and young women may not grasp this as part of women's history. Can you discuss the importance of stating this, of remembering our recent pasts?

MC: It is important, because as women we have to reinvent the wheel on a regular basis. These days, we simply have to look around to see how viciously 'reality' is mediated and reinvented minute-by-minute, algorithm by algorithm. Rape is not rape; torture is not torture; abuse is not abuse; everything is just banter.

It's important because otherwise, if as women we are not *actively* putting ourselves in the picture, in the frame, in the text, we run the ever-present risk of being written out, or of simply sliding away from it completely, to become silent and invisible. Susan Calman, the writer and comedian, in response to the question: What has been your biggest disappointment? wrote, 'That I'm still having the same discussion about women in comedy as I was having 12 years ago. Are we funny? Will anyone watch us? Can I have my own sitcom?' (*The Guardian*, 24th November 2018)

It's particularly important for women and activists to be consciously aware of the importance of making our own histories. The nineteenth and early twentieth century labour and suffrage movements had people who were dedicated to having agency in their narratives. There are collections and archives all around the country which testify to this and embody this, and into which young people can delve today to bring things to light.

It's important to do this because women really are written out. I've mentioned the flowering of women's publishing houses in England in the late 70s early 80s. This came about partly because women who'd benefitted from the increased accessibility to university education enshrined in the 1948 Education Act, had discovered from university libraries that there'd been an astonishing number of women writers whose books *were simply no longer in print*. The message was: women writers are simply not good enough to be reprinted – never mind that the presses had been owned by men.

So colonised by patriarchy was my own young mind, that I distinctly recall the extraordinary moment when I realised I could use the pronoun 'she' as the protagonist of her own story. Before that light-bulb moment, practically everything I'd written had had, in my head, a male narrator. When, as a child, I began to write for the first time, ideas of fiction – of naming, of tracing with the point of a pencil the pronouns 'I' and 'he' and of wondering who they might be – never included 'she'. Until I was in my early thirties, I internalised the misogyny which said that only men could be writers; only then did I use the pronoun 'she' and only then did the narrator 'I' embody a female or a male identity, depending.

MM: You make the interesting point that you were writing about a period (the 1960s) during the 1980s, which was a very dark time to be Irish in England. How did this shape and direct your writing (or not)?

MC: This double vision is behind the fictional 1960s of *Over the Water*. My own 1960s, until the Civil Rights marches in 1968, took place without much anti-Irish incident. I never experienced my school friends as racist. We had fun, just being young women, dressing up, causing mischief. It was the roar and rush of state intervention in our lives much later that was the impulse behind the novel. The fear and anxiety; the paranoia and silencing. Of course, these lenses had always been there, as Cecil Woodham Smith pointed out in the early 1960s:

So completely is the history of one country the reverse of the history of the other, that the very names which to any Englishman mean glory, victory and prosperity, to an Irishman spell degradation, misery and ruin. (1962:19)

I re-read *Over the Water* recently, and was struck by how it feels like a historical document, like a text of grief and rage and loss, and I was struck by how hard I was working to find reasons for hope. Mary herself senses that her initial nostalgia for the 'cosy … Englishness of crumpets and tea, of evening fires and Agatha Christie' (Casey, 1987;15) with which she is internalising the racism directed at her, would be a denial of hope in her own process of becoming.

For me, hope emerged from writings by bell hooks, Angela Davis, Maya Angelou, N'gugi wa Thiongo, Hannah Arendt, Toni Morrison, Audre Lord, Edward Said, Stuart Hall, Bob Marley. Their words accompanied me like talismans: Decolonise your mind. Emancipate yourself from mental slavery; and so on. They still do. We still haven't come to where we should be. We keep on being interrupted.

In the 1980s, I was struck by how much the abuse perpetrated by colonialism targets the body, particularly the body of colour, the labouring body, the female body, the LGBTQ+ body: how it zones in on what we might call the intimacies. There's a chilling sense that what we're looking at here is seriously barbaric. In 1958 in *The Human Condition*, Hannah Arendt explores the nature of evil and makes the point:

> Thought, … no other human capacity is so vulnerable, and it is in fact, far easier to act under conditions of tyranny than it is to think. (Arendt, 1998:324)

Elsewhere, she notes:

> The sad truth of the matter is that most evil is done by people who never made up their minds to be either bad or good. (Arendt: 1971:438)

I feel Arendt is right: we need to do our best to use the power of thought, actively, to resist indifference to tyranny and abuse.

As I wrote, I sensed that the effects of this abuse echo down the generations, so that the unvoiced grief and loss of one generation trickles down and is felt in the sorrows of another. It seems to me that writing is a kind of yearning: it's a grieving for that which was lost, and an aspiration for that which is almost about to be said.

It was this which lay behind my decision to include those things which had been unsayable in my own life, such as references to menstruation, because of the shame imbued in Irish women about our bodies, by the abusive indoctrination of the Roman Catholic church. Equally it was necessary for me to include the voices of the women whose endurance ensured the survival of the Irish people. I feel these stories are crucial in keeping alive the sense of where we came from, so that we can keep alert to where we are going.

The naming of my narrator-protagonist, Mary, invoking the Blessed Virgin Mary, created by patriarchy, came from a wish to interrogate ideas of womanhood being given to Irish girls and women at that time. I wanted to try to deconstruct these ideas and re-appropriate them, using the Irish goddess Bridget, clann-chief Mebh, and tales from Tir na nOg. It makes me happy that these continue to be re-appropriated by women, for example in the campaign to repeal the Eighth Amendment in Eire, and in the video installation *BRIDGIT* by the winner of the 2018 Turner Prize, Charlotte Prodger. So, I placed Mary in the landscape of her grandmothers, and gave her agency in her journey, as she rides off on a young horse. It was important that Mary was not controlling him with a metal bit and reins. I wanted to convey something of the importance of respect, of intuition and of our connectedness to the elements, to our physical landscapes and to the life of the natural world, without which we are all doomed.

I'm honoured to be a small part of the continuum of writing, which for me is a process of bringing into the present – of giving voice – to so much that has been broken, and of reparation, of repair.

Bibliography

Arendt, Hannah (1998) *The Human Condition*, Chicago, University of Chicago Press (1958).

Arendt, Hannah (1971) Thinking and Moral Considerations: A Lecture. *Social*

Research, Autumn, 71.

Burchfield, E.W. (ed) (1986) *A Supplement to the Oxford English Dictionary*, Volume IV, Oxford, Clarendon Press.

Casey, Maude (1987) *Over The Water*, London, The Women's Press.

Casey, Maude (2017) 'Writing as Survival' in Dawson, Dover & Hopkins (eds) *The Northern Ireland Troubles in Britain: Impacts, Engagements, Legacies and Memories*, Manchester, Manchester University Press.

Ngugi, wa Thiong'o (1986) *Decolonising the Mind*, London, James Currey.

Woodham-Smith, Cecil (1962) *The Great Hunger: Ireland 1845–9*, New York, Harper & Row.

John O'Donoghue
The Place of Asylum

've been writing poetry seriously since I was fourteen. Along with this very private, secret discipline has come deep reflection on my personality. But this personality and this reflection hasn't been formed in a vacuum. I'm a product of a variety of forces, and I'd like to examine these in this essay, and try to say how they have affected me, and the work I've been at for over forty years. I'd also like to outline how I feel about how these forces have shaped my identity, and where I feel they have left me.

My parents were part of the post-war Brawn Drain. My father came over from Ireland after the Second World War and worked as a builder's labourer first of all, then as a fitter's mate on the railways, and finally, when British Rail made him redundant in the early 70s, as a road sweeper, but only at night, when I like to think he swept the moonlight along the dark and dusty roads of the parish.

My mother was everything from a nippy in Joe Lyons Corner House, to a nurse emptying bedpans, to a dinner lady, to, finally, a cleaner in a local factory. That's when she wasn't shopping, cooking, cleaning, washing, in our small flat in East London. We had the upstairs of a terraced house in Leyton, one remove from the East End, where the Irish had landed in the mid-nineteenth century. We were not quite the murphoisie, but we weren't culchies off the boat either.

That my parents were country people was always there. My father, as the surname suggests, was from Kerry, from Killorglin, off a thirty acre farm, and Puck Fair, and wildness, and sometimes even, when the moonshine hit him, madness, never left him. But he had the good luck or the good sense to avoid the asylum. My mother wasn't so lucky or perhaps so sensible. He was a native speaker, but I have from him only the baby words he left me: *bainne agus sucre*, perhaps his way of telling me we had arrived in a land of milk and sugar. My mother, he said, was the one I should pay attention to, as she had passed the Leaving, which sounds to me to this day like the test every Irish person faces as the boat sails out of Dun Laoghaire. The Leaving … The test you take in order to emigrate…

My Irish formation took place not in my father's county, on the farm, within spitting distance of Puck Fair, but in my mother's place, up in Monaghan, in a small post-war settlement built in Lemass's Ireland: Cappog Ballinode, an adjunct to the old village up the road, past the creamery, and over the bridge. It was to her brother's house, to Uncle Tommy the postman, to Auntie Lizzie and my six Murphy cousins, we came. It was in Ballinode that I realised home was where your people were, and that made the parish of St Joseph's in Leyton a much more provisional place for me. It was as if I was learning to be amphibious, to acquire Irish ways and even a brogue as well as a Cockney hardness you needed on the playgrounds, parks, and precincts of East London.

My parents' deaths before I was twenty left many unanswered questions.

What now was I? Officially I was a Ward of the State, fostered at fifteen, sectioned at sixteen, orphaned at nineteen. But what was I to myself?

My father's death at fourteen bruised me into poetry. I'd had exposure to poetry way before this, from Mother Goose to the rhyming riddles my aunt would recite, to the classic nonsense old John Traenor, a relative and neighbour, who would tickle our fancies with: 'One fine day in the middle of the night/Two dead men got up to fight/A blind man came to see fair play/A dumb man came to shout hurray...', to the subversive versions of carols we all told one another on those hard London playgrounds: 'We three kings of Orient are/Wearing Batman's underwear/How fantastic/No elastic/In our motor car'.

But these were rhymes – the first, funny, distracting, naughty – and thus especially appealing – words we ever knew shaped into verses and designed to make you laugh, kinetic, as Joyce would say, not lyric. It was when my English teacher, Mrs Puncheon, played us Dylan Thomas reading his own work that something deeper stirred within me. This would be at that tender age of 14, and as well as exposure to Thomas's voice which seemed to come all the way from another galaxy, she also showed us the internal workings of English poetry, the horsepower of the pentameter.

I then started to do the real homework every poet has to do. Not the sort Mrs Puncheon set me, the learning by heart of speeches from Shakespeare, the pen portraits, the stories, the compositions, the ecker, as my cousins called it, but what Thomas himself set about, before homework that was never done. Kavanagh called this dabbling in verses, and in four red exercise books that took less than six months each to fill dabbling was what I did.

In my solitary pursuit of the call of poetry I worked away at all sorts of experiments, setting myself to follow the countryman's lope of Ted Hughes, the slippered amblings of Auden about his City Without Walls, the solemn processions of early Dylan Thomas, the lyrical hwyl of late Dylan Thomas, the climb up the winding stair of late, stately WB Yeats.

And then – midway this life, as it were – I was sectioned, aged 16. My inner life, the life that had been a stay against grief, collapsed in on me.

It's at this point that I wish to turn to one of the founding myths of Irish poetry, Mad Sweeney. The legend has it that Sweeney is rude to a cleric, and is cursed into a bird, who haunts tree and canopy and sky, bereft of family, of status, indeed of humanity. In return he is gifted, like Orpheus, with song, with flight, with a curious kind of freedom. Sweeney challenges power, and because of that he is cursed. I too came up against a cleric, as Sectioned tells, not, I hasten to add, one of the priests I was taught to hold in respect and reverence, but a cleric of the Other Persuasion.

Unlike Sweeney, I hadn't been cursed by this cleric into my poetry – that, as I say, had already come after my father's death; however I was cursed into something I shared with Sweeney – I was cursed into madness.

I spoke earlier of the legacy my parents had left me, and it is here that I come to the nub of what I want to say to you. Before I entered the asylum, the old Victorian county asylum of Claybury, I had already entered inside myself into another kind of asylum, the asylum of poetry. In the grounds I came upon others there who were also astray: Kavanagh on a bench, Yeats by the lake, Hopkins in the chapel, Keats in a sunlit meadow. In my asylum I had begun to develop an inner life that tried to make sense of the deepest aspects of our condition, of the mysteries the priests advised me to accept, as if closing off the temporal from the eternal. Where have we come from? What are we? Where are we going? Those questions – Gauguin's questions inscribed on his famous Tahitian painting – haunted me. A print of the painting hung on the wall of one of the small rooms where I went for Group Therapy in Claybury aged 16. You couldn't miss them.

I do not say that I have plumbed these mysteries, that I have the answers to the questions Gauguin asks. But in the midst of my confusion and trauma, in the wounding curse I had received from the cleric, I was like Mad Sweeney. I was free. In that first asylum I was free. I was clean cracked, but through the cracks daylight gradually started to appear. I had been admitted to a different class of experience altogether, I had seen how suffering could be shared, and overcome, but I was also aware of the depths from which something beyond adolescence and its fumbling articulations might emerge. My inner and my outer worlds suddenly coincided, in an orbit at once terrible, and liberating. Sweeney remains a potent figure because he represents dissent – dissent from authority, from family, from sanity. And this is why I think the mad are so fascinating and so troubling – the ultimate dissent is the dissent from reality.

It took a long while to recover. Three times on that first admission I came back to sanity, and three times I slipped back. But in doing so I found in myself that place all poets go, a place of refuge, of calm, of asylum, and I was given time and space to explore its airy green grounds. It seems like a dirty word now, asylum, the place where the mad were carted off to, what all those freeloading foreigners are seeking, what dictators look for when they flee the countries they once ruled. But the word means more than that – it should mean a place of safety, of calm, of sanctuary, and God knows we have need of such places.

For me poetry and this inward sense of asylum have always gone together. I don't of course mean the institutions I was placed in – I mean the place where the mind can come up against those mysteries I referred to earlier and find enough imaginative space to countenance them without being overwhelmed. I'm not making a case here for poetry as therapy, as a cure for soul-sickness as Kavanagh's brother Peter called it. I'm talking about a place where inspiration may blow in, and like grace transfigure reality with some small fall of beauty. I think poetry is an outward sign of an inward grace, that poetry is an art that is essentially inspired, and that the poet must find some kind of asylum in order to catch the wind that blows about their head.

Which brings me back to that earlier unanswered question, the one I was left with after my parents' death: who was I to myself? I grew up in London at a time when to be Irish, to identify yourself as Irish, to proclaim your heritage, was asking for trouble. The Birmingham Six, the Guildford Four, the Maguire Seven – these served as examples to instil fear in the Irish in the Britain. It would have been easy for me to hide or deny my identity. Indeed, my dealings with the State and its system of protection and punishment as I went in out of the old Victorian asylums – I was in Claybury,

Friern, and Banstead – were not always what you might call caring.

But if to be sane is to know who you are, what you are, where you are from, then these two aspects of my identity, my Irishness and my sense of myself as a poet – an unpublished, unheard of, unknown poet – kept me going. For poetry helped me to work out the answers to these questions I asked myself after my father died. Who am I now, who am I to myself? The answer I found is that I am Irish, London Irish, as Irish in my way as the Dublin Irish, the Galway Irish, the Cork Irish, even the Kerry and the Monaghan Irish. I am as Irish as the Liverpool Irish, the Boston Irish, the Sydney Irish. I am a child of the Diaspora, not of an imaginary Fifth Province but of a city as big and as real and as dirty as London. I am at home wherever Green in worn. Or, for that matter, White, or Gold.

As John Hume, one of the great political leaders who helped broker peace in the North of Ireland, said, 'Over the years, the barriers of the past – the distrust and prejudices of the past – will be eroded, and a new society will evolve, a new Ireland based on agreement and respect for difference.'

I like to think that the boundaries of this Ireland extend to all those places I've cited beyond these shores, and to the others where the Irish have settled, or are indeed yet to settle, just as my own mother and father set off on their journey to become something more, not something less, than the Irish they had been all those years ago. For Ireland may be the mainland, the mother country, home, but I think the condition of twenty-first-century Irishness is not one of exclusive essentialism, as it was in the tome of De Velara, but of inclusive internationalism. And it's here, finally, that I seek my asylum, and claim it for all us children of the poor immigrant.

Truth, Lies and Memory

Moy McCrory
Memory and Authenticity
Imagining the past to understand the present

n this essay I explore how newer explorations for narrative which merge fact and fiction might still be interpreted as expressions of experience, and I consider how the role of imagination and embellishment in storytelling contributes towards how we view the past as it challenges ideas of authenticity and belonging.

As a writer from what has been called the second generation Irish experience, I find this this needs clarification. There is a problem with this description, when claiming an Irish background might include a distant or American sense of nationality, where Irishness is claimed four or five generations removed with no practical experience in an individual's day to day living. This is not the case for me. I was born in England of Irish parentage. This is what I mean here by the phrase 'second generation'. What this implies in terms of how I belong to a particular culture has been profound.

Writers from this background describe themselves, and have been described in sleeve notes, in different manners; an 'Irish woman living in (a named English town)' of an author born and brought up in southern England, 'Irish, born in England' on an author's webpages, and the one which I describe myself by, 'of Irish parentage'. This shows there is no common description nor even agreement about who we are. But we probably all know that we are not English, at least not in any straightforward way.

In this essay I examine how individual tales and memories show not only how I belong to, but how I differ from, my background cultural source. As we engage in re-imagination and reconsideration of individual selves, how far can those writers amongst us venture from public memory without that projected memory resulting in distortions, and are these distortions part of our authentic need to communicate creatively and otherwise as writers?

Examination of writers' work reveals different uses and methods for accessing a past. Authors who write about their experience of place and/or identity often merge fact with fiction, but such newer forms of telling stories, which work as self-documentaries merge the real with the memoried and the re-remembered to produce an 'authentic' version of events, to occupy a place in writing that has been difficult to label. Authenticity can be at variance from factual truth. Primo Levi, who did not swerve from the reality of his experience, said if one did not alter the way of telling, either by structure or method, then this was not storytelling. Why storytelling was as important as documentation was central to Levi's desire to communicate his experience:

'Levi believed in stories as paths to truth, and in particular truths about human nature' (Magavern 2009:138) but Levi aims for something, which while historically accurate, has to go deeper – he employs a literary truth where, in order for characters to be memorable – to survive in literature – they need exaggeration, otherwise he complained in an interview, 'one is not writing stories, but merely accounts.' (Magavern 2009:139) (McCrory: 2013:89)

One problem that I encounter is that as soon as someone writes from this little accounted for group which I will for brevity call the second generation (of Irish in Britain), their work is taken to stand in for everyone and the work is always assumed to be the author's individual experience. The implication of this is that we are unable or unwilling to fictionalise, at worst that we do not create, but simply observe, in effect that we lack agency.

One of the first responses towards such Irish culturally formed writing was that of inauthenticity. Aidan Arrowsmith's article to the *Irish Studies Review* where he employed the term 'Plastic Paddy', a term which had become popular post the Peace Agreement in Northern Ireland, was one of the first papers which attempted to discuss the authentic/inauthentic seriously and examine this problematized term. (2000)

Maude Casey's 1989, *Over the Water*, reads like thinly disguised autobiography masquerading as fiction, much in the manner of Jean Rhy's writings, an author who famously claimed her fictions were all about herself. However, if Casey describes herself as Irish, the subject of her Young Adult novel does not have to be herself. It is significant that Rhys's memories of Dominica and the use of her own life in her fiction was never examined for authenticity. If Levi's testimony stands in for those who did not survive the Holocaust, his version of European assimilated Jewry shows one aspect to Jewish life out of many. Interestingly he felt free to tell the best account of what were essential truths of observed detail.

Rather than take sides, or swipes at national identities, I want to examine the way being of the generation born away from Ireland reveals itself in creative writing, which up till now has been a poorly examined area. This is becoming part of the expanding field of Irish Studies, (e.g. Murray, T. *London Irish Narratives*, 2012, which treats one aspect of the Diaspora) and hopefully will provide new avenues for exploration.

Because of this problem of being seen to be authentic, have Irish-parented-authors who want to represent their own pasts had to stick clearly to their experiences? For myself this would mean adhering to the oddness of reality, rather than creating a fictional, but more believable reality. This raises questions about the role of memory and imagination. Just how free are we to evolve? What risks can we take? Arrowsmith calls the past 'a constant and elusive presence' which is often 'driven by fantasy'. (2006:166).

The Role of Memory and Imagination

Peter Schneider, a German who became an 'East German' due to the allies division of the country, wrote about his childhood and coming of age in this new state claiming that the country he calls Germany is neither east nor west (BRD, DDR) and his nationality belongs 'to a country which exists only in my memory or my imagination.' (Schneider, 1990:126) He offers a model of a shifting country, but it applies equally to a shifting people such as the Irish.

> If I respond to queries about my nationality by saying without hesitation that I'm German, I am clearly opting not for a state, but for a people that no longer has a state identity. At the same time, however I assert that my national identity does not depend on either of the German states. (1990:126)

Although not stateless in Britain and afforded equal privileges in the U.K. where many Irish live and work, with the route always open for return, this land of 'memory & imagination' is the construct into which the first generation of Irish in Britain are thrown. When I wrote in 'Identity and Belonging in the Irish Diaspora' how the Irish community had been invisible, I was not ignoring the anti-Irish attitudes this group experienced. (Commission of Racial Equality, first major study of Irish in Britain, Hickman and Walter: 1995)

Possibly admitting that memory is variable, and imagination exists to fill gaps, that there is no clear authentic version of any one life, might enable a more honest take on our shifting sense of self as the generations age. This sense of otherness and of difficulty in nationality and of belonging, seems to resonate solely with those where one, or both parents are Irish. The difficulty is experienced amongst those who were the first to be born in Britain.

Sebastian Barry has a character say, 'It is very stupefying to be Irish and have none of the traits or the memories or even a recognizable bloody accent. No one on the earth has ever confused me for an Irishman, and yet that is what I am, as far as I know' (2008:46)

And as far as most of us who go through this route into consciousness of our difference in Britain know, we share what can only be called lodestones of identity. While individual perspectives shape interpretations of events, those lodestones of group identities shape us.

It was while working with a targeted group when I taught Creative Writing at the London Irish Women's Centre in the mid 1980s that I began to see how a common heritage informed and directed our writing and inhabited our imaginations. That there was a rich, culturally driven image-bank from a shared background also often meant that the difficulties we experienced were things we held in common, a repository of misadventures and wrongs.

Family life was rife for unpicking, as was religion, education, and sadly, intolerance, small mindedness, a very persistent state of what has been called Irish begrudgery (Witoszek & Sheeran 1991:11–27) which at least elevates the subject matter from the Irish always seeing themselves as victims, to examining those behaviours of a shared heritage. Speaking ill of others, name calling and cursing generally to bring bad luck on one's enemies has a long heritage. Under Brehon Law (The Ancient Laws of Ireland) an entire section is reserved for penalties for such a one who uses 'spells, slander and verbal abuse' while a classification of 'crimes of the tongue' includes both satire and insult (1991:15).

'The dispossessed, having nothing left but words, might curse freely.' (McCrory:2012:183) and we examined the many spoken forms of insult, some humorous, some genuinely disturbing, but all idiom-rich. At the time it felt as if it was very much a first naming of the shared wrongs we had experienced on account of being women. And the 1980s were hard on all of us.

The 1980s were seen as being dreadful times to be female in Ireland as many educated women left, viewing the referenda on abortion in this decade as attacks on women's rights. The 1983 Referendum stated that abortion was illegal, in 1986 the High Court ruled that the availability to women in Ireland of information on abortion outside the State was in breach of the Constitution, as under the 1983 amendment this would also undermine the right to life. This decision was affirmed by the Supreme Court two years later. (*The Irish Times* Archive)

It was not a great time to be Irish identified in England either, with the IRA targeting England, and London in particular. The Prevention of Terrorism Act (a new security law introduced in 1974) led to heavy handed policing and a situation where 'Irishness became … synonymous with subversion and criminality' (Whelan 2002:20). The infamous Jak cartoon in the *London Evening Standard* (29.09.1982) used racist stereotypes to show 'The Irish' as a race of killers. Sub-captioned 'The Ultimate in Psychopathic Horror' it expanded the definition of racism to employ such tropes to whites. After a history of colonisation and 'othering' (Curtis:1984) the Irish were again being seen in relation to a contemporary civilized England as the 'other'. (Arrowsmith:2006). The Commission for Racial Equality's research project found that assimilation was not as widespread as had been held, a fact assumed by whiteness, which gave the second generation its 'unreadable nature' (McCrory 2012:170) and which created further problems, not least the chilling statistics regarding mental health and the high level of admissions to psychiatric hospitals from this community. (Leavey, Gerald et al, King's Fund London Commission, 1997)

But there had to be something to celebrate, and there was an ownership of our own national identity, no matter how fragmented this was, it was not diluted, as in the manner of claiming past generations, but had been an active formation of those identities.

However, we not only came from different social classes and had experienced different educational opportunities, but the Protestant-identified Irish throughout this time felt they were the wrong sort of Irish on account of Loyalism in Ulster, while those who were Catholic-identified felt disgusted by, yet responsible for, the harsh laws directed against women and the church's control over their bodies in the Republic. What we shared was that we had lived our lives differently amongst the English. And that was my starting point for all subsequent examinations.

I wrote previously about the difficulty of claiming an identity from which there is no 'one size fits all' but rather a fluid construction, responsive to background but defying definition. (McCrory: 2012) Engaging and challenging the inherited visions of our backgrounds meant accepting and naming those less attractive attributes such as racism and fear of the other. In the 1980s it was difficult to have such discussions, and the personal and divisive arguments excluded many women, split groups and silenced voices, and can only be compared to the early days of the women's movement (1970s in the UK) with the bruising encounters experienced among 'sisters' split along class, race and education into zones of privilege against which it was difficult to speak.

It was for instance difficult as a second generation person to claim in public that Ireland suffered from racism, that attitudes were entrenched, that conservative attitudes held sway in the country. It was difficult to acknowledge one's own parents' racism, but there was a subtler difficulty of hearing unconsidered views expressed in terms which were compromised – especially as language shifts were slowest to be taken up in working class districts with limited access to education. However, if the middle classes shifted terms, this was often simply a masking of attitudes rather than a shift of view. Yet it was not the accepted view of the Irish, long considered as 'other' to take into account the community's own difficulties with negotiating 'otherness'.

The Act of Forgetting

There is a constant claim that one's life cannot be authentic, that errors of memory make everything a tissue of fabrications, and that someone other than the author will be the arbiter of the experience. To not be allowed to own one's own life has to be a particular violence felt by anyone who works creatively. To be told that one has got it right, as approval, implies one could get one's life wrong, presumably, without ever realising this.

Willfully getting it wrong is fine. No one asked authors to stand in for national attributes. But what can we forget? What have we had to omit, in order to maintain our lives? What have we had to omit in order to tell a good story (don't let the facts get in the way)?

Who are we protecting?

When I consider my formative years and what has informed my own writing, such background was implicit, and like oxygen, all around but hardly perceived. When I remember incidents of hostility, exclusion and insults on account of Irishness, it is with the sense of this being a forgotten part of social history – of just how bad it was.

People not from this background are always amongst the first to state that other groups had it worse, which of course is true. Equally wrong-headed are those who project their consciousness of difference to claim they experience direct anti-Irishness without giving an account of how they are recognised. If our parents encountered difficulties through their speech in public, we have been like plain-clothes detectives slipping through the meetings and the crowds to eavesdrop. But this is an under-documented group of people, whose parents suffered in the 50s and 60s, and who themselves suffered in the 80s as another Irish spike in emigration occurred. This time the newer Irish arrivals did not recognise the generation born in England. Not only were we not Irish, we never had been. This generation were told that they had no history and at best an incorrect sense of identity. Now, when the more recent immigrants experienced anti-Irish attitudes for the first time, it was claimed that the generation of British-born were part of the problem. By proximity to anti-Irish attitudes we had simultaneously absorbed them rather than suffered on account of them.

This was a time when well established Irish communities in Britain were routinely mocked, their attitudes towards their pasts belittled. This was the setting in which I published my first book, which although fictional, was nonetheless heavily reliant on my experience of growing up Irish in England. In this straightened atmosphere I was expected to be relieved at the Camden Irish Centre when a group of anonymous Irish women (literary critics?) told me my work was 'real'. Because apparently it may not have been. My life may have been a dream after all, a figment.

Imagining the Past to Understand the Present

Was it easier to imagine the past and to create imagery from out of an older form? Referring to literature, Frank O'Connor noted that no country can discard what he called the 'backwards look', relating to historic literary sources, stating that in Ireland without this 'we have nothing and are nothing.' (1968:230) The importance of such literary models are paramount, offering a window back towards a distant history and in turn a sense of ownership. Liam Harte notes the 'inordinate power of storytelling over the second-generation imagination' suggesting that here we might find a coherence. (2003:298)

If real events lock mentalities to that time, the older forms are still relevant, often providing models to illustrate current situations. It was a political act to claim Irishness back in the 1970s and 1980s due to the increased hostility to all things Irish unleashed after the IRA bombing campaign was exported to London, while the volatile situation in Ulster with an army of occupation and stop and search and the deaths of the Hunger Strikers who campaigned for political prisoner status, sent shock waves through the Irish communities.

During the referendum in the 1980s and the situation regarding abortion law, there were incidents in the Republic which made international coverage that centred on single women with unwanted pregnancies and tragic ends, the Kerry Babies case being one of the best known of these.

In my first book I wrote a reworked section of the myth about Macha, into a story about a young woman whose sense of difference is expressed through the images which follow her. Frank O'Connor had earlier written that when something went wrong with early Irish literature 'it did not get corrected, but was rationalised over until it established a minor mythology of its own' (1968:16) and as part of this he dismisses the 'childbirth sickness' that afflicted the Ulaid, cursed into them by Macha, an early horse goddess figure. But at this time (the 1980s), I needed the small myth more than a scholarly working back into the medieval manuscript. Isn't literature about such happy accidents? When the weight of

Catholicism was falling onto the control of Irish women's fertility, wasn't this time to remember (misremember) how powerful men might be served a taste of their own medicine?

> The men of Ulster were low with their pangs, five days and four nights the curse of Macha upon them. Weak as women in their labour. Who dared to shed their blood now would suffer from the same affliction (McCrory,1989:126)

This becomes part of the daydreaming word the character of the story exists in, in which she sees the sean bean bhoct – a personification or Ireland as an old woman mourning for a past, but playing back to historic funeral practices as at times this old woman is shown such as when she 'wrung her hands over the corpse and began to caoin' (128)

In my experience of what was an Irish working-class family in Britain there was an emphasis on storytelling. In this manner was a way of remembering and passing a history along which could not be pulled apart as being 'incorrect' by the more educated. However the way these details were revealed tend to the piecemeal and partial.

If a crisis of identity besets modern Ireland, then possibly its diaspora exports are the most Irish of its people, this contradiction Eagleton expresses as 'nostalgic for a dying culture yet eager for industrial development' (1995:287)

This nostalgia is something which accounts for the sentimental and the backward look to a time when everything was better – the mythic golden past. But if it was so good, as I wrote in an early story, why were the Irish all over here? I put these words into the mouth of an English child, whose anti-Irish parents express their hostility and ignorance on the page.

> 'Why do the Irish all come to England if they're all so proud to be Irish?' her daughter asked over-loudly. 'England must be better if they all end up over here, mustn't it, mum?'

> 'They come over here to work,' said her mother.

> 'I thought no one worked in Ireland. Isn't that why the country's poor? Because they're all lazy and won't work. That's what dad said.'

'Of course not', said her mother embarrassed, quickly turning to mine. 'Your husband is from Belfast isn't he?'

To us children she explained 'That's British. He's not really Irish you see. Of course it's different for you,' and she smiled at my mother. 'A wife's place is with her husband. You have as much right to be here as … well … as me', she finished doubtfully.

My mother's face set awkwardly, the distance between them too great.

'It's time I got on with my work,' she said retreating…
(McCrory:1989:76)

However in the perception of self as 'other' a sentimental version of events can arise in which there is the promulgation of the eternal victim. There is a historic source for this. Noting the shock of what was nineteenth century Ireland's cataclysm (which Eagleton summarises as famine /agrarian revolution/ decline of native language,) Eagleton calls this the 'transformation within living memory of a social order' in what is 'a peculiarly shocking collision of the customary and the contemporary'. (1995:279)

Authenticity

The term 'Plastic Paddy' became popular towards the end of the 1980s and was in part given spurs (to follow my horse-goddess mis-use of an early Celtic image) by the new influx of educated and highly skilled Irish who encountered the seismic shock of how openly hostile they found their new neighbours on re-location to Britain. When we were lumped in together as 'English' we were made invisible. In this way, a group who had been barely perceived and described were being excluded and silenced.

What is authentic about the background? Are we on shifting ground when we begin to question where memory leaves us and storytelling takes over? Might it be that as well as documenting a past we also recreate it for ourselves? In a time of 'false news' we need more than ever to maintain factual details, histories, but in this area of identity, for those like me can there ever be just one version of a culture, arising out of a past to which we look for our touchstones?

In a chapter 'Coming out of Hibernation'? The Myth of Modernity in Irish Culture' Luke Gibbons writes that 'much of what is now taken to be traditional Irish values is of fairly recent vintage' (cited in Eagleton:1995:279).

When people claim they have this common allegiance because of being Irish-born in Britain, an acknowledgement about the Ireland they view might be the starting point. Modern Ireland is largely beyond the grasp of this group. Their homeland is a state of memory, and memory passes freely between countries.

Is there still the need to be the victims of this? As long as there are a generation of those born of their parental exodus, there will be second generation identities. However, such a generation if borne of a freer choice (rather than economic need) might set up expatriate communities but generally such communities do not seek to establish themselves as part of the new country, but remain apart. (Eavan Boland's time in America as the child of an Irish diplomat stationed in New York for example.) All paths without immigration at their core do not destabilise national identities; those born to diplomats or military families stationed abroad would not be encouraged to imagine themselves as other than parental identity. At an Irish in Britain Representative Group (IBRG) meeting in Manchester an English sounding young man announced that nationality was defined by place of birth – which suited him, as he had been born in Ireland, (and left at the age of three months). An elderly man who had spent all his life in Limerick until his 80s when he came to Manchester to live with his adult children, announced that he must therefore be Egyptian, as his father had been stationed there and he had been born outside Cairo. In the end people craft their identities, including their relationship to their nations and those of their parental nations, through lived experience.

Possibly admitting that memory is variable and imagination exists to fill gaps, and there is no clear authentic version of any one life, might enable a more honest take on our shifting sense of self as generations age.

If I had not been brought up in this Irish manner, without ever once glimpsing that it was different to the life of those around

143

me, I would not have reason to reflect on it. Things we took for granted as a culture were suddenly obvious to me when I worked at the Irish Women's Centre. It was a dawning realisation that my background had not been English.

It was only when I started to write creatively that I understood the immersion in a tradition that was spoken, loved storytelling, made connections with a past and survived hostility on a daily basis due to the proximity of the host nation. If according to Medhurst, proximity to strangers increases the need to emphasise difference this surely also creates the need to maintain traditions? Medhurst gives the example of 'English comedians' ... devot(ion)to the Irish Joke' while he finds they 'have no need for Portuguese jokes' (Medhurst 2007:28) as a way of showing the products of such tension.

The sensibility of otherness is central to my writing. Is this purely about the individual or is the individual framed and moulded by their experience? I plump for the latter. It is partly the denial of the individual in the collective view that grates most sharply. We are not homogenous. My own background was especially poor in educated and literary awareness. Those homes where everyone played music and sat round in sessions, seemed to me to reflect a more educated sector of the community, as it was inside the more privileged homes of the Irish in England that as a teenager I discovered these activities, often made possible via private music lessons. I have since learnt this was not the case for many; those who were instinctively musical for example and many who learnt from relatives. If my parents were lumpen, their neglect of such attributes from our background demonstrates another disruption to culture that mid-century economic developments fostered. However, what replaced these outward forms of cultural expression?

There was still an ethos into which my family's Catholicism played a central role. I am relieved sometimes to think that the world was a place with altars and candles and incense and time spent kneeling, if only that the thin forms of 'culture' which might be left available to me as a working class person, and today could be reality TV and the X Factor, pale in comparison. And there was the Irish way of death.

Cultural Ties: Death & Mourning, Education, The Miraculous

Never were our differences so marked as in our mourning practices, and I spent a childhood aware of death largely due to personal circumstances in which the experience of bereavement was frequent, so much so that when my father died while I was at grammar school, although I was singled out for a time, as 'the girl whose father had died', losing a family member was not in itself a new experience. When I wrote a chapter for the book *End Notes* (2017) about death rites I looked specifically at the role of women in the Irish community in Britain. It was important to sketch out my own family's history, where the memory which has been kept alive is maternal – of my father there were no documents, or so we always thought.

Later, it was during the unexpected race for Irish identifiers to claim passports to allow myself and my family to remain as part of the EU in a Britain fast isolating itself from Europe, that these missing details were to prove crucial. The elusive birth details of my father annoyingly became necessary as my mother, it turned out, had in fact been born in Liverpool, likewise her own father. No matter if they returned, no matter their background and culture, the paperwork set them apart and proof was necessary through a paternal line, accessing a history long denied by my own father.

My conclusion at the time was simply that he must have been illegitimate. Somewhere in that past most likely was a story about a woman cast out in Catholic shame and a bastard child brought into a family who neither wanted, nor needed an extra mouth to feed.

Of this, he had had nothing to say when alive, maintaining he had been an 'orphan', brought up by strangers with no knowledge who his real parents were.

I used to trouble myself about his name, where had it come from? Why such an odd hybrid for a devout Catholic – who had hated him enough to name him Billy? Was this name taken from a roster of benefactors from the orphanage? Whatever it was, it showed a lack of concern. And that surname, the one I have retained despite marriage, was it ever part of my 'genuine' history, or was that too a random name pulled from a list at baptism? There were no documents for that either.

I decided he had been a foundling, probably from a Presbyterian background as he showed all the zeal and attachment to Catholic principles of the convert.

How wrong I was.

His eradication of his own past, the loss of evidence, and his failure to maintain the memories by speaking them, was a wilful act of forgetting. Of his birth certificate, there is no trace, but here he is, traceable via a residency card to allow him to travel between Belfast and England just after the war, and there is a date of birth (we have three different dates) however there is his place of birth – we had him – Belfast. On the census of 1911, he also appears, making him four years older than his permit, but it's him, with a named father who reappears (by now deceased) on his marriage license to our mother, and in the census he also has a mother and siblings. He had family. Clearly, he didn't want them.

His past was an act of omission. This lack of memorial was conscious. And throughout our memorials for the dead he was tight lipped, and believed he took his past with him to the grave when it was time to memorialise him.

I wrote in my initial exploration in *End Notes* how these deaths set us apart, but it was more than that – this absence of a father's history, along with his lack of spoken memories and stories, created silences and gaps. Odder than the deaths we experienced was this strange emptiness surrounding him that troubled. He sought out no one, made no friends and made our home a no-go area for all but the most essential visitors; the doctor, the priest and the man from the Prudential. By his insistence on always being right and his general bad humour our father drove off most of our mother's friends. He had no time for our maternal relatives, dividing people up into those who were 'no good' and those who were dead. In the light of the recent discoveries, I suppose he had made this judgement on his own relatives and cut them out of circulation, so why stop there?

When I wrote that he was silent about his childhood, I imagined it was an unpleasant place, but now I see this eradication of the past was highly organised, efficient. If no evidence of his birth remains, he was able to use this to reinvent himself, to escape a history, but there was baggage. And there he is, aged five, unable to read or write, the pen of his father filling in the names of his siblings and mother, and the family religion. Roman Catholic.

While my father's intention was to never speak of his own past, the maternal line unofficially provided a link to our dead, in stories and memories. Even while grieving, the stories could still make us laugh. This is how those ancestors and the relatives who died before my birth were spoken about, so they lived in my imagination, while those I had known were kept present through this manner of storytelling.

And throughout, my father maintained his silence. In time my mother grew to accept his version of himself and decided (wrongly it now transpires) that he was illegitimate and would have agreed that this was a disgrace, akin to suicide, of which there was an example in my maternal line, and like suicide, it was better kept silent. We inherited a past of shadows.

There was an ancient tradition of professional mourners, women who were paid to caoin (keen) and to cry, and there were even 'sin eaters' who went round from village to village taking on the sins of the deceased. As we gathered back at the house after burying my father, there was an odd silence that only a professional mourner could have filled, and so it was left.

I wrote at the time, how '…it is in the construction of the past that we remember our dead, and with nothing to guide us, his life seems to have less substance now than those remembered relatives whom I never got to meet, but who were so fondly remembered that they took on a shape and impression, as the women spoke their stories. Because in the end, that is what we remember and what we take with us.' (2017:57)

Education

The types of schools we attended were part of convents and mo-

147

nastic orders. Although I know very few practising Catholics today many of us who grew up in the tradition have an interest in religious paraphernalia. Images of the Virgin Mary still move me, offering a link towards childhood, the way someone might regard their Action-Man, when a copy of a once much loved toy is discovered in Oxfam.

I never understood the narratives of working class improvement or support, except that these focused on talented young men, from DH Lawrence's Paul Morell to Billy Elliot, whose dead mother nonetheless supports him. My mother believed educating girls was a waste of time and claimed all forms of education were dangerous. Time spent at school was unnecessary. It was as simple as that.

As for authority, I was to respect both priests and the Pope, who was an infallible fount of wisdom. My mother would reply that intelligent 'men' had already decided the answers to questions I wanted to ask about religious belief and faith. There was a non-intellectual, anti-questioning authority at work. So, cowed, bowed, silenced and unquestioning, many of us second generation were told to accept the world as it stood. However, it stood differently. Consider the miraculous.

The Miraculous

I grew up among stories of saints and their properties. These hagiographies are still of interest me; real people who walked this earth and dedicated their lives to a cause and the miraculous which accompanied them. In many the prosaic and the marvellous coexist which I consider a feature of existing differently – a common practical sense and the hope or expectation of something better, which may as well be the product of magic, so far removed from reality is the dream. It is a sort of Gothic knife edge on which we poise.

My mother's experience of the banshee (beansíbh) is a case, where she came in one night looking shaken up, describing the position of the supernatural woman she had just seen, on the threshold sitting under the back window in the yard, and then complained that the window cleaner hadn't touched that same window for months. (2017:45–58) But the mixture of the real and the supernatural is why Magic Realism could only have developed out of Catholic countries. A good example of this is Joseph of Cupertino, whose story exemplifies the switch between prosaic and marvel.

Of this saint it is told how he was so stupid that he could not memorise the catechism, so for his examination for the priesthood he could only learn one passage. When this was the question he was asked on the day, it was declared as evidence of a miracle. And of the marvellous; this same figure was thrown out of the monastery choir, when the other monks complained that his habit of levitating when the spirit moved him, was putting them off their plainsong. Rather than be ashamed of this quant medieval story, the Catholic Church has him enshrined as the patron saint of airline pilots.

Such stories offer a shifting view of reality. Things which cannot be, yet are a necessary part of a narrative. My own employment of reality and the uncanny worked its way through an early story using that most Irish of tropes, the potato, when I turned a woman's husband into that same vegetable, reworking a model from Kafka,

> When Bernadette Lynch woke up in the morning an enormous
> potato the size of a small man lay next to her wearing her
> husband's pyjamas. It was the first thing she saw. She rubbed
> her eyes furiously. She did not want any lingering nightmares,
> she had no time for them; it was washday and she had to do the
> sheets. (1988:9)

Frank O'Connor writes that the differences in consciousness are shown in religious attitudes – the Greeks, he finds, triumph in the glory of man, the Jews, to use O'Connor's phrase, 'abase themselves before the glory of god' but the Irish, are 'fascinated by the mystery'. (243)

Surely the point is that there is no return to the auld ways, which were never ours, but only our echoes. If our mythologies can be bought and studied, why does that make them ours any more than yours? When I was busy using the birth-pang elements of what appears to now be a mistranslated or gleaned element in the Macha story, (according to O'Connor) I found this appropriate to tell of an Irish woman's route into England. Written about the time I had moved from Ireland to London, the time was ripe for me to exert such background tales. In this like all authors I am guilty of embellishment.

This urge to embellish is everywhere – we extend and expand our daily lives Indeed I overheard recently on a train a man on a phone saying: "I told him, 'I choose when to work.' He can't just say 'come in on Saturday'. I told him: 'I'll let *you* know when *I* can work, not the other way round'."

In a time of zero-hour contracts, this surely is the fantasy. What, I wonder was the reality of the conversation with his boss? A pitfall for the Irish in Britain is to see ourselves, not as this gentleman, as victor, but as victim. This was something I did not want to provide more images towards. This I feel, is what led me towards Irish new gothic, via the woman who now sees other women's husbands turning slowly into root vegetables, like her own, ('Transubstantiation') or 'The Strange Case of the Vanishing Woman' (1989:97–107) which more or less does as its title suggests.

If this reflects the tension in the generations and the belief systems which were being questioned by the generation removed from the grip of the church, then the tension in belief and what is seen, what is told and what is actual, plays out in our lives. The division between the expectations and the reality is certainly what caused me as an individual to write and caused me as a teenager to question how we lived and were perceived by our neighbours.

The gulf that opened up between us across the generations and left many of us reacting to and escaping from a background which we would simultaneously want to preserve and yet quit, was not easily resolved.

Those writers from a shifting background such as this can hardly fail to recognise this oscillation in their own work. If the close family group is one which is exposed to hostility, then the need to maintain the security of that background, and aspects of it, also becomes a focus.

It was as if we, the children born on English/British soil, who were the first in our families to be brought up away from Ireland, were setting out on an unexplored highway without signposts or maps, and at the time we were setting out, none of us had any intentions of returning. And then I began to write, and the images and dreams I saw, and those things which moved me to white hot rage, those things which stuck out then, as they still do now, were all part of that background, of that strange place, the shifting ground I occupied, where nothing was as it first appeared, but the writing was leading me home.

Bibliography

Arrowsmith, Aidan (2000) Plastic Paddy: Negotiating Identity in Second Generation Irish–English Writing. *Irish Studies Review* **8(1)**:35–43.

Arrowsmith, Aidan (2006) The Significance of Irishness. *Irish Studies Review* **14(2)**:163–168.

Barry, Sebastian (2008) *The Secret Scripture*, London, Penguin.

Casey, Maude (1987) *Over the Water*, London, Women's Press.

Curtis, Liz (1984) *Nothing but the Same old Story: the Roots of Anti-Irish Racism.* London, Information on Ireland Publishing.

Eagleton, T. (1995) *Heathcliffe and the Great Hunger: Studies in Irish Culture*, Verso, London.

Harte, Liam (2010) Somewhere Between England & Ireland: Narratives of 'home' in second-generation Irish autobiography. *Irish Studies Review*, **11(3)**:293–305.

Hickman, Mary J. & Walter, Bronwen (1995) Deconstructing Whiteness: Irish Women in Britain. *Feminist Review* **50**:5–19.

Hickman, Mary J. & Walter, Bronwen, et al. (2002) *The Hidden Irish in Multi-Ethnic Britain* (ESRC Report).

Hoppen, K. Theodore (1998) *Ireland since 1800: Conflict & Conformity*, Routledge, London & New York (2nd edition).

Levi, Primo (2000) *The Periodic Table,* London, Penguin Classics.

Levi, Primo (1991) *If This is a Man*, London, Abacus.

Jones, Kathleen (ed.) (2000) *Butler's Lives of the Saints*, Collegeville, MN, The Liturgical Press.

Magavern, Sam (2009) *Primo Levi's Universe. A Writer's Journey*, New York: Palgrave Macmillan.

McCrory, Moy (1989) 'The Water's Edge' (pp.119–127) and 'Touring Holiday' (pp.65–77) in *The Water's Edge and Other Stories*, London, Sheba Feminist Press.

McCrory, Moy (1989) 'Transubstantiation' in *Bleeding Sinners*, London, Methuen (pp.9–28).

McCrory, Moy (2013) Primo Levi as storyteller: the uses of fiction, creative non-fiction and the hard to classify in Levi's narrative of the Holocaust, *Short Fiction in Theory & Practice* **3(1)**:85–96.

McCrory, Moy (2012) 'This Time and Now: Identity & Belonging in the Irish Diaspora', in *Land & Identity. Theory, Memory and Practice*, Berberich, C., Campbell, N. & Hudson, R. (eds) Amsterdam, Editionas Rodopi (pp.165–190).

McCrory, Moy (2017) 'A Time to Grieve: Women Mourning and Remembrance in the Irish Diaspora Community' in *End Notes:Ten Storioes About Loss, Mourning and Commemoration,* French, R. & Mckay, K. (eds) (pp.45–58) (http://endnotes.ypsweb.co.uk/wp-content/uploads/sites/12/2017/05/End-Notes.pdf).

Medhurst, Andy (2007) *A National Joke: Popular Comedy & English Cultural Identities*, New York, Routledge.

O'Connor, Frank (1968) *A Short History of Irish Literature : A Backward Look*, New York, Capricorn Books.

Schneider, Peter (1990) *The Wall Jumper: A Berlin Story*, Chicago, University of Chicago Press.

Walter, Bronwen & Hickman, Mary J. (1997) *Discrimination and the Irish Community in Britain. A Report of Research undertaken for the Commission of Racial Equality*, http://hdl.handle.net/10068/377594

Whelan, Bernadette (2005) 'Famine & Fortune' in *When Irish I's are Writing*, PhD Thesis, University of London.

Witoszek & Sheeran (1991) 'The Tradition in Vernacular Hatred' (pp.11–27) *The Crows Behind the Plough: History & Violence in Anglo Irish Poetry and Drama*, ed. Lernout, Amsterdam/Atlanta, GA: Rodopi.

Kath Mckay
Under the Influence of Liverpool,
an Irish city: a 'very close first cousin'
Home

When I mistype 'Irishness' for this chapter, the spell-checker says 'Not in dictionary' and instead offers me 'Rashness/Girlishness/Richness/Apishness/Brashness/Freshness'. I mistype 'Englishness' and it self-corrects no problem. Rashness to define Irishness, like digging a hole, and the soil collapsing back around the hole as you continue digging.

I was not born in Ireland; my parents were not born in Ireland. I'm not living in Ireland. Brought up without religion, I'm not Catholic. Yet it's been said to me 'If you were American, you'd be Irish.' The editor's blurb on my first poetry collection read 'And the sense of Ireland at the back of it all', while a publisher's reader described my stories as having a 'distinctly Irish edge'.

Coming from Liverpool, and with my name, people have always presumed I'm Irish, and as I often feel more comfortable with people from Irish backgrounds than English often I've said nothing. Many people from an Irish background have said I look very familiar, or 'You've got the look of the Irish about you', or 'that Irish Scouse look', and that 'It must be your Irish ancestry'.

But what's the look of things got to do with anything? Pale face, freckles, a reddish tinge to the hair. Blue eyes. Unlike in the myths, there's no one way of looking Irish. I've never claimed Irishness, but others have thrust it on me, and I've had a toe in Ireland.

As a child, you accept whatever is around you. There was always a sense that Ireland was there in the background, which of course it was, as the boats from Liverpool went to Belfast and Dublin. On the rare occasions we left Liverpool, when people found out where we'd come from,

'Ah' they'd say. 'Liverpool. The capital of Ireland.'

In an article in the Liverpool Irish Festival Programme 2018, Mary Hickman quotes estimates from the Office of National Statistics that say that '50% of the Liverpool population have Irish heritage, while the Liverpool Echo puts it higher, at over 75%' (2018:4)

John Belcham, Professor of History at the University of Liverpool, has talked of the 'Celticism' of Liverpool being its 'essence'.

There was always the sense of being slightly apart. A Liverpool friend asked in all seriousness once whether she could put Scouse on her passport. The Hickman article on Migration also quotes a remark from Simon Rattle, the conductor, in support of this: 'Liverpool is off the side of the known universe, and it always was. New York is the only place comparable'. (2018:5)

A while back, my brother, who has lived in Ireland for many years, and has an Irish partner and Irish-born children, phoned up and said he now had the family tree, and the feeling we have always had that we were Irish is brought into focus by official certificates and figures.

Lies, half-truths and stories

I grew up thinking my father was Irish, but it turns out he was more of a wannabe. He would sing to us what I thought were

Irish songs –'I'll take you home again, Kathleen'; 'With a shillelagh under my (pronounced 'me') arm and a twinkle in my eye', and of course 'Danny Boy'. My mother joined in with 'When Irish eyes are smiling' and 'If you're Irish, come into the parlour'. This was released in 1912, written by Irish – born comedian and songwriter Shaun Glenville, and Frank Miller, and is now available in the Irish traditional music archives.[22] (For a very funny rendering of this song, see this 2009 version.[23])

'When Irish eyes are smiling' was written in 1912 in the States, by Chauncey Olcott, whose mother was Irish, and George Graff and Ernest Bell –neither of whom were Irish. Many of these songs were examples of what has been called 'Tin Pan Irish', or 'cod-ethnic', hugely popular ballads and ditties specifically written by skilled songwriters for the Irish American market.

The lyrics to Danny Boy were written by an English lawyer who allegedly never set foot in Ireland, and only achieved success with the song in 1913 when he matched the lyrics to The Londonderry Air, based on an ancient Irish melody, and supplied by his Irish born sister-in-law.

There are countless renderings of Danny Boy, e.g. Shane McGowan; Elvis; and a version at the Last Night of the Proms at Belfast City Hall. Northern Ireland was represented in the opening ceremony of the 2012 Olympics by a choir of children singing Danny Boy, standing on the Giant's Causeway on the Antrim coast. And during Derry's Year of Culture 2013 they held a mass sing-in of Danny Boy in the city. Barry McGuigan's father often sang it at his boxing matches, with McGuigan saying he wanted a song that belonged to both communities.

The oddest version of 'I'll take you home again Kathleen' (written by Thomas P Bettendorf, a German American) featured in a Star Trek episode, when a crewman who fancies himself as a descendent of Irish kings repeatedly sings the song as the ship plummets out of orbit after the crew are affected by a substance

22 The link to the traditional IRISH MUSIC Archive referred to n p.2 can be found at https://www.itma.ie/digital-library/text/915-sm.)

23 A modern version of 'If you're Irish, come into the parlour.' https://www.youtube.com/watch?v=cw9vazexg7c

that brings repressed feelings and behaviour to the surface.[24] Such is the power of song.

Interesting that these songs, mostly written for the Irish immigrant market in the States, crossed the Atlantic to England and Ireland and became popular in some parts of Liverpool, a city heavily influenced by the States.

Over the years there has been a lot of debate about whether these are 'authentic' or bastardized versions of 'Irishness', but as Fintan O'Toole, the Irish journalist and commentator, has said 'Everything gets washed up in Ireland ... it has this habit from very early on of absorbing everybody's influences ... and then reprocessing them and turning them into something distinctive ... (there is an) incredible capacity to take in whatever's going and try to make something new of it.' (2014)

And I like these comments posted by 'O'Donnell, the fiddler' on an American music site, *The Session*, in a debate about the worth or otherwise of this music:

> 'Growing up, I knew these songs simply as "Irish songs". I was given no frame of reference for their context, and culturally, I think this is where it stops for most people (Americans, at least) ... Only after I became enamored with actual Irish songs from actual Ireland did I go back and learn the true origins of these songs.
>
> Are they valuable? Yes. Do they have a place in any sort of authentic Irish tradition? No. Are they important to the history of the Irish people and the diaspora? I think so. Should we associate them with Irish culture? Maybe. Kind of. Sort of. It's all about context'.

I absorbed stories that my father had been left wing in his youth, active in his trade union and that he was the black sheep of a family, but his idealism had disintegrated. He told us stories about Kitty Wilkinson, an Irish migrant to Liverpool, who campaigned for public washhouses and baths, the first built in the country in 1842, ten years after a terrible cholera epidemic. I was intrigued to read in the Hickman article in the 2018 Liverpool Irish Festival

---

24 https://www.youtube.com/watch?v=PToL4mNwS84

Programme about a new social enterprise community laundrette being launched in the same part of Liverpool as the original wash-house, to be called 'Kitty's Laundrette'.

My father told us he had fought for Ireland and against Franco, in the International Brigade. I fantasized about getting Spanish citizenship, but have found no proof of his involvement, although when I wrote to Jack Jones, a trade union leader, he said that my father 'certainly supported Spanish progressive forces', and could have been in an Irish branch of the International Brigade. Again, I have found no evidence.

My father, a man of mystery, spun us tales. I thought this was normal.

Truths

During the Great Hunger, between 1846 and 1852, 1.3 million Irish people passed through Liverpool. Many headed west towards America, in the infamous 'coffin ships'. By the end of 1851 90,000 Irish-born people were living in Liverpool, making up over 22% of the city's population (although this had declined to 15.6% by 1871). My ancestors were amongst them, as were those of Stephen McGann, actor, who has written about discovering his Irish roots, in *Flesh and Blood: A History of My Family in Seven Maladies*, and having relatives who starved in Liverpool after escaping the famine in Ireland. Many Irish immigrants were grouped in awful conditions around the docks, and disease and ill-health were widespread. If in one year, 1847, 7000 paupers were buried in common graves, in the same year, under new powers under the Poor Law, 15,000 Irish people were deported back to Ireland.

McGann talks of how seeing refugees in fragile boats puts him in mind of his ancestors fleeing Ireland during The Great Hunger. As Fintan O'Toole says, 'Memory goes on and on. It stays for incredibly long periods of time'.

My mother was brought up in a Liverpool orphanage after her mother died and her merchant seaman father went back to sea. She escaped becoming a child migrant. But one day a friend of hers disappeared from the orphanage: my mother was told she'd gone to Australia. Migration, back and forth across the oceans.

I was born in Liverpool 8. When I was a toddler, our family, like thousands of others, were moved out from the inner city slums to the supposedly new lands of Kirkby, a six mile, expensive bus ride away. We shopped in mobile vans (mobiles). At the time, giving people bathrooms and inside toilets seemed more important than providing shops, which came later, alongside pubs.

My father bussed it to his job at the docks, taking his hook with him, and occasionally took us for a Saturday afternoon trip to the docks, still busy then, with the river full of traffic.

My mother meanwhile was bringing up seven kids, working in the newly open frozen food factories of Kraft and Birds Eye and acting as the first secretary of the local Labour Party.

In an interview, Belcham has pointed out that when people lived in the inner city, and life revolved round 'the pub, the parish and so on, there was an immediate geographical thing which strengthened your ethno confessional or sectarian allegiance – that sort of disappeared when tens of thousands were decanted out to outer estates that didn't have that type of infrastructure based on particular confessional allegiance'. (2011)

The divisions were still in the education system. There were four comprehensive schools in Kirkby – two Catholic schools – the all-girls St Gregory's and the all-boys St Kevin's – and Brookfield and Ruffwood for the others.

However, a kind of tribal allegiance united us. One summer there was a 'leprechaun scare' and hundreds of us converged on local churchyards, hunting for leprechauns after rumours flew round that the little people had been seen. The hunt lasted two days. I thought I'd made up this story, but now I know it followed a similar eruption of leprechaun hunters in central Liverpool a few weeks before. Children interviewed by local newspapers spoke of creatures eight inches high with red and green tunics and knee-high breeches, speaking with a strong Irish brogue.

I thought my mother was straight Liverpudlian. After my father's death, I said something about him being Irish. My mother laughed and said 'I'm more Irish than him.' He was an often taciturn man, who I was also told was an 'orator', speaking at the dock gates to try and rouse men into action. Whereas she was a sociable, lively person, who according to him was always 'gabbing' at the garden gate with the neighbours. Straight away I think of the register of language. So while he hauled and orated at the docks, she 'gabbed'. 'Gabbing' was 'talking indiscreetly, foolishly'. There may be an etymological link to the Irish Gaelic colloquial word for mouth or beak: 'gob'.

When my mother brought her new lover back home after my dad died, we found out he was a member of the Orange Lodge. Growing up with our father's socialist values, and my mother's involvement in the Labour Party, we felt ashamed.

'It's only a day out in Southport,' she said as she went off on the coach with him on The Twelfth of July. We knew it wasn't, so my brother Kevin and I toppled the plaster King Billy he'd put up in the window of our front room. With his plumed hat and long boots, he cracked clean across his upturned sword and we swept him up.

When my mother died, she had a Catholic medal in her purse.

If I was going to claim any kind of Irishness, it would be fifth generation, on my mother's side, which provokes splutters of disbelief and laughter and remarks about Irish Americans and how sentimental and nostalgic they are, claiming to be more Irish than the Irish

My mother's family, like thousands of others, left Ireland for Liverpool during The Famine. They were in the Liverpool census in 1851, but not in 1841.

Their names were Robert Phipps and Margaret Phipps. They were Catholic. Their son John married Ellen, who was Scottish, and also Catholic. He died, leaving her with five kids, and one was Charles Phipps, my granddad, who I never met. They all had Catholic baptisms. In the family were paperhangers and decorators. There was time spent in the workhouse for some. 'There was a lot of institutionalism in your family,' said my sister-in-law, on seeing the family records. Charles was a merchant seaman who, after his wife died, left my mother to be cared for in an orphanage. At some point, I don't know when, and I don't know why, her family stopped being Catholic

Football

Football mad as a teenager, I supported Liverpool and attended matches with a mate. We were passionate fans, going on the Kop, which in those days was a standing terrace. I remember bawling our eyes out as we watched Liverpool lose. We were fanatics.

Since I left Liverpool people have said to me that Liverpool used to be the Protestant club, and Everton the Catholic, but when I was a supporter sectarian divisions had faded away.

For an interesting article about the background and history of the two clubs, showing how both clubs had a tradition of trying to 'cement good fellowship', and not cultivate divisive practices, see David Kennedy's 'Red Blue Green Orange' discussion site.

In the same interview, Belcham (2011) has lauded the fact that 'You don't have to be a particular type to support one or other of the football teams, which is marvellous about Liverpool, which wouldn't apply elsewhere, where it would be a straightforward sectarian association.'

And Bill Shankly, the socialist manager who ignored the sectarian divisions between Celtic and Rangers when living in Scotland, and divided his loyalties between the two teams, had plenty to say about football on Merseyside:

'I've seen supporters on Merseyside going to the ground together, one wearing red and white and the other blue and white, which is unusual elsewhere. You get families in Liverpool in which half support Liverpool and the other half Everton. They support rival teams but they have the same temperament and they know each other. They are unique in the sense that their rivalry is so great but there is no real aggro between them ... I've never seen a fight at a derby game. Shouting and bawling ... yes. But they don't fight each other. And that says a lot for them.' (2015:03)

Talk

Ireland was never very far away. It was there in the names in my family – Maureen, Michael, Colin, Kathleen, Kevin, Patricia. It was there in the surnames, in the numbers of 'Macs' on the school register. Belcham has talked about the Irishness of Liverpool being its distinguishing feature: 'in England, but not of England ... The Irish presence really explains what Liverpool was about,' he says. It was there in the way people spoke to each other, as if talk was a form of entertainment, or craic, as if a conversation was meant to be carried on, that stories should be told.

The Irish writer, Kevin Barry, lived in Liverpool for three years, where he set his prize-winning story 'Beer Trip to Llandudno'. In an interview on *Thresholds*, the short story site (2016) he speaks of how 'there's a way in for an Irish writer with the Liverpool accent-it seems like a very close first cousin.'

Away

I went to Queen's University, Belfast, at the height of The Troubles, living in the North for four years. On the surface, Belfast didn't strike me as much different from Liverpool – the same terraced housing, the same dark humour, the same delight in telling stories. But with the British Army in occupation, high tension and sectarian assassinations, I rethought Liverpool, and realized how to some extent I had been brought up outside defined lines. I remember a discussion with a girl from a Protestant background, and she referred to 'the proper English, not like you.' She was referring to class, but was also voicing her perception of people from Liverpool. For the first time, I met middle class people, and became alert to the nuances of different accents. When one middle class student said that they said they were going 'home', I had presumed from their voice that they were English, and thought they meant England, not the Antrim Road.

There were two philosophy departments at Queen's – Philosophy, and Scholastic Philosophy. I studied Scholastic Philosophy for a year, zooming through centuries of thinkers, examining the nature of existence. A perception amongst some Protestant students was that Scholastic Philosophy was 'philosophy for Catholics', a too easy (and inaccurate) shortcut of an answer. Everything was political.

I was taught literature by Seamus Heaney, nicknamed the 'poet of the root vegetable' by his wife, as at the time he often wrote about turnips and potatoes. Even vegetable shops were political, with a local fruiterer gunned down. David Park's title story 'Oranges from Spain' fictionalises such an incident in his first collection of stories (1990). Heaney took us out to cairns and read his poetry over ancient stones. We had a seminar shortly after Bloody Sunday, everyone in shock, him with his head in his hands.

His writing, and that of other Northern Ireland writers, rooted in the local, but, with universal resonances picked up by others far away, bedded down in me, superimposed on what I'd brought from Liverpool. So when I came to study Joyce and Frank O'Connor, and later Chekhov's stories, with his focus on the little person, characters in a world of matter, with usually unfulfilled spiritual longings, I saw connections.

I've always liked this quotation from Heaney's essay The Sense of Place, in *Preoccupations*, and it makes me think of the layers of places we have lived in and places that we have dreamed of that we carry around within us:

'I think there are two ways in which place is known and cherished, two ways which may be complementary, but which are just as likely to be antipathetic. One is lived, illiterate and unconscious, the other learned, literate and conscious'. (2005:131)

The influence of Belfast and the contradictory nature of the place made me sceptical of 'truth'. Abortion laws (like now) were very restrictive, and male gay homosexuality was a criminal offence until 1982, with gay male friends in danger of prejudice, abuse and jail. I was in a women's group, and at one point we joined friends on a train to Dublin to attend a meeting of a newly formed 'Union for Sexual Freedoms in Ireland.' There was a long way to go.

When I moved to London in the mid-70s, my life was coloured by the experience of Queen's, and Belfast. An Irish friend working at an abortion charity told me of the numbers of Irish women who arrived at their door. And the 'proper English' in the establishment were jailing innocent Irish people in convictions that took years to reverse. Like many, I helped on one of the Irish miscarriage of justice campaigns. Later, in the 80s, I taught at the North London Irish Women's Centre, meeting women who had come over in the fifties and women who had recently left Ireland, finding London a more amenable place for Irish women.

Death

I've had a few people die on me in the last fifteen years. A second generation Irish friend reminded me of the Irish way of shaking your hand and saying 'I'm sorry for your trouble' and the aptness of this. How it acknowledged your loss, out in the world, and gave you the option of saying more, or not. As opposed to experiences I had with some of the 'proper English' crossing the road to avoid me, and not wanting to bring up the topic of death, 'in case it upsets you'.

When my mother died on Christmas Day in a Liverpool hospital, with the world outside snowed up and me the only one of seven children able to get there in time, I asked the nurse if I could take my mother home.

'A lot of people in Liverpool still do,' he said.

'Have you got a car?'

'No.'

But eventually we did take my mother home to the cosy flat she was so proud of, and she lay in her bedroom surrounded by Christmas presents she'd been stashing for her family for months. My sisters and brothers and I sat up all night drinking and talking (and arguing), knowing we shouldn't leave her alone. And how touched I was the next day as people stood in the street in respect and men removed their hats. Living in London, I had forgotten people still did that.

The Irish way of the wake before and the drink and the talk, and the 'aye, he went quick at the end' even if it took them weeks to die, makes perfect sense. Laughter and sorrow are often very close together.

We do a good funeral in my family. I've had to speak at several funerals over the last few years.

We played Wandering Aengus, at my brother's request, by Christy Moore (1984), at his funeral, and another brother, Kevin, sang an unaccompanied song he wrote himself. I spoke of my brother suffering his final illness mainly with 'stoical good humour, except for the occasional melancholy, which is the other half of his heritage'. A year later, we threw his ashes in the Mersey, where we'd already thrown my mother's and my sister's, into the river my father worked on, that widens out into the Irish Sea, where I took the boat to Belfast when I left Liverpool for university.

Writing

Fintan O'Toole reminds us that in Ireland writing matters, and that poets and writers have always had a sense of a public role. That for a country of six million people, it has been disproportionally represented in the literary culture. And a memory comes back of fighting in the primary school playground with a group of girls over which was the best story we'd ever read. And at aged nine, of queuing all night for the opening of Kirkby Library.

Writing matters. Music matters. Death exists.

Silence can be as important as language. I have stayed silent for a long time, not facing up to the contradictions of my position, more comfortable in letting people presume things.

As O'Toole says, 'Art doesn't give you answers –it gives people courage-if there are deep seated tensions, allows us to experience those things'. (2014) There are deep seated tensions in being an 'outsider', feeling more comfortable around Irish identified people but not wanting to be classed as a fraud. Others have picked up on resonances in my writing that I didn't even know were there.

O'Toole talks in the same interview about how art gives you the 'capacity to deal with contradictions' and of the 'extraordinary dialogue between past and present'; how in a diaspora culture things don't get lost, but sometimes go into a 'dormant state', ready to be picked up again. ' (O'Toole 2014)

It's like I have been in a dormant state, ready to pick up things again.

I'm not claiming Irishness; I am claiming a little dilution of Irishness, a part.

Belchem and others have spoken of 'ethnic fade', especially amongst Protestant Irish, with identities becoming fainter as people assimilate. My ancestors must have made that decision to assimilate when they stopped being Catholic. But something, no matter how diluted, remained and bubbles up.

O'Toole has also spoken of the capacity to imagine 'something different' and to 'tell stories about your place … your own people'. Through telling stories you 'make it new'.

As Gary Younge, in a nuanced exploration of Self-defining wrote after the Rachel Dolezal affair, 'It is a cardinal rule of social identity that people have the right to call themselves whatever they want. That's as true for Dolezal as it is for Caitlyn Jenner. But … what you call yourself must be comprehensible to others.' (Younge: 2015)

It is comprehensible that my ancestors were Irish. It is comprehensible that I grew up in a city heavily influenced by Ireland. So what did it do to me? It made me not 'proper English'.

I have spent my working life writing and teaching, mostly short stories and poetry, much of it Irish literature. Always it comes back to words. Anne Enright has spoken about how the Irish short story has been dominated by stories of childhood and the repercussions of childhood. It interests me how patterns laid down early cast long shadows and set up mysteries, engendering silences we try to fill.

You get on with your life and you don't think about identity. But then you keep an eye on Ireland and at conferences you gravitate towards the Irish and you talk and find yourself wondering 'Why did she have a Catholic medal? Where did that come from? Why did she keep her options open?'

I'm in an Alice in Wonderland situation with the word 'Irish'

> "When I use a word," Humpty Dumpty said in rather a scornful tone, "it means just what I choose it to mean – neither more nor less."

> "The question is," said Alice, "whether you can make words mean so many different things. (1934:205)

And I think of my mother in her flat, surrounded by the objects she gathered around her ('company'): an electric fish, a plastic parrot that played Born Free, a rotating multi-coloured Father

Christmas, and the switch that turned on the electric dog, a disembodied bark she used to scare off burglars, happy as anything with her make believe, her glitter and gauze, taking double exposed photos of bins and tower blocks, so that the tower blocks floated high in the sky, in the world, but not.

And what have I got left? A few ornaments of my mother's. A leprechaun house. A music box that plays 'When Irish eyes are smiling.' This essay. My pen hovering over official forms, when it asks for 'Ethnic background'.

Bibliography

Akenson, Donald (1993) *The Irish Diaspora: A primer*, Toronto: P.D. Meany Company; Belfast: Institute of Irish Studies, Queen's University Belfast.

Barry, Kevin (2012) *Dark Lies the Island*, London, Vintage.

Barry, Kevin (2016) Masterclass with Barry on the short story http://thresholds.chi.ac.uk/wp-content/uploads/2016/11/PODCAST_Kevin-Barry-Masterclass.mp3

Belcham, John (2007) *Irish, Catholic and Scouse*, Liverpool, Liverpool University Press.

Belcham, John (2006) *Merseypride*, Liverpool, Liverpool University Press.

Belcham, John (2011) Interview on the effects of Irish culture and immigration on Liverpool https://www.youtube.com/watch?v=rSx46rfw6yw

Carroll, Lewis (1934) *Through the Looking-Glass*, London, Macmillan.

Heaney, S (1980) *Preoccupations 1968–78*, London, Faber. https://www.irishtimes.com/culture/books/seamus-heaney-if-i-described-myself-as-an-ulsterman-i-d-have-thought-i-was-selling-a-bit-of-my-birthright-1.2077002

Hickman, Mary (2018) 'Migration' in Liverpool Irish Festival 2018 programme https://www.liverpoolirishfestival.com/wp-content/uploads/2018/09/2018-brochure-1.pdf

Park, David (1990) *Oranges from Spain*, London: Cape.

McGann, Stephen (2017) *Flesh and Blood: A History Of My Family in Seven Maladies*, London: Simon and Schuster.

Moore, Christy (1984) *Wandering Aengus*, Ireland, WEA Ireland; USA Roadrunner.

O'Toole, Fintan (2014) 'Imagine Ireland: The Irish State of Mind', Fintan O'Toole in conversation with Margaret Spillane https://www.youtube.com/watch?v=7CWEfyWRgOs

Younge, Gary (2015) https://www.theguardian.com/world/commentisfree/2015/jun/12/rachel-dolezal-black-identity-civil-rights-leader

http://www.academia.edu/566121/The_English_Poor_Law_The_Irish_Migrant_and_The_Laws_of_Removal_and_Settlement_1819-1879

http://research.ie/what-we-do/loveirishresearch/blog/loveirishresearch-blog-senator-david-norris-on-gay-rights-and-reform-in-ireland-a-personal-history/

The Session, a music discussion site https://thesession.org/discussions/33780

Shankly, Bill '30 Great Bill Shankly Quotes Every Liverpool FC Fan Should Read' https://www.pastemagazine.com/articles/2015/03/bill-shankly-quotes.html

Kennedy, David 'Red and Blue and Orange and Green?' http://toffeeweb.com/season/09-10/comment/fan/RedBlueGreenOrange.pdf

Fiction and Poetry

Elizabeth Baines
Family Story

Part I

Guidelines for a Daughter at her Irish Father's Funeral

Paint your mouth Coral Blush, the colour of discretion. Keep it closed.

Smile, sadly, at the relatives gathering at the house beforehand –
your mother's, the Welsh ones. Act the loving, grieving daughter
and offer them tea in the rose-printed cups. There'll be none there
Irish, not even the nun, the ex-nun, the only one of your father's
relatives you met, the only one of his scattered siblings whose
names you couldn't remember or always muddled.

Don't bother wondering why she hasn't come. As with every-
thing else, you'll never know. You'll never know why she lost touch.

Once upon a time she threw herself on your father's mercy, turned up on the doorstep in Leeds when you were ten, standing there beneath the windchimes in an old outdated coat the convent had given her, stockings wrinkled round her ankles, her shorn black hair growing out in tufts. She brought a whiff – just a whiff, before she went off to a different, distant life – of the world that your father had put behind him long ago.

It was a world of tall tales: *Daddy, Daddy, tell us about Ireland; Ah well now, so poor we were, we hadn't a table, just a board on the floor, a beaten-earth floor with holes dug all around for our legs.* And he'd grin, he'd fooled you; you thought he must be lying but still you felt he'd fooled you: he'd blocked you, you were a fool, a Welsh, Welsh–English fool, you didn't have his gift of the gab, you couldn't make strangers love you instantly, with a lilt in your voice and a story, and with a promise you never meant for more than that moment to be their lifelong friend. That world, that place, didn't even have a name in the big leather atlas. You asked him once to point it out, and surprisingly he complied, flapped his big yellow smoker's finger on an empty green space in the centre of the map, a blank. The one letter your grandmother there ever sent you, which you forced her to send by writing one to her: *You lead a very different life from us, and you would not like it here.* The brush-off that you, Welsh Protestant brat that you were, didn't understand at the time. You got little from the nun; like your father, she was vague, as if she found it impossible to put into words or had even forgotten: after all, when she entered the convent long before, she too had left it all behind.

There's not much point in wondering if something went wrong between her and your father. You do know, though, that your father hated the quiet Englishman she met at church and soon married. She brought him to visit, and you thought your father simply despised him, but you've wondered, looking back, if what he didn't like was the staring, watchful eyes. You know your father hated being watched and wondered about. You know it's why he had it especially in for you.

You will think of this, of course, that he had it in for you, as you look at him in his coffin, at his big right hand laid over the other. You won't avoid remembering its sting, the flick as you passed, across your ear, your bare arm, the flex of his wrist as he wielded the slipper, the belt like a cutting blow from the past. You were the one who asked too many questions; unlike your sister, you dared to challenge. You complained when he hit you (so he hit you more), you couldn't keep your mouth closed. *You watch your bloody mouth,* he'd boom as he leapt for the cane. His car would pull up in the yard outside, the weatherfront of a scowl coming down on the face he gave to world, and the others would turn to you in alarm. *Now watch what you say,* your mother would warn; *Don't rattle his cage!* your sister would hiss, her black curls shaking with passion and fear. And when, after all, you'd both had a beating, *You make us all suffer,* your sister would sob.

Hold you tongue. Hold your back straight, polish your shoes, wear nice clothes. Smile. No one will ever know. No one did, no one does, not even the closest Welsh relations arriving just now.

Don't breathe a word of any of it now. You'll have your guide: your sister will have warned you, anxious and intent on the phone beforehand, as she's done every time you were due to visit down the years since you left, desperate to get away from it all.

Regard him in the coffin, brought back to the house just as he'd have wanted, to lie in state in the house he dreamed of and got in the end, the Georgian mansion high on the hill, businessman pillar of a small-town English community, rags to riches success. Surrounded in death by the trappings that proved it: the Chippendale chairs, the antique revolvers in cases, the silver. Take in the black jacket, the grey pin-striped trousers, the tie with Masonic symbol. As you do, you'll think of the time, as an adult, you decided to join a class in Family History Research. You happened to tell your mother, and she rang you back, anxious, to tell you: Your father doesn't want you to do it. He can't stop me, you told her (and made her more anxious, panicky even): there are records, such things are in the public domain. But you didn't do it: you thought, Fuck him, fuck him and his past you're shut out of, you'd got your own life, a life without secrets or prejudice or shame, his past was nothing to you. But what you felt, what you know, is that in fact you'd been forbidden, it was taboo.

Was it only the Masons, you wondered then, and will wonder now, or was it you he didn't want knowing? What was it exactly he didn't want you digging up? The Catholic background, your mother told you at the time, the Catholics and the Masons hating each other. You'll think about the other things she told you, at other times. His flight from Ireland at the age of sixteen, vowing never to be an Irish Paddy, never to get his hands dirty again, but still ending up unloading ships on the dock and swilling ships' decks and digging foundations on land. When she met him during the war, she told you, he asked her to correct him whenever he came out with any Irish phrase, or if ever he said *filum* instead of *film*. But he never lost his accent (*you* corrected him once, and he clouted you round the ear); it couldn't be hidden when he and your mother went looking for lodgings after the war, past the signs in the windows, *No coloureds, no dogs, no Irish*. The excommunication from the Church, all in his absence, news of which came only indirectly, from an aunt in Australia, for failing to bring his children up Catholic. The children, you, the cause of his secret pain and shame.

You especially, the lippy one, always ready to challenge the illusion, the one with a mouth that must be stopped with a firm, hard hand.

As you stand at the coffin, you'll think about his illusions and contradictions: the silent brooder and talkative charmer, sober man of business and lovable professional Irishman. You'll want to laugh. Don't laugh. Don't scowl either (another thing he would hit you for: it gives the game away). Don't tax yourself with the paradox, you'll never understand. After all, he made sure it was nothing to do with you.

Except that it's everything to do with you.

You never thought of yourself as half-Irish; you always wished it wasn't so, but he was alien to you and you were alien to him. But you never felt truly Welsh, either, nor, in the places you moved to in England, could you ever feel English. The secrets and uncertainty cut you off from the world outside the household, and what you felt, all the time, was odd. You weren't Catholic, but you didn't want to be the thing he saw as a threat and despised, so in the end you weren't Protestant either, you were nothing, no religion; religion to you was a throbbing sore, a matter of strife and pain.

You were nothing, belonging nowhere, and it did still your tongue.

When it came to your turn in the classroom roll-call, you found it impossible to say your name, the *l*s tripping over the *n*s, a knot, a jumble, the Irish surname and the English first name two dissonant chords crashing together, your impossible identity rolling under and over and tangling your tongue. You flinched at everything. You flinched when he neared, and he'd hit you for flinching, and you cringed in the outside world at all the things you didn't fit and couldn't fathom: the confidence and ease of other kids in the playground, their unconscious accents, their long-established and agreed traditions, their taken-for-granted sense of belonging. You were terrified, long into adulthood, of walking into a crowded room, afraid to speak in a group, scared you didn't know the codes, worried that what you might say was wrong. Ever unable to account for yourself.

He did that to you, you'll think, as you follow the hearse in the car to the church (Church of England, establishment church for an establishment man), as you find it packed with black-coated Masons from all over the country and beyond, and all the people of the town, purple-nosed men and their fat wives in pearls from the Rotary Club and the bridge-playing circle, the whole community turned out for a legendary, generous, affable man.

You'll feel negated. You'll feel angry.

You'll think for a moment: I could spill it all with a word.

Don't. As the first hymn starts up, as the church vibrates with the deep hollow sound of establishment men singing, remember the one time you did.

You were six years old, you hadn't yet grasped it was not to be spoken. You let it out to a girl who had come to tea, you said, No, no, we can't jump on the chairs, my daddy'll hit me with the stick.

She told her mother. Her mother took your mother to task.

You heard her mother say the word *Irish*.

You will never forget it: your mother standing as the woman stalked off, on the prom in the place where you lived at the time but moved away from soon after, you'll wonder now if this was why. The superior disgusted air of the woman; your mother's coat – a hand-me-down from one of her aunts – flapping helpless in the wind, her hand on the icy handle of the secondhand pram. And all around the air breaking, seagulls falling and screaming – *shame, shame* – and the wind coming in from the Irish sea to blow forever through your life.

Part 2

Conversation Between a Writer and her Mother and Sister

WRITER (*tentative*): So, Mum … did you read the story?

The mother, who is usually enthusiastic about her daughter's writing, pauses, serious and troubled.

MOTHER: Well, I found it upsetting.

SISTER (*to Writer*): I *told* you she would be.

MOTHER: The way you present us all. The way you present *me*: a bad mother, telling you off all the time! And you've made it all so miserable. You've left out all the happy times, the times I took you walking and biking, all those sing-songs and laughs!

SISTER (*unsmiling*): Yes, no laughs. I *told* you to make it funny.

MOTHER: All those trips your dad took us on, those picnics on Sunday afternoons…

The writer is filled with shame and horror and remorse.

WRITER (*recovering*): But Mum, it's not *you*, it's not really us, it's a *story*!

MOTHER: Of course it's us! But you've made it all seem different from the way it was. And I'm really very sad you see it like that.

WRITER: Mum, I don't. It's just – you know, the way stories take you over … It's not meant to be the *reality*! It's fiction! And anyway, look at how I've written it: it's not *I*, it's *You*, second person; I'm not claiming it's *me*, it's someone else, or anyone. And it's not claiming to be a historical truth: it's framed in a future tense, it's conditional!

The sister is looking cynical.

SISTER: But everyone will know it's us. The house on the hill! You've described my hair! You've even put the china with roses in. You've got the wind chimes on the door when we lived in Leeds!

WRITER (*all at once feeling hilarity, if not hysteria*): How many people know we had wind chimes when we lived in Leeds? Or even that we ever *lived* in Leeds?

The writer's sister is still not smiling.

WRITER (*hastily*): Well, I can change those things. I can take out the china and the wind chimes. I can give you red hair. I can change Leeds to York. Or Glasgow, even…

MOTHER (*looking happier*): Yes, and put the house in a hollow. And put in those things I told you: all those picnics and walks in the country…

SISTER: But you've put Annie Renshaw in! She'll recognise herself straightaway!

WRITER: What? Who?

SISTER: *Annie Renshaw*!!!

WRITER: Who's Annie Renshaw?

SISTER: You *know* Annie Renshaw! From the bridge club! You've even got her *in* the bridge club!

WRITER (*remembering the name now vaguely, wondering if her sister has forgotten she left home at eighteen, before they ever moved to this town*): But I've never even *met* Annie Renshaw!

SISTER: You must have, you've described her exactly! Fat, with pearls! She always wears pearls!

WRITER: But it's generic, a *type* – a stereotype, even! It's not meant to be any specific person!

SISTER: Well, if Annie Renshaw reads that, or any of the other bridge club members, or anyone in the Rotary, they'll recognise it as her. And then everyone will make the connection with us, and all that awful stuff you've written there!

MOTHER (*having come around now*): Oh, Sally, it's just a *story*! Like I said, she hasn't got it right, it isn't the truth.

SISTER: So why would she lead people to think it might be? No one reads fiction just as fiction! Why would you do that to your family?

Maude Casey
Extract from
Over The Water[25]

We live in England, but. We live in England, but all year long we are preparing for the journey home.

When we grow out of bits of our clothing, Mammy folds them in the careful way she has, and adds them to her bundles. She says, 'I'll take these with us, when we go home. They'll do grand for Carmel and Siobhan. They'll be delighted with them, sure.'

Sometimes, Mammy buys things specially, men's suits or shirts, mostly, at the church bazaars or at jumble sales, and these too she puts away in her bundles, for her brothers who work the land at home.

We snigger and we pester her:

'Mammy, why is it they have so few things at home? Mammy don't they work hard on the land at home? Wouldn't you think

---

25 Chapter One.

they'd have money to buy their own clothes?'

'Mammy, Siobhan didn't even know what a toothbrush was, when I was brushing my teeth at the well at home!'

'Whisht yer owld cod!' she says, and gives one of us a clout round the ear-hole. I hate it when she sounds so Irish.

Carmel and Siobhan are two of our cousins at home. They are younger than us, but older too, in some ways. They are able to do a full day's work on the farm, every day, during the school holidays. And so they are used to going about on their own and making their own decisions about things.

Whereas us lot here in England, Anne and John and me we make no decisions about anything. Mammy and Daddy see to that.

We go to school each day and we return each afternoon. On Saturdays, we go to Confession at the church, and on Sundays we go back there twice, in the morning for Mass and in the afternoon for Benediction. That is the sum total of the things we do. Daddy says, 'The family that stays together, prays together.' I feel as though I am drowning, drowning and suffocating.

Sometimes, some of the girls at school invite me out, to go round the shops on Saturday. Mammy says, 'What do you want to be doing that for, wasting your time like a shreel?' I say, 'Can I go?' She says, 'You can not.' Sometimes, one of the girls asks me to go bowling with her, on Saturday night. Saturday night! I don't even bother to ask my mother. 'No thanks. I'm busy Saturday night,' I say, and turn away.

I'm becoming clever at lying. On Monday mornings at school, I invent outings that I've been on with my family over the weekend. I invent boyfriends, and tell the girls at school of how they pop in for a coffee before Sunday lunch. I don't dare tell the truth.

Mammy knows no-one in our road. She is so afraid of scornful glances at her Irish voice that she opens her mouth to no-one. She says that we should do the same. 'Keep your business to yourself,' she says. 'Don't get involved with anyone,' she says. We have something to hide.

She looks over her shoulder the whole time, scanning the air for danger. She watches herself and us all the time when we are out of the house, to make sure we're all doing the right thing. To make sure that we don't stand out as aliens in this foreign land.

Except, for us, it's not a foreign land. We were born here, and every day we go to school.

At school, the girls are all English. They're often telling jokes about how thick the Irish are. I'm supposed to laugh. They watch me with eyes like knives, ready to strike if I show the slightest flicker of embarrassment. I want to laugh with them. I want to be one of them. But I turn my head away when I feel wild waves of anger and prickles behind my eyes.

Daddy says, 'Show them you're *not* thick.' So I work late into the night on my homework, hot and heavy with exhaustion. But then they call me names if I become top in any of the tests. I have to be careful.

I'd like to talk about all this with my brother and my sister. But John is too little, still, only nine, busy with his mice and his bike and his football. And Anne, well, Anne is beautiful. And if you are beautiful it seems that you can often get away with anything. She is always surrounded by friends, with her big blue eyes, and her thick blond curls that never seem to look lank or greasy. It never seems to matter when she doesn't bother to do her homework.

A lot of the time, I'm so afraid. Afraid that my lies will get found out in the end, and afraid that I'll never make friends, that I'll always be alone.

I say to Anne, 'I feel as though I don't fit in anywhere.' She turns her head towards me, and her eyes are so clear and blue that there's nothing in them. She hasn't got a clue what I'm on about. She's only two years younger than me but we're so far apart.

Mammy sets us to work, Anne and John and me. We each pack a box with the clothes from her bundle. I wonder whether our cousins really will be delighted with our cast-off clothes. Myself, I hate the things that Mammy buys us, twice a year in the sales. She never lets us choose them. And when I give my opinion on what I'd like to wear, she makes me feel as though anything I might like is wrong. I have started to make a few clothes for myself this year, simple things like mini-skirts. But she makes such a fuss, whenever I try to get her to buy me some material.

We tie the boxes with twine and seal them with wax, ready for the journey. Our hands sting with the memory of how the string of each of those boxes will sting itself into red welts in the palms of our hands, as we carry them through trains and boat in the endless hours of darkness. I decide to wear my newest mini-skirt on the journey. Such a fight I have, with Mammy.

'Sure, Granny'll have a heart attack, seeing the spread of you, showing the brazen legs on you up to your behind!'

'The way you go on, Mammy, you'd think it was a mortal sin for people even to *have* legs in Ireland!'

'God forgive you for your blaspheming talk! Sure what have I done wrong to be rearing such a pig-headed strap of a girl!'

In the end, we reach a compromise. I will wear the mini-skirt until we are on the boat. Then I will change into my old tweed skirt, 'smart and sensible' and well below knee length. When I set foot in Ireland, I will be in disguise.

In the meantime, I watch Mammy, preparing to go home. Here, in her own house, the wild excitement is building to a frenzy. I wonder, for the hundredth time of wondering, why it is that she never thinks of *this* house as being her home. And why she should feel so foreign here, when she's been here for years and Ireland is so near. And I wonder, for the hundredth time of wondering, in which of them is *my* true home, and whether I'll ever find it, one fine day.

Ray French
The Two Funerals of Patrick Cullen

The first one was held in St Christopher's, the church in Newport that Luke and Ellen went to as kids. Built with money raised by the Irish who worked on the buildings and docks, the priests were imported from County Wexford, Waterford or Tipperary. They were robust, rural men who always looked out of place in that grimy industrial town. One of them, Father Hayes, became famous for claiming in one of his sermons, 'We are a tiny island of Catholics, surrounded by a sea of Methodists.' So Luke was surprised when he saw the priest waiting for them at the church door on the cold February night they went to discuss the funeral arrangements. He wore a stylish black Crombie, single stud earring and shiny oxblood doc martens.

'Ellen and Luke?'

He was Welsh, softly spoken, from somewhere in the industrial south, but without the harsh edge to his voice you often got in

Newport and Cardiff. Though still relatively young, mid-thirties at most guessed Luke, he already had the weary expression of a man battling against the odds.

'I'm Father Michael.'

He shook their hands, ushered them inside. Ellen had already spoken to him on the phone and now took the lead, while Luke, only half-listening, gazed around. He hadn't been inside St Christopher's for over thirty years. The huge stained glass windows were still impressive, the same dark, grisly paintings depicting the Stations of the Cross lined the walls, but the place looked smaller, shabbier. The plaster was cracked and flaking, the benches worn and chipped, the high-vaulted ceiling badly in need of repair. The powerful sense of loss took him by surprise. Memories surged up: the priest rubbing ashes on his forehead at Easter; the altar boys swinging incense on chains; being marched from primary school to mass here on Holy Days, and ushered brusquely into benches by their form teachers. Ellen, four years older, sat near the front, never once looking around to see if he was there.

He sometimes felt that distance between them had never been bridged.

'It's a lovely church,' said the priest, when he saw Luke gazing up at the ceiling, 'but as you can see it could do with some investment.'

'It was always full when I came here with my parents.'

'We probably get about thirty for Sunday mass now.'

Luke tried to imagine how small that would look in a church this size. There must have been three or four hundred here for mass in the 1970s and 80s. His father stopped going years ago, but his mother continued to attend twice a week until the dementia took hold and they found her a place in a home two years before. He suspected she'd gone to get a break from their father, to sit quietly in a place where nothing was demanded of her except to rise and sit at the appointed times, and let the quiet, calm voice of Father Michael drift over her. She was still in the home, unaware her husband had died, rarely recognising them when they visited.

'Most of the congregation were Irish back then,' Luke replied.

Father Michael squinted up at a damp patch in the ceiling.

'A lot of those will have died or gone back home. It's the Poles that keep this place going now.'

They moved on to the question of favourite hymns and prayers. This was an awkward moment, their father was not a man who ever talked about hymns, took Holy Communion, or offered any opinions about a sermon, unless it was to complain it went on too fecking long. He liked a priest who got through mass quickly, so he could get home and change, go to his allotment while their mother cooked Sunday lunch. He'd come back just as she was taking the chicken out of the oven, bursting through the door and shouting, 'The working man is home! Jayzus, great grub.'

'The usual hymns will do,' said Luke, waving a hand vaguely. Father Michael took this in his stride, never missing a beat as he moved on to ask if there was any other music they'd like played. Ellen opened her bag and took out a CD, *Come To The Bower*.

'The last track, 'Fields Of Athenry', was his favourite song.'

Father Michael took it from her.

'If we could have it played at the end.'

'Yes, of course. And will you be wanting to say anything?'

'I'd like to read a poem,' said Ellen.

The priest looked at her expectantly.

'I haven't decided which one yet.'

'I'd like to say something, Luke told him, 'I won't take more than a few minutes.'

One thing he and Ellen shared was an aversion to people who went on and on at funerals and weddings.

'And it's a cremation after the funeral?'

'That's right, we're taking his ashes to Ireland to be buried.'

Father Michael nodded, the migrant returning home in a box a familiar routine. Probably a lot of the Poles did the same.

Father Michael took down details about their father's life, and made bullet points next to them, Luke noticed. When they'd finished he slipped the notebook into his pocket and asked if they'd chosen a place for refreshments after the service was over?

'That's next on our list,' said Ellen.

'The Golf and Country Club just down the road from the crem

might work, that's the place a lot of people use. It saves everyone driving back into town and finding a place to park. They won't be busy on a Tuesday afternoon.'

'Thank you, we'll check it out.'

Luke could tell that Ellen wanted to go, that she needed to move onto the next thing, her way of coping. She looked pale, exhausted. On the way there in the car she told him how she kept waking in the early hours with a start, sure that something terrible was about to happen, then remembered that it already had. But Luke was touched by the priest's thoughtfulness, his honesty, and it felt rude to rush off. He thought it would be polite to show some interest in his work, and asked him about the notices in the entrance, advertising other services, meetings, drop-ins.

He told them about the eight clock mass he held in the week for a handful of elderly people who had trouble sleeping; the parent and toddler sessions on Mondays and Wednesdays; the drop-ins on Tuesdays and Thursdays for the unemployed and retired – tea, coffee, biscuits and a chit-chat. A shame their father hadn't attended these, but he'd never been a joiner. He'd have had no idea how to chat to strangers over tea and biscuits, and any attempts to do so would have ended in disaster. Luke imagined him, those green eyes glaring, standing far too close as he roared, 'Grand tea missus! Christ it's great to get out of the house once in a while, ain't it?'

Luke could imagine the priest as a social worker, or running a hostel for the homeless. It didn't seemed possible that someone like him actually believed that the Son of God died for our sins. He was young, had missed out on the glory days of packed congregations, reached adulthood in an era of plummeting attendances, leaky roofs, sex scandals and the risk of sequestration. A good man in a rotting institution trying to do the right thing in a dead end town. It would make a good midweek Channel 4 drama, barely scraping an audience but gathering respectful reviews in *The Guardian* and *Observer*.

Later, over a drink, he asked Ellen what she'd made of Father Michael. 'Very nice', she replied and returned to discussing arrangements for the lunch at the Golf and Country Club. Even after all these years he was still taken aback by how uninterested she could be in other people sometimes. 'That's all very good,' she would say, if he drifted away from the main topic too long for her liking, as if they only met to discuss action points, 'But which of us is going to visit mam next week?'

They counted up the number of people coming, how many to the lunch afterwards. Discussed sandwich fillings, whether to have sausage rolls, samosas, or both, and which types of quiche. When they'd finished Ellen looked out of the window, and for a moment he thought she would cry. He was about to reach out and take her hand when she said, 'Right! What's next?'

She nipped off to ring Des, and Luke stared out of the rainy window at the cars zipping past on the M4, on their way to somewhere more interesting. He wondered what a hip priest like Father Michael did with himself at night in a place like Newport? His cropped hair, that stylish coat and earring – was the One Holy And Apostolic Church comfortable with that kind of thing now? He doubted it. The posting to Newport was obviously their way of showing their disapproval.

The funeral went smoothly. Father Michael was respectful, understated and professional. There was no attempt to sound as though he knew their father well, but he made the most of what Luke and Ellen had told him. In his way he was a storyteller, constructing a coherent narrative from a jumble of snatched memories, fleeting impressions, and anecdotes. Luke liked the way he emphasized that this had been a church which welcomed people from different communities, both in the past and now, and, he hoped, in the future. There had been a mix of races in Luke's class – the Italians, some Asians and Ayo, the class comic, the black girl who wound up the teachers and cracked them all up with her whiplash replies. What had happened to them all? Had they got out as soon as they could, like him, or were they still living here, still meeting up with their old school friends, telling the old stories?

Their Irish cousin Katy and their cousins from Liverpool and Manchester had come. Luke noticed some old school friends and neighbours dotted around the pews. A few unknown elderly people sat the back. Maybe thirty people or so in all, not a bad turn out.

At the Golf club there was tea, sandwiches and drinks. This was posh Newport, plush red carpet, fake beams, on the walls photos of golfers, trophies in glass cabinets. Luke had brought a collection of old photos: him and Ellen as kids, then teenagers. Their parents at different stages – their mother at eighteen, a shock of frizzy hair, face bright with expectation. Their father in his Royal Navy uniform, strikingly handsome, a dangerous glint in his eyes, looking a little like Robert Ryan, one of his favourite actors.

'No wonder your mother fell for him,' said Brenda, one of the Liverpool cousins.

Their father in the garden in summer, wearing just a pair of shorts and an Australian bush hat, mugging at the camera, looking like one of those grotesque Irish apes in a *Punch* cartoon from the nineteenth century. Katy burst out laughing.

'*That's* the Pat I remember. Oh god, he was a gas.'

Des, Ellen's husband was a quiet man, but something in the photos made him turn philosophical, and during a lull he said, 'That's all we are in the end. A jarful of ashes.'

He seemed not to notice the uncomfortable silence. Then he added, 'I liked Paddy, there aren't many left like him.'

Luke had always thought the sober, thoughtful Des found his father crude.

'In another culture he'd be revered as an elder, and kids brought to meet him so they could learn the old ways.'

Luke thought that was laying it on a bit thick. But then Des never had him as a father, hadn't experienced the roaring, the swearing, the blood-curdling threats. Once, when Luke was about eight or nine, a couple of boys a little younger than him were playing football in the back lane. Twice the ball flew over the wall into their garden, twice his father had flung it back when they'd asked. After the second time he warned, 'If you send that over here again I'll put my fecking axe in it.' He had an axe to hand, as he was chopping wood, and he showed it to them.

A few minutes later the ball soared over the wall for a third time, and his father made good on his promise, puncturing their ball, then tossing it back over the wall.

'There's your fecking ball. Are you happy now?'

There was a brief, stunned silence. Then one of the boys shouted, 'Mister, you're a bastard.'

Their father pushed open the gate and, axe in hand, chased the two of them down the lane.

'I'll fecking kill ya, ya little bastards.'

Father Michael mingled briefly. He shook a few hands, said a few words, had a cup of tea, left.

'A nice looking man,' said Brenda, nibbling a samosa. 'A bit of a waste.' She laughed at herself in case anyone made fun of her. Luke relaxed, accepted that it was going well, so grateful that people came, and behaved themselves. When the last guest had left he found Ellen pouring herself a large glass of white wine.

'Do you think it went okay?' she asked.

'Yeah, very well I reckon.'

For a moment she looked at Luke as though she'd remembered something about him that she'd been trying to forget, then tipped back the glass, her eyes closed. For a moment he thought that was it, then she said something that shocked him.

'I'm glad you're here. I couldn't have done it without you.'

This was a rare compliment, and he wasn't sure how to take it. She looked at Des picking away at the last of the sausage rolls.

'He'll get fat again, after all that time he spent in the gym last year.'

She turned back to Luke, and now he saw how exhausted she was, her face drawn, those four extra years really showing. She looked ready to collapse.

'You really think everyone was okay?'

'Yes, I do. Actually, I think they enjoyed themselves – you know, the stories about dad.'

Katy had told them how patient their father had been with her when she was young, taking her out on mushroom hunts, showing her the best places to look, never once getting irritated by how clueless she'd been. Luke had no idea his father was capable of patience, or knew where to find mushrooms. Brenda remembered the time he'd visited them in Liverpool, telling them war stories, terrible things, men on fire in the sea, men screaming for their mothers as they died, and the terror of being a stoker in the bowels of the ship, knowing you'd go down with it if a torpedo struck. Luke had never heard any of this. Or about the time he and one of his brothers had got drunk in Ireland and tried to steal a pig, and staggered home, pigless, covered in shit. All these different versions of him, unknown to him, and to Ellen.

Ellen nodded faintly, pulling at her watch strap. She was somewhere else, far away from him. That distance, always there. On his first day in school he'd ran up to her in the playground, desperate to speak to her about something. She had grabbed his arm, pulled him to one side and warned him never, ever to do it again. Even now he remembered the shock of her anger, how it froze him to the spot, and knew this was something they'd be locked into forever.

Still, they needed to find a way of working together now.

'They had a good laugh at the photos.'

'Yes, they did, didn't they? It was a good idea, bringing those.'

She stopped pulling at her strap, and sighed.

'Well, that's over.'

Luke raised his glass, desperate to raise her spirits.

'Here's to the auld fella.'

She smiled faintly, they clinked glasses and drank, then leant back against the wall in silence, shoulder to shoulder. Luke closed his eyes; the worry, the lack of sleep, that hideous moment, the one he'd been dreading, when the coffin disappeared through the curtain to the sounds of 'The Fields of Athenry', all finally fading into the background. They had no father, their mother didn't know who they were anymore; now they only had each other. But right then, he thought they'd be okay.

Ellen turned to him and said, 'It's the one in Ireland I'm really worried about.'

Luke carried the ashes in his backpack on the boat to Ireland, Fishguard to Rosslare, the route they'd taken so many times in the summer. When he collected them from the funeral director the day before he'd been shocked by how warm the urn was. Hard not to feel this was his father's spirit enduring – the rage still burning. They waited till they were halfway across, and there was just one man left leaning on the railings at the back of the boat before they made their move. He unscrewed the lid and each of them took a handful of ashes and flung them into the Irish Sea. They put their arms around each other and watched the flakes dance madly before the wind suddenly changed and the ashes flew back, spraying their clothes, blowing into their faces.

Luke started laughing.

'*The Big Lebowski.*'

'What?'

Ellen looked at him as if he'd gone mad. He shook his head.

'Nothing.'

Ellen picked a flake from her top lip with her finger and slowly swallowed, closing her eyes as if she were taking communion. Luke tried to think of something memorable to say, but felt his throat tighten and the bitterness rising.

'A drink,' said Ellen.

They drove to Katy's, Des behind the wheel, Ellen next to him, Luke squeezed in between their teenagers, Christopher and Alannah. Luke remembered their Uncle Mike picking them up at Rosslare in what called his *Flintstones* car, how it shook and rattled as they navigated the potholes. Mike would laugh when he saw Luke staring through the holes in the floor at the road beneath.

'Don't be worrying now, Luke, boy, you're safe with me.'

Now, in Ellen and Des's Volvo estate, he gazed out the window. White cottages with thatched roofs, auld ones sitting on benches watching the world go by, cheerless looking pubs advertising Sky Sports, bungalows, a standing stone in an empty field, bungalows, a ruined abbey, more bungalows.

Christopher and Alannah had spotted one of his paintings in the Premier Inn at Newport, and plied him with questions. This was a sore point. Liam had never made money as an artist, who did? His debts had been escalating until a friend introduced him to the hotel chain scene a few years ago. Now he churned out bland landscapes, seascapes and lifeless abstracts to help relax budget travellers in their cut-price hotel rooms.

'Is it well paid?' asked Christopher.

'Leave him alone,' said Des.

'No, it's alright,' said Luke, not wanting to appear defensive. 'Yes, it does pay well, as long as you carry on churning out the crap and don't gag.'

'It pays the rent though,' cut in Ellen.

This was one of her regular reminders about how he'd finally fallen on his feet, and should be grateful. Of how, before that, she had bailed him out numerous times.

'When we were growing up he was the special one, the golden boy. Whenever we came back to Ireland people begged him to draw them.'

'*Jealous*,' cried Alannah.

Des shot her a warning look.

'Oh, I was – nothing I ever did could compare with Luke's art. It seemed like magic, he never seemed to work at it, it just came naturally, as if he'd got the gift at Lourdes.'

He played, she did the hard work. He had talent but frittered it away. She set herself goals and now ran her own business, had raised a family.

'One of his paintings is still hanging up in The Atlantic Bar,' she told them.

'We'll have to see it!'

It was something he'd done in the sixth form, a crowd pleaser, the little old Irish bar at night, glowing with warm, inviting light. But Luke's favourite piece was about his dad. A recording of *The High Part Of The Road* by Tommy Peoples and Paul Brady playing next to a painting of him sitting on a stool in his allotment in Newport, staring into space. In the background the steelworks and docks, on the next allotment a West Indian man, plucking a sweet potato from the earth.

When they reached Katy's house she, her husband and their daughter ran out to meet them with the usual cry of, 'Welcome home!'

The house had been old, run down when they'd bought it, the last owners an elderly couple who'd been there since the 1940s. Katy's husband had transformed it – sanded floorboards, put in new plastic doors and windows, modern furniture, an enormous TV in the living room. Luke missed his aunt and uncle's house, ramshackle, messy, the dog lying in front of the fire, the hall strewn with things Mike planned to fix but never got round to.

Katy put on a spread: chicken, roast spuds, gravy, followed by apple pie and ice cream. After a decent interval, out came the drink. When they'd had a few Katy broke it to them, explaining that last year the priest had stopped people from speaking at funerals.

'Why?'

'He said they often went on too long, and got upset, and some of them broke down at the altar.'

Luke started laughing.

'They got upset at a funeral, how inconsiderate. Who is this joker?'

Katy looked uncomfortable. She explained that they'd had a lot of trouble getting a replacement when Father Dunne retired.

'He was lovely, but he wasn't able for it anymore, he had terrible arthritis. Sure it's hard to get priests in a parish like this now. Father Dunne lived over 20 miles away. He had to do a mass here in the morning, then get into his car and drive to Castlebar for the midday mass. He kept it up for nearly a year, but he was too old.'

'We were hoping for a Polish priest,' said her husband, 'They have one over in Kilmore, they love him, they say he can't do enough for people. But we ended up with this fella.' He gave Luke a sympathetic look. 'I don't think anyone else would have him.'

'Hang on, are you saying he actually won't allow us to take part in our own father's funeral? That we have to leave it up to him – to the church? What century is this?'

Ellen shot him a look. Something clicked into place. He remembered her and Katy huddled in a corner at the hotel, talking in low voices, Ellen giving him a look that shut him out.

'We can be quick', said Ellen.

Katy looked embarrassed.

'We were quick in Newport', she added. 'We already know what we're going to say. We've already said it once – you were there, you can tell him how it went.'

He couldn't believe she was talking like this, Ellen of all people, pleading for permission to say a few words at her own father's funeral.

'Let me speak to him,' said Luke.

'No.'

Luke was shocked by the fear in Katy's eyes. He could feel Ellen watching him.

'It's better if I do it. I know how to talk to him. I'll go see him tomorrow.'

'I'll come with you,' said Luke, then excused himself and walked to the bottom of the garden, and cried, 'Fuck, fuck, fuck!'

Later, when the others had gone to bed, Luke and Ellen sat on the bench in the front, shivering in their coats, cradling whiskeys.

'You knew about this already.'

Ellen nodded, pulled her collar tighter.

'Why didn't you tell me?'

'You were right, the funeral in Newport went well. I didn't want to let this spoil it for you.'

Luke shook his head.

'You should have told me.'

'Katy might talk him round. She lives here, she knows how to talk to someone like him, we don't.'

'It's bloody feudal.'

'This is not Dublin. Dublin is not Ireland.'

'Thanks for that.'

Luke took a slug of whiskey, cringed.

'Christ, I just remembered why I don't usually drink this stuff.'

Faintly, in the distance, they heard the sea. The deep silence of the countryside at night something Luke always remembered from his family holidays.

'Screw him, let's do it anyhow, we don't need his permission. We'll just walk up there and say our piece. I'd' like to see him try and stop us.'

'Then we'd be gone the next day, and Katy would be left to face the music. We don't have to live here. Katy does.'

Katy's husband told them how their neighbour, Tom Keghoe, once questioned whether conducting a raffle for the local Hurley team in mass was really appropriate. The priest had glared at him and walked off. He gave a sermon the following week about arrogant busybodies who thought they knew better than him, a priest, how to conduct mass.

The next afternoon Luke and Ellen went with Katy to the village. They sat in the empty church waiting for the priest to turn up at 4. By 4.15 the conversation had petered out.

Katy had brought some fresh soda bread as an offering, Luke noted with disgust. Eventually the priest emerged from the back, a tall, distracted looking man, moving briskly, not looking their way. Luke remembered the story about the Hurley team and imagined thwarted sporting ambitions. Katy fidgeted with the bread in her lap. The priest disappeared, his head down. There was no telling if he'd seen them or not. Katy waited another couple of minutes, then got to her feet and said, 'Right, here we go. I'll do my best.'

'I know you will, said Ellen.

They watched her walk down the aisle, skirt the altar and disappear into the back. Ellen took out her mobile, Luke sat with his hands in his pockets, slumped on the bench, staring straight ahead. After about fifteen minutes Katy returned. She shook her head.

'He said you could say something at the graveside. That was the best I could get.'

'The Fields Of Athenry?' asked Ellen.

'No, I'm sorry. I really am.'

The second funeral took place on a Sunday morning. The church was larger than St Christopher's, in much better condition, and it was packed. Luke recognised some of his father's family, but there had been so many rows down the years that he could no longer remember which of them his father had made it up with. None of them caught his eye.

Katy had supplied the priest with a lot of information about their father, but he only offered a few sentences about where he was born, the names of his parents and the year he left Ireland. This, thought Luke, was the crucial factor for this priest, that he'd left and not come back, had chosen to live out his last days in another country. At one point he got his name wrong, calling him Callaghan before quickly correcting himself.

Half way through the service the altar boys carried on a picnic hamper, boxes of chocolates and sweets, some toys and a DVD recorder, and the priest conducted a raffle for the local Hurley team. Luke reached for Ellen's hand and gripped it.

At the graveyard the priest blessed the grave and prayed for the soul of the deceased and all the other souls buried there, then left. Luke had planned to repeat the speech he'd made in Newport. How his father had had Ireland tattooed on his arm when he was serving in the British Navy in the war; how he'd never stopped talking about how he was going to return one day. How different he'd seemed to other people's fathers when he'd been growing up, and how embarrassing that was at the time. But how, over the years, as friends listened to his stories about him, and laughed, laughed so hard, and demanded more, he began to realise just how extraordinary he was. And how now, at last, he was finally going back to Ireland, just as he'd wished. But that didn't feel appropriate anymore. Instead he stood over his grave in silence for a long time, then simply said, 'He was loved.'

Then Ellen read 'The Emigrant Irish', by Eavan Boland.

Just as they were about to walk away the grave digger, an ancient man with a ravaged face, dressed in a threadbare black suit, produced a tin whistle and played 'The Fields of Athenry'. For a moment Luke thought he was having a supernatural experience, then realised that Katy must have asked him.

On the way to the car Ellen gripped his arm and said, 'I won't cry, not here, not now,' though she clearly was.

On the boat back the next day, after several drinks, Luke was floating. He was enjoying the sway and dip of the boat, the vastness of the sea and sky. Ellen, exhausted, had drifted off to sleep on the seat next to him. Her features had relaxed, her mouth slackened and open, and she looked shockingly vulnerable.

There was only the slightest of swells and he knew, without looking, that the Welsh coast was already visible to his left, a thin grey strip. Home, not home. He thought about his visit to the registrar's office in Newport. The thin, middle-aged woman sitting at a desk, a huge ledger in front of her, taking down his father's details in fountain pen as he spoke. There was something comfortingly timeless about it. And he thought how appropriate it was that she recorded births, marriages and deaths all in that quiet, surprisingly cosy little room. She had blue-tacked children's drawings on the walls – new baby brothers and sisters in bright felt pens and crayons. His attention has been caught by one in particular, in which the young daughter was a twin of the mother – same size, same hairstyle, same stance, the only difference was the mother held a new born baby. Both women towered over the husband, who looked more like their child. Another showed a couple getting married, bringing a string of children from previous relationships to the church. Another depicted someone's grandma, hands clasped, smiling down at the still living from a fluffy cloud.

He'd felt puzzled by the wave of euphoria that gripped him as the registrar scratched away in the ledger, but now he grasped why. It was one of those moments when something you'd dismissed as a cliché suddenly felt profoundly true, and he was now certain that nothing ever truly ends. We are all part of an endless cycle of dreaming, living, remembering, the past, present and future all mixed up together. Yes, his father had died, and was gone, but in another way he had multiplied. New versions of him had sprung up over the last couple of weeks that Luke had never known existed. The tender Paddy who'd taken Katy out mushroom hunting; the terrified Paddy in the bowels of the British Navy destroyer; the Paddy who'd tried to steal a pig and staggered home covered in shit. There were many more versions to come, he was sure. He'd ring Katy, Brenda and the others and collect their stories, their most precious memories, and piece together the future Paddy, the one he would celebrate in his paintings. His father had always been his best subject. He would paint him standing upright in his coffin, ready to face the rising sun, like the ancient Irish. He would paint him trying to catch a pig, shovelling coal in that British destroyer, patiently hunting mushrooms with his tiny niece. He would collect more stories, more memories, and there would be more paintings, another, then another, then another.

Maria C. McCarthy
More Katharine than Audrey

C *ome Dancing* is on Tuesday. Some lose track, but it's mince and potatoes on Monday, *Come Dancing* on Tuesday, sheets changed Wednesday and so on. I'm not supposed to watch it – the lights go off at nine – but I turn the volume low so the staff won't hear. I close my eyes and I dance around the room, then I'm in the black taffeta, and the skirt and my hips are swinging. If the nurses catch me, when they're doing their rounds, their eyes smile above the masks. The flickering of the screen reflects on the walls. My room is a dancehall.

Mrs Davies left the ward today. There are two of us left, so it won't be long until it's my turn. I asked Rankin how far it is to London on the train. It takes half an hour, she said; half an hour from Epsom to Waterloo, and a little longer to Victoria. It seemed to take as long as that to walk the corridors when I first came here. Windows either side, so I could see the grounds and the buildings with the other wards, the laundry and the kitchens. The kitchens are a long way off: sometimes there's porridge, sometimes corn-

197

flakes, but always tea and toast, and the toast is cold.

I have my own telly, now that most of the others have gone. There are films in the afternoon: Humphrey Bogart and Katharine Hepburn in *The African Queen*, she as ugly as me, and a film star. It was the other Hepburn, Audrey, that I would have liked to be: petite and pretty, like a fairy gone to live in the world of men. She was a nurse in *The Nun's Story*, tempted by a handsome doctor in a hospital in the Congo; Peter Finch played the doctor. She didn't succumb, but she wasn't for the convent in the end. 'You are a worldly nun' the Reverend Mother said, or was it the Mother Superior? The times I saw that film, and each time the tightness in my chest, a hankie at the ready when she goes into that room at the end of the film, to leave the convent, and she gets her old clothes back, the ones she came in with, and there's no one there to say goodbye, as if it's a disgrace, wanting to go back into the world.

I could never be like Audrey Hepburn; my hips are too wide.

We had the cowboys back in Mitchelstown – Randolph Scott, Gary Cooper, John Wayne; he was a favourite of Molly's. And I loved Jimmy Stewart. They have them on the telly, too, and it's as if I'm in the middle rows of the picture house with Molly.

I'm like Audrey Hepburn after all, a worldly woman kept apart from the world. She got sick in that film: tuberculosis was it? She was isolated in a beautiful treehouse, given the 'gold cure' and tended to by Peter Finch. And here's me in Long Grove with Rosina Bryars and the nurses. No gold cure for me. No Peter Finch. But it won't be long before they find the right combination of drugs for me, as they did for the others.

Pea soup it said in the books: *six to eight motions a day, and it looks like pea soup.* That's just how it was when I had the fever. I can't eat it to this day: that and rhubarb. Mammy used to boil it up to clean the pans; I worried it would strip the lining of my stomach.

Rankin cut me some roses on Sunday. She brought red and white, but a nurse will always arrange them separately, or there will be blood and bandages before the day's out, so the white went to Rosina and I have the red. They were in bud, so they'd last longer.

I've been watching them unfurl. They smell like summer, like the outdoors as I remember it. When the petals drop onto the bed-side table, I want them left there to darken, then brown. I want the leaves left to wither on the stem, to watch them shrivel; but the cleaner comes in every day, gloved, overalled, and changes the water, wipes the fallen from the bedside table with a cloth dipped in disinfectant, and it masks the scent of the roses. I close my eyes, and I see the roses in the garden blossom, fade and drop. I walk on a carpet of withered petals, and pinch them between my toes. Then I'm in the field back home with Molly, and we're running fast towards the sun.

Rosina isn't up to much now; she'd as soon eat a rose as smell it.

I was used to the smell of disinfectant when I was nursing, and the way it changes colour in the bucket when you add water. Sid offered me Pernod once, added a dash of water. It clouded in the glass like disinfectant; smelled of the aniseed balls that they tipped into paper bags from the teardrop-shaped bowl of the scales in the sweetshop in Mitchelstown. Disinfectant would do it, if I could get hold of some; I could mix it with the water in my bedside glass and pretend it was Pernod.

There's no wildness in these gardens, just straight lines and fresh mown and leaves piled up in the autumn. Nothing like the fields back home with the brambles and crab apples. Off we'd go: Molly and me, with bowls to fill, and our arms and our clothes would be torn and purple-bruised with juice. The sweetest would always be the furthest in, and didn't we always want the sweetest, the juiciest, to reach for the best, not to settle?

The first time I offered a brimming bowl to Da, I was so small I had to raise it to reach his hands, hanging like shovel-ends from his arms. He said No; he wouldn't touch those things, full of spiders and flies. I never offered them again. I gave them up to Mammy for the crumble. His was made separate with crab apples and lots of sugar. He didn't like the black stain on the apples' flesh.

Da thought it was the boys I was after when I went to England. Jesus, with what I've seen of men's parts, what's there to get ex-cited about? Like snails tucked in a hood, and sometimes, sick as they were, it would rear up at the feel of the sponge. God, the first time I saw one at full length I called for Sister. I thought something awful had happened. Shrub came running at my shrieks, and when she saw what had alarmed me, she pursed her lips to stop the giggles. Sister said, 'I think Mr Ericson is well enough to wash himself.' Shrub dragged me into the sluice room and collapsed, tears rolling down her cheeks. Oh, she took me off something rotten: *Sister, come quick it's Mr Ericson's* ... I couldn't even find a word to describe it at the time. And we were both in stitches, with her attempt at my accent.

It was last names, even off duty. It was Shrub, Gates, McCallion, and so on. You'd say, 'Is Shrub on tonight?' or, 'I've the same shifts as McCallion.' Then the crowd I went round with called me Josie, as there was another Noreen. I forgot I was Noreen at all until I came here; it was in my notes, and that's what they go by. I still think of her as Shrub, though she'd a beautiful Christian name – Annette. But that's how it was, and that's how I remember.

You didn't have to choose what to wear, to be as good as, to have a style. You just wore the uniform, maybe dressed with a frilled cuff if Sister would allow. Rankin wears a cuff and a fob-watch like I had, pinned to the chest. I can see it through the plastic apron. She's my favourite, Rankin; she listens, really listens. Some of them just talk to each other. I suppose we did, too, me and Shrub: tipped the patients forward like they were one of the pillows we were tidying, eased them back, talking over them the whole time. As long as the ward was spick and span, that's what Sister was after.

The fool I was, falling for a woman. I'd study Shrub's lips, the soft hairs on the nape of her neck below her pinned-up hair when she was on the ward, the curl of her hair when it was down, when we went dancing or to the pictures. She hadn't a notion that I dreamed of her, dreams from which I woke with the sheets twisted, dreams of parting her lips with mine, her face cupped in my hands, of slipping a satin nightdress from her shoulders, like the ones they wear in the films, watching it fall to the floor. Sometimes, on the ward, she'd brush against my bosom in passing, and the heat of those dreams would flush my face and neck.

When I first arrived at Euston station from the boat train, no one smiled or allowed me to catch their eye; no one said hello. It was just after the war – we weren't involved, in Ireland, so I'd no experience of what they'd been through. Nice enough people, but there was this reserve, and not just because I was Irish. It was as if they'd had something removed, like patients recovering from an operation, trying to get back to normal, but no longer sure what normal felt like. But the nurses, there was a spark in them; they knew how to dance, to drink, to let go. You never knew what you'd encounter on the next shift: a motorbike accident; a patient with a tumour; a family gathered to hear bad news about their father; and the bedpans and bottles, everything scrubbed and sterilised. So it was living for the moment.

There weren't always men to dance with, so the women danced together, and if there were any men, the women would flutter round them like moths to an old suit. A man could have a different woman for each dance. I wasn't bothered; if a man asked, I'd dance with him, but I was happiest with Shrub.

So when I went home to Mitchelstown I was full of stories, of the hospital and the friends and the dancing. Mammy clapped her hands and wrung them in turn. She was in envy of me, for getting away and making something of myself; but another part of her was afraid I'd go to the bad. She was wearing her thousand-times-washed dress with the faded paisley swirls of pink and mauve, the lace of her slip peeking out from the hem, and there I was talking of taffeta and satin and the new coat I'd bought for the winter. As for Da, he was all hard edges, and as broad as he was tall, with no softening at my touch or my words.

I tapped a cigarette from the packet, and tried to light it with the matches from my coat pocket. It had rained on the walk from the bus stop in town, and they were damp, so I put a spill into the embers of the fire. It was as if I'd stripped naked and danced on the table, the blustering and the language from Da, how I'd been ruined by England and nursing. How I was setting a bad example to my sister Molly. I wasn't to smoke either in or out of the house. And when I laid in late he said, 'There's no holiday here, my girl,' expecting me to go back to my old chores.

I went to a dance at the Mayflower with some of the old crowd, and Jimmy O'Gorman walked me home. He'd been disappointed by a girl he liked; she was dancing with another boy the whole evening. We were great friends, Jimmy and me, and I linked arms with him on the way up the hill. He'd had a drink, and it was as much me holding him up as him walking me home. We parted at the fork in the road below the house.

Da was waiting at the gate, late as it was. 'Are the men in England not enough for ye?' He slapped me round the head. I reeled, but I stood my ground.

'It's only Jimmy. He walked me home.'

'Walking, is it, with everything on show?' We'd had words about how I was dressed before I left the house. I'd wrapped a stole around me to placate him, pinned it with a brooch, but I'd whipped it off at the dancehall. He went for my head again, but I ducked from his open palm. He slapped me round the back of the thighs as he had when I was a child. 'There'll be a different fella every night in London, the hoor you are.'

I flung my head back, the offending bosom thrust forward. I picked up the yard broom and held it in front of me; handle up, to hit him should he come at me again. But Mammy ran out and bundled me inside with Molly. I could hear his old clichés: *no daughter of mine*, and the like. They wouldn't find house room in a decent film script. And I was as bad, battering against the bedroom door with my fists, rattling the handle to get out.

'Mammy locks the door when he has a temper', Molly said. She looked so small in her nightdress. Her hair hung in waves, released from the plaits they were tied in by day. I came away from the door and sat next to her on the bed. My hands shook as Molly took hold of them. 'Da says I'm not to go to England, but as soon as I've finished school I'll be away. I want to go to the dances, have all the lovely clothes.' Her hand dropped to my dress, and she rubbed the fabric of the hem between her fingers and thumb. I undressed and got into the bed with her.

'It wasn't so bad when you were here,' she said. 'Could you stay, do you think, until I'm ready to go with you?' I didn't answer. I stroked her hair until she fell asleep, as I used to when we'd shared the bed before I left for England. I lay awake until I heard Mammy making the breakfast for Da, heard him leave for the fields, and heard the turn of the key in the bedroom door, and Mammy going out to draw water from the well.

I slipped from beneath the curve of Molly's arm, gathered my clothes and left. Why would I stay and be beaten and called a whore? Or end up like Mammy, chopping the vegetables, cutting the meat for the stockpot, sweeping the floor, taking out the ashes and sitting on the doorstep waiting for a passing neighbour to bring a bit of gossip.

I sent money home, as was expected, and Mammy wrote letters, begging me to make my peace with Da. I didn't write back, just sent the money. When I came here there was no more money to send.

You'd think, with her being a nurse that she'd know, but they're as prone to such foolishness as anyone, and Annette Shrub fell for a baby. She asked me what should she do, about being in trouble. I said what Mammy would have said: she should get the man to do the right thing.

She asked if I'd be her maid of honour, but I said 'Can you see me in a froth of a dress with these lumbering hips?' Truth is, I couldn't face the wedding at all. I prayed that that her husband-to-be would have a terrible accident and there would be a funeral, not a wedding. Then I hoped that I would break a leg, so I couldn't walk into the church; but the day came and the fella and me were both intact, so the ceremony went ahead. I sat in the front row and stared at her soft neck through the stiffness of her veil. Thinking I might get the chance should her hair become unpinned, and I could caress the stray strands into place, a hair grip in my mouth, press her hair to the back of her head for a second while I reached for the grip. But all went off as planned, not a hair or a word out of place, and Shrub became Mrs Someone-else.

Paper and pen, pen and paper: I ask for them when Rankin brings my dinner – fish pie, as it's Friday – and I start to write home. Someone in the town will know Molly, will recognise the name, even though she might be married now. Someone will know where she lives if she's left Mitchelstown. I keep the letter short, just telling Molly where I am and asking would she like to get in touch, and I ask Rankin to post it. It might take Molly a month or two to write back after a shock like that, a letter after so long.

My hair was good, thick and wavy and almost black, and there was never a problem with my skin. Just those lumbering hips and the bosoms I didn't know what to do with. Cover them up, Mammy would say, though the devil in me said show off your assets. The men had a fair love of them. When I wore the black taffeta with the red roses and a glimpse of cleavage – a glimpse was all they needed – some of them couldn't keep their eyes away as they asked for a dance. I wanted to tilt their chins with the heel of my hand, so their eyes would be level with mine. How they'd have loved to get their hands on my chest. It wasn't *their* hands I wanted.

Annette gave me a photo: bride and groom, beauty and the beast. I cried over it every night until I could bear it no more. I burned it in the sink, watched the faces blacken and curl, and then rinsed the ashes down the plughole.

Shrub gave up on the dancing, so I went with McCallion instead. I wore the black taffeta with roses again that night, black stockings, heels, my hair up with a mother of pearl clip, and red lipstick to match the roses on the dress. This man came over, and it was me he was interested in, not McCallion, though she was the slimmer and prettier of the two of us. I danced with him, but it was Shrub I thought of: how I would tuck my hand close around her fingers as I swung her, pull her close, push her back, the lightest of touches as she twirled beneath my arm, her finger looped in my finger and thumb, and her skirt flying, her hair streaming behind her and the set of her mouth as she concentrated on the steps, and the click of her heels on the dance floor; the lightest of clicks – click-click – and the flush of her cheeks as we fell back to the table for our drinks.

He was kind, this man, Sid – older than me, well spoken; a

proper English gentleman – and we fell into a courtship of sorts.

When I get out of here I'll take a flat in Tooting Bec, be close to things. I'll wander round the market with my basket in the morning, stop for a cup of tea and a slice of toast and jam at Luigi's cafe, maybe look up Shrub, if I can remember her last name (what was the name of that fella she married?). Or just sit in the café and wait for Godot. He took me, that Sid who courted me, took me to the theatre to see it. Hadn't a clue what it was about – two old tramps talking and waiting for a man that never turned up. I didn't get it. Much preferred a bit of a musical when I went to see a show, or to go for a meal and a swing round the dance floor.

I could do that, too: take a look at a dancehall in Kentish Town, go and watch the young ones, maybe show them a few moves myself! I'll need a new wardrobe. It won't be like Audrey Hepburn in *The Nun's Story*, they won't give me back the same clothes that I came in with. They'll have been incinerated. And decades out of fashion in any case. Any old rags, they give you here; the Lord only knows where they find them. But I keep up with the trends in the magazines that Rankin gives me after she's read them. I suppose she's not allowed to take them out of here anyhow, but it's good of her nonetheless.

The food came and it was grand: steak, fried, fancy potatoes done with cream and thin slices of onion, a little salad of lettuce and tomatoes and cucumber in a glass dish of its own at the side of the main plate, and cloth serviettes embossed with an ivy leaf motif. I dove in with my fork turned the wrong way. Sid smiled, turned it round in my hand and showed me how to push the peas onto the fork, to soak the gravy with a little potato on the prongs. He ate like a lady, little bites. And he stared at me, a shine in his pupils, but it was the food that got me going, not him. It was all I could do to stop lifting the plate and licking it clean. After Shrub married, I got so thin that my curves all but straightened, but my appetite returned that night. And a hand on my knee beneath the table, which did nothing for me, but I let him.

He took me dancing in Kentish Town, fingers pressing into my back in the slow dances, his cheek to mine, and his cigarette breath on my neck. We twirled round the hall, and my frock swirled and flicked, and he smiled.

That was the night he gave me Pernod. I wasn't much of a drinker, in spite of what Da thought of me, and I warmed to Sid with the drink inside me. I placed a hand at his back as we walked from the taxi, leaned my head on his shoulder. He turned to kiss me. His moustache scratched at my top lip. It was cold, raining; we sneaked past his landlady's door. There were drips coming through the ceiling in the attic room, pots and pans laid out to catch them. He drew me onto the bed beside him, slipped the dress from my shoulders and kissed my neck. His face was red; he was breathless. I shouldn't have led him on, so.

That was the night that did for me: someone in the kitchen of that restaurant. Someone that was a typhoid carrier like I am now, not washing their hands, passing it on to all that ate there.

The daylight is fading. I have to wait for the lights to go on. I'm down to the last page of the *Daily Mail* with those pictures: men on the moon, looking like they're underwater in diving suits, and more men at Houston staring at screens, pencils dangling from their fingers like cigarettes.

If I had a suit like that I could go into town and shop for myself at Woolworth's instead of asking Rankin to get bits and bobs for me. I could get a cup of tea and a jam tart at a cafe. Last night I dreamt of cafes and pubs and shops and crowds, of sliding into a seat on the top deck of a bus, arms and thighs butted up against the woman in the window seat, carrier bags arranged around my feet. A bit of food from the International Stores, a pair of tights, a new blouse, a lipstick, tickets in my handbag for the stalls at the Odeon from the night before, a dab of perfume behind my ears.

I wouldn't be able to drink the tea, I suppose, in a spaceman's suit.

I asked for some knitting needles and wool, and I am clicking my way through a scarf, russet and green, to match the coat I have picked out from the *News of the World* magazine. I don't want to order it; I'll wait till I can try it on. I could try knitting gloves, but they're tricky.

Rankin brought me a box of Christmas cards. I've written one for Rosina, one for Rankin, some for the other nurses and for Mavis the cleaner. There's been no reply to the note I sent Molly in the summer. I'll try again, with a card. I choose a holy one with the blessed Virgin and the infant Jesus, haloes lighting their faces. I give it to Rankin to post.

Moy McCrory
Combustible World

The night the bomb went off in the phone box down our street I'd been up the road, drinking Guinness with Loyalists. Everyone thought it was the IRA. It was only a frightener, not meant to kill anyone, but a girl we knew had been making a call. Some man she'd never seen before turned up banging on the phone box windows and she got out fast in case he was a lunatic. Whether he was or not, that madman saved her life. It's the details you remember. She'd been ringing the speaking clock.

Someone asked me when it all started, the weird stuff, and I said it was then, that night. But the truth is it had started well before. But no one's interested in that. They seem to want to pinpoint a moment of drama, as if that alone will provide the key, because then you can look back and understand why. Problem solved. But it's not that simple. Nothing ever is. I tell them, it could all start again tomorrow. I tell them I'm not trying to be difficult. All of those statements could be true, and all of them could be false.

I was a student then, in my second year. And if I've learnt anything it's how reality exists in feelings, while the events which demonstrate it, like most things we attempt to put into words, surround it in a kind of limbo. Who was it said, never let truth get in the way of a good story?

Let me explain something about myself. I am a person of no importance. I don't mean on a global level. I mean that I've always been insignificant even in small, individual details; those places where anecdotes are born. In my own, tight life I cut no figure. For as long as I can remember I have felt that there is always something better going on somewhere else, that I will always be in the wrong place. If I go to a party, most folks go elsewhere.

To my family I am like those odd cousins no one remembers, or in-laws who show up at funerals and no one knows their names. They try to figure me out, but can't. Relatives can make you feel awkward just for living. It's not as if you have to do anything.

Maybe it's because I only had brothers and they were involved in things I couldn't fathom; aeronautical engineering, combustion engines, the offside rule. I wasn't worth the explanation. When the last of my brothers left home he would come back at the end of term to look bored, regaling me with interminable stories of drink and dope fuelled escapades. There was no one else to listen to him. Yet when I visited his college as a gauche sixth former because he'd said he'd take me to some student publishing party, the night was a total washout.

He vanished leaving me in a room where everyone was older than me and purposeful. He returned two hours later, in which time I'd experienced terror and boredom in equal measure. He wanted me to feel overawed. What he didn't expect was to find me struggling to stay awake.

I had sat for eternity on a hard desk watching people fret over pages of type (*that's* how long ago it was). People were making corrections with *Tipp-Ex*! Biggest excitement was when everyone went to wave the copy off in the printer's van. I stood watching it drive away and a girl said -It's thrilling isn't it? I just wanted to go back to the halls and sleep.

The next morning my brother was full of tales about the high jinks they had got up to once the paper was 'put to bed'. It was some technical term people used then because print was set in a frame called a bed, but I heard in that phrase how anything interesting would only start once I was also safely in mine and I imagined life forever eluding me while I would be doomed to hear endless stories of what I had missed.

In my second year five of us rented a house with an Arctic wind that howled through it. Good Times! With the exception of the living room, where it was possible to light a fire in the tiny grate, the house was unheated. On wintry days if the sun shone it was warmer out on the street because the house stood in shadow. Nothing thawed. Coats left hanging in the hall grew stiff with frost overnight.

We equipped ourselves with hot water bottles and would nurse these on our laps while we debated if we could afford to light a fire. Then one of the group – a short girl called Bernie who had grown up in the Republic, started staying out most nights, and when the spring came she showed little sign of wanting to return, so we reckoned it wasn't just the temperature. Over that dark, disconsolate winter as we had huddled together like hens, Bernie decided she wanted nothing to do with us and carved out a new social life.

We felt like outcasts while she was having this whale of a time, or if not a whale exactly, something large like a shark maybe, circling in dark waters. Bernie was in a hurry. In those long, slow days of student-hood she seemed to splash in a race from one thing to another. She was never home now that she had bigger fish to swim with. And then *that* night, she had them, all these *important* people, back to *our* house, for some party which she hadn't even mentioned. She was surprised when she saw us in the kitchen. She said she had told us. *Told us*? And that was that.

We had realised she was planning something because she spent days cleaning and wouldn't let us in to use the cooker on the Saturday morning. The day before I had walked across a washed patch of lino to where my shoes had been marooned like castaways and hurriedly left for a lecture before she discovered the footprints and went ballistic. But in that week, before we knew what she was doing, I watched as she transformed into the harridan of a mother she claimed to hate. Her mother was a god-fearing convert who had moved to Cork and had nine children after seeing the error of her Protestant ways. She used to send her daughter regular missives about the perils of drink and to be mindful of her virginity. She would have had Bernie tarred and feathered if she'd know the half of it. Bernie always said she was never going back, but that week I could see this iron core of her resolve which must have been inherited. I guess the party was part of some strategic plan now that she had moved away from our circle. There was something determined and anxious about her as if she was preparing for an interview.

It was only after that I thought how odd it was for all her guests to come from the year above. There was no one from her cohort. She had invited lecturers as well, including the visiting lecturer, a performance artist making a name for himself in the relatively new field of video, which in those days was all about cutting edge art work, Warholesque. No one could have predicted video's collapse into the mundane once people realised they could use it to record episodes of Stars in Their Eyes.

Although Bernie always claimed to have no money, that week the kitchen filled up with foodstuff in boxes with 'Do not Touch' written on the sides. So Big Marcia wrote our names in felt tip on the individual eggs in a tray. Of course Bernie said we were being petty. And so we found ourselves arguing about eggs, because we couldn't have put into words what it was that was driving us.

On the afternoon of the party – when she finally admitted to us there *was* to be a party in our house – she had been lugging bottles of cola for mixers and paper plates from the V.G store home on the bus when The Misery got on.

The Misery was one of the few final year students whom Bernie had not considered inviting. She was a strange girl, who always wore knee length socks like she was still at the convent and spoke in this whiney voice that made everything sound like a complaint, even if she was just ordering coffee in the canteen.

Apparently she'd spied the bags of stuff and said, – Arre ye haavin' ah perty? (She was from somewhere up the coast.) When Bernie told us this, and did the accent, we shuddered with her at the idea of The Misery finding out that all the final year were off to a party, except for her and Wall-Eye-Brian who later became a successful film maker, but whom Bernie considered a loser back then.

Imagine The Misery turning up uninvited, we said. But weren't we were doing the same? Bernie had turned us into uninvited guests.

That evening at the close of summer term there was a yellow light bathing the city. You could be suckered into thinking this peace was real. Cave Hill in the distance looked shadowy as it softly began to recede into the oncoming night.

The four of us didn't know what to do so we stood around downstairs as an entire faculty's worth of seniors and the odd lecturer poured into the house. She had spent her food allowance for the month on this single night and had admitted, after Big Marcia collared her, that she was hosting the party 'because the final year students had all been working *so* hard' and, she said they 'deserved something as a reward'. She blushed, because we all knew it didn't make sense. There was something bogus about the event which none of us could figure.

The music was lousy. It sucked. She didn't have anything decent of her own but after letting us know how bored she was with our company none of us would consider loaning her anything from our boring collections. In those days we loaned vinyl and risked its annihilation, so none of us offered.

It was as well because the place was jammed and any form of dancing would have been dangerous. It was an oddly stilted event. Guests stayed in their own groups and apart from the free food, no one seemed to know why they were there.

Bernie hovered behind people, flapping her arms to get their attention in order to offer food and pour drinks. She was rushed off her feet. She snapped at Marcia who was filling a kettle just as a couple of guests walked into the kitchen and she tried to turn her bad temper into a laugh, as if she was being ironic. She gave Marcia a hard smile as she knocked past her to the corridor.

What else to do? There were people everywhere. We had to join in so I attempted a conversation with a girl in a green frock but she turned her back. My second attempt got me stuck with a lumpy girl, Ethel who was bewildered to be there and whose invitation was probably a mistake. When I extricated myself I saw my housemates standing in the corridor. They looked lost. Bernie had told them that none of the food was for us. Odd the things you remember: a redheaded girl being passed some fruity looking pudding in a plastic disposable bowl and looking at the hostess and pulling one of these faces that middle aged women make, the naughty-me look, the one that says – I shouldn't really. Why? Will the world stop because you ate a slice of cake? Well yes it will, that's the point, when you are the centre of the universe you are its gravitational pull, your every move impacts on the rest of us small planets. Bernie was smiling shyly and urging her – Oh Go on, and she blushed as the redheaded girl acquiesced, like she was doing Bernie a favour.

So the four of us walked up the road to the local pub, a Loyalist stronghold we avoided, but we were too dispirited to care. Then I thought I saw someone pass me, look my way, and keep moving.

– Jesus, Ethne said, – I've just seen The Misery making down the road. I hope she's not going to our house!

– She'll get a bloody shock if she does, Big Marcia said. Then she called,

– Hi Barbara! (That was her real name) – Barbara! Are you off out?

Instead of being relieved to be acknowledged, because she so seldom was, The Misery kept on walking, although she glanced up and we knew she'd heard.

Barbara? We couldn't tell if she was Protestant or Catholic with a name like that. Saint Barbara the patron saint of munitions workers and those handling explosives. Great name to have in Belfast.

We sent Shirley up to the bar because she was from Birmingham and no one would bother her. We sat in a huddle nursing Guinness.

– I hope you know this is a Catholic drink, Ethne said. – If any trouble kicks off we're for it.

– How can you tell it's a Catholic drink?

Shirley never understood the invisible lines which divided the city. But the songs they sang that night were an indication.

– But they're pop songs, she said.

And Big Marcia whose brother was in the Kesh had to explain it was the *absence* of songs which were an indication.

– If you got up and sang the Croppy Boy now, you'd be lynched.

– I'd expect to be anyhow. You've heard me sing.

But we watched as floor singers stood up unaided by backing tracks or instruments and belted out pop songs. This was the formative days of Karaoke – they'll try to tell you it's a Japanese invention but those Ulster Unionists had it down pat. Singers accompanied themselves on spoons and combs and paper. An old feller in a coat down to his ankles roared 'My Boy Lollipop', giving it the Millie treatment if not the vowels. People all around were crying with laughter. Then a woman stood and started in on 'Rose of Spanish Harlem' in an unhealthily high treble and a man jumped up and began cod flamenco dancing, using his false teeth as castanets.

For a rare moment the party I was *not* at was not the place to be. Maybe that's why I remember that evening so well. How different that night felt.

When we drew back to our street we knew something had gone wrong. Fire engines and people standing round on corners. We were headed off by an RUC man who wouldn't let us go any further, and women were nursing children with coats thrown hurriedly over pyjamas. The lower half of the street had been evacuated. The bomb disposal squad crept up on a parked car with English number plates.

An incendiary device had gone off in the phone booth which was a smoking hull of molten glass and twisted metal. An 'Out of Order' sign still clung to the wreckage.

– That was working earlier, Shirley said in all seriousness, and despite ourselves we cracked up. Then we saw Bernie running with this big tall fellow, the visiting lecturer she had a bit of a thing about, and he was striding ahead of her, straightening his clothes. He looked irritated and she was trying to keep up. People came spilling from our front door, even though that end of the street and the corner shop was declared 'out of range' but they all stood round gawking as the lecturer explained it was his car after all, and the soldiers got up from the pavement where they were looking under the bodywork with mirrors.

– What sort of a country is it? he asked one of the RUC men.

– What kind of people are *they*?

He spat what a bloody awful place it was, how he'd be glad to get back to *civilisation*.

– I've had enough of all this stupidity.

A Geordie soldier agreed with him.

Now he was full of it, having been inconvenienced by The Troubles. We got a lot of visiting lecturers like that – turned-on by being in a danger zone, good for their C.V sort of thing, the 'making it real' types, but come the first power cut, they'd be off.

The RUC man said they'd had an anonymous tip off from a public phone, about an unfamiliar car with foreign number plates parked in the street on the same night a resident had complained about the volume of strangers going in and out of a house. The squaddies arrived just as the phone box blew.

– We had no warning about that, they said. Then they told him to move his car for fear of reprisal. He didn't need to be asked twice. After a couple of false starts he roared off without saying anything to Bernie who stood watching his brake lights.

When we were allowed back down the street it was cold, the party guests who first went to look had just kept on walking to their homes. Except for a few stragglers who lived too far away to get home there were only us. It was the time of curfews and military patrols. It was common for people to end up stranded at each other's houses. You wouldn't send anyone out after the pubs shut, even if you hated them. This tight circle of the abandoned huddled round the small fire downstairs drinking whiskey. Bernie looked as if she had been crying, but when she saw us she straightened up and told us what a roaring success, what a wild night it had been, apparently from the exact moment we had left and prior to the bomb scare.

A couple of years after that night I ran into her at a party in London where we were both doing post graduate work. She discovered that I was friendly with someone who was one of her tutors, and went mad to know where I had met this person, what my relationship was with them exactly? They were the sort of questions you just wouldn't ask. Not if you had any sense. And her politeness teetered on the edge of rage. As if that spoilt night long ago still rankled.

When I asked if she saw anybody from back then she looked startled as if she barely remembered and then she said something, that there was a girl she never trusted, who was jealous, and I listened as she described me. In her version I had managed to slip out, set fire to a phone box, cause a scare and have the house evacuated on an important night when her future might have been decided. It was all bunkum, but the terrifying thing was she had no idea I was the girl around whom she had constructed this story.

— Don't you remember her? she asked me. — She used to live in that freezing house in second year. Can't remember her name. Didn't you do the same subject as her?

— What happened to them? I asked her, Those girls?

She didn't know. But I could have told her. Two of us were in London, one was in New York, Marcia got married in a hurry and had a kid.

— Hey, I said at last. — Remember Barbara?

But of course she didn't, just as she didn't know which girl I had been.

All those years ago, I had wandered off that night to queue for the ladies in the pub. It was across a yard where all the barrels were stacked and there was a public phone on the outside wall. I remember the floor was swimming. And I had overheard a man shouting at someone saying it was far too late to do anything about it now.

When I went through the door to cross the yard to the toilet I saw him, a small grey man in a Mac, the kind of man who worked all day in an office, a shipping clerk, a wages clerk, or on an assembly line, semi skilled, and he was puffed up with his importance.

– We don't want that type round here! I heard him say.

– Bloody foreigners, taking our jobs. A houseful of them, ye say? Dave Macann's been keeping an eye out.

Macann's was our corner shop.

– Drop the load in the box. And scarper. Make sure no one tries to use it.

He covered the mouthpiece with his hand.

Later I tried to think what he looked like, but I had only the sketchiest of ideas, I couldn't have described him. And it was all conjecture. Like the story that Bernie had told herself about some spiteful housemate who had made a hoax call, this is how rumours start and in Ulster then, rumours could cost a life.

Maybe it's because I felt something then, that night of the party, something which had been coming to a slow boil in her mistreatment of us, and along the way all those other times began to flicker up as memories, that I can remember her now. Details surface; like the tea towels she bought specially, or how hard the desk top was that I sat another party out on, before that night.

I think that must have been the night when I got an inkling that the best times weren't always elsewhere. Nowadays I get away fast from anyone who makes me feel like that. I see my family rarely, my brothers at Christmas, and Colin (the youngest of them) is still being difficult. My folks died many years ago now, after a lifetime of silently sitting together in contempt, and I am still the unknown face at funerals.

I probably am scared of commitment – I become anxious that I won't be able to handle another rejection, which stops me ever getting too comfortable in case I need to escape all over again. Along the way things have attached to me, husbands, houses, but I have let them all go.

Shortly after meeting Bernie in London that time, I saw her on Tottenham Court Road when I was sitting waiting for someone in a falafel house. It was dark outside and I saw this figure crossing the road, bundled up in a coat. I was sitting along a window bench, she only had to look up and she would see me there, lit up by the house lights like an advert. I panicked and ducked beneath the window until I estimated she had passed. When I came up the waitress was staring at me. I had to pretend I had dropped my pen.

I suppose we crop up in everyone's version of events. At some point we are all The Misery, the girl no one wants. And I think about her that night, crossing the road, going towards our street. She was the last person to use the phone box, once she'd noted the number plate. An anonymous tip off.

She was lucky to escape with her life.

That's what she kept saying on Monday back in college, that she'd been in the phone box minutes before it blew. Marcia asked her who she'd been ringing and Misery shot back without thinking – The speaking clock.

She didn't know the booth had been rigged, or that the man hammering to use it was trying to save her. Just like he couldn't have said the precise time it would happen.

– Just bloody make sure no one tries to use it.

When I saw the fire engines that night I began making the connections. Too many connections are dangerous. It's not clever to know all the pieces. But we were all young then and simple feelings could spark out of control, jealousy could erupt. Better to remain cold than risk everything bursting into flames.

When you are young you think you are missing out on all those good times someone else is having, but as you get older you realise that even those times you missed are now over for everyone, and you end up living as if you are cursed, like that man shouting down the phone – always knowing something bad is about to take place, but never knowing the moment it will occur.

Kath Mckay
Specimens

There were a lot of dead things that summer. A seal washed up in the Narrows, its body bloated like a slug, and the papers were full of people all over the North getting shot or blown up, as they settled into their car, or walked down steps from one area into another to buy cigarettes or crisps, or sat in the pub for a drink.

And then there was the car crash. My friend Jinny and I had taken a notion to go up to the folk night at a pub in Kirkubbin. The bar looked like a public urinal, and was about as comfortless. Painted snot green, it had red leather banquette seating and a few bar stools, which meant most of us had to stand up. The Guinness tasted watered down, the beer was piss weak, the peanuts felt like they had been handled before, and the crisps were stale. There were a couple of country and western bands on that night as well as the usual folk musicians: some woman called Philomena Begley, and her band, the Country Flavour, alongside a local band.

The older locals, swaying in time with the music, and staring glassy-eyed, loved Philomena. All I could hear were words like

'Mother' … 'Lonely' … 'Rambling'. Then she launched into 'Truck driving Woman -'*my daddy taught me everything I knew / and this woman's gonna fill her daddy's shoes*'. People smiled in amusement. As if.

Her band left the stage, and then the audience decamped to the bar and rushed back with full glasses. A teenage girl cleared her throat and sang a lament in Gaelic in a high pure voice. We stilled ourselves, not even lifting our drinks to our mouths. A local show band broke the spell, and soon people were up dancing and clapping. We carried on slurping and swallowing and tapping our feet and then we too were up and moving, and everything became fuzzy. At one point in the evening, a space cleared around an elderly couple as they inched across the dance floor. Bone thin, with sparse white hair, hers pulled into an untidy bun, his greased back from an almost translucent forehead, they held each other as if they might break. We didn't know it then, but a fortnight later they would be dead.

How we ended up with two young turds that night I'm not sure, but the lads sidled up to us, and bought us a drink and I suppose in the dim light they looked OK, it wasn't like they were ugly or anything, and we were the youngest on the floor by a decade. They both had dark curls and blue-green eyes, not unhandsome the pair of them, but I'd heard them shouting and carrying on earlier, and the older men taking them aside warning them. Yet it was the most natural thing in the world after the pub closed for them to offer us a lift home: the alternative a walk of eight miles along dark country roads, with the buses long finished, and there being no taxi firms for miles. Not that we would even think of getting a taxi in those days anyway, taxis were out of our league. The night would grow colder, and we'd be at the mercy of whatever drunken drivers went past. Better the devil you know. We got in their car.

About a mile from the village, the driver, who'd been smoking and humming tunelessly, suddenly braked. There was a loud bang, the sound of stones shattering and I was flung forward, winding myself against the front seat. Jinny fell sideways and the door flew open, and then she was on the ground, moaning and crying, scratched and bleeding.

'Jeezus,' said the lad.

'That was close.'

I unfolded from the seat, and creaked my neck, moving it gingerly from side to side. There was a grating sound, and a pain down the back of my left shoulder. The lad pushed the door open. The sudden cold hit me. The front wheels, surrounded by bits of wall, were in a ditch, the windscreen was cracked, and two curious cows lumbered up to us through the dark, staring with gentle eyes. Jinny was hopping round. The cuts on her leg weren't deep. She was OK.

'Good job we were so drunk,' I said to the driver. We didn't know the lads' names.

He looked blank.

'We were so relaxed we didn't hurt ourselves much.'

'Oh.' He nodded.

With the aid of a torch, the driver's mate inspected the dent in the front of the car. He shook his head. There were no marks on him.

'I'll come back for it tomorrow,' said the suddenly sober driver.

'I'll tell me da a cow ran out in front of it.'

His mate snorted. Even me, no countrywoman, knew his da wouldn't believe him. Cars were valuable in the country.

'Only some old banger, sure.'

The driver kept on, as if rehearsing his speech to his dad.

'Insurance.'

We ignored him. Jinny and I linked arms, and began walking, and the lads followed behind. The summer night was cool against my thin jacket. We were all sober now, Jinny and I in charge, the lads seeming much younger than us now, just lads. I knew we had the upper hand. They were scared of us, in awe. They'd never been out of the province in their lives, while we were other, from over the water. We weren't stuck in this place, like them. We didn't have to answer to a father.

After about half a mile, they began asking us questions:

'What were the Beatles like?'

'Did you know them?'

I hinted that I'd met John Lennon, and mentioned 'family connections'.

It was like the year before when I went to the Soviet Union as part of my course, and young Russians asked me did we always have afternoon tea. I realized then I could make up any old shite. 'Yes,' I told the Russians: 'Earl Grey in a teapot, and home-made scones.'

We arrived home at dawn and fell into bed.

Two hours later the sun streaming through bare attic windows woke us. We were quickly up and out. I'd promised Jinny I'd help her down at the Marine Biology Station, labelling samples. Her PhD research was on creatures that lived between the grains of sand. She spent a lot of time at the edge of the lough in wellies, collecting samples, a lot of time peering into salt water, and filling specimen jars, or whirring sand around in a centrifugal spinner. When she wasn't working she was always fiddling: planting up seedlings; collecting fungi; bird watching; snipping bunches of flowers. Now she rushed in and thrust a pile of sample jars and sticky labels into my hand.

'Got to finish an experiment,' she said, and was off.

I dutifully began writing out labels. I had a terrible headache, and my neck felt stiffer than the day before, so I was glad to do something mindless. In those days my writing was neat, legible, I wanted people to see what I meant. There was something soothing about the Greek and Latin words: nematoda, copepoda, polychaeta, gastropoda, rotifer, ciliate. I had no idea what any of the words meant, and I couldn't grasp the idea of something so small you couldn't see it, even though Jinny had shown me fantastic sci-fi creatures under the microscope, with their bug-eyed heads, their segmented bodies and their curling tails. Quietened by the words, I wrote away.

And then the phone rang, and there was a short, terse conversation.

'Yes,' I heard her say.

She handed me a waterproof.

'Come on.'

We piled into the Land Rover driven by Michael, her boss, a wiry man who said little. Pat, the round, red-faced boatman, joined us. He had a rolling walk, from his years on boats, liked a drink, and favoured pungent filterless cigarettes. Aidan, the new lab assistant, a shy and muscular young man, made up the party. They threw ropes and ladders into the back of the Land Rover, and we were off.

The day had started off sunny, but as we neared the coast the sky darkened, the temperature dropped and waves grew ferocious, with a wind off the sea. Sea mist hugged the rocky coast: it was difficult to make things out. Everything looked ghostly and insubstantial. I could imagine shipwrecks washing up on this shore. Word would travel that a boat had struck the rocks, and country people materialize from the isolated cottages around, milking the stricken boats after checking for survivors. Bloated bodies still turned up occasionally, driven by the tides, sometimes with a bullet in their head.

We were collecting a dolphin: something bigger than meiofaunae, their usual specimens.

'The coastguard saw it this morning when he was doing his rounds,' said Pat, directing.

'Up this way.'

We climbed over rocks encrusted with limpets and suckered with kelp, over dark green pools where small fish swam and crabs scuttled under stones.

We trudged on. I regretted wearing plimsolls, and not the heavy duty boots of the others. Jinny had that look of the scientist on the hunt. I was just another pair of hands, with no specific knowledge, no noteworthy skills.

'Storm's coming.' Pat cupped his hand to light a match. He pushed his hood up. I felt the first gash of rain on my face.

And then we rounded the point. The dead dolphin lay near the water's edge, flurries of water moistening it as if to draw it back in the sea, its upturned side nibbled ragged. Blue grey, with a snub nose, a dribble of white chalk fell from its mouth, its dead eye stared. So still, so flat on the greyish sand, the sight winded us.

We drew in breath and bowed our heads. Jinny's specimens under the microscope were wriggly and alive. Here was a salty, sweetish smell. Seagulls squawked overhead.

Then the others kicked into work mode: 'Bottlenose dolphin,' said Jinny, circling it, making notes in a plastic covered notebook. In a quiet precise voice, Michael spoke into a small tape recorder, as if he was testifying in a court of law. Aidan took out a tape measure, and held out a length to Jenny. They put on gloves, and peered at the gash on the dolphin's side. I stared at lashing waves, and imagined living in this place. Occasionally you'd hear of an old woman or man found wandering the roads, or clambering over rocks. Some said the sea drove you mad in the end: that twice a day ebb and flow of the tides, the waves coming in, and the waves going out, no matter what.

'We have to be quick, so,' said Pat, ever practical.

'The tide's turned. It'll be coming in soon, sure.'

So they covered the dolphin with a tarpaulin, and laid it on a board and roped it to the ladder, and Michael and Aidan hoisted it up between their shoulders and Pat gathered up the rest of the stuff. The mist hovered as we hugged the rocky cost. The rain grew heavier, soaking through my trousers. At one point, I fell behind, slipping and sliding, no grip in my inadequate shoes. When I lifted my head as they rounded the point and headed inland, I could see the whole funeral procession – Pat, like a stocky priest, ahead – Michael and Aidan shouldering the dolphin, Jinny at the rear.

At the Marine Station, I left them to unload the land rover. We'd be falling over each other, and I had no skills to offer them. Reading Dostoevsky and Aristotle didn't count. The dolphin would be put in the giant freezer, and the next day Jinny and Michael and Aidan would dissect it, making careful notes about their findings. I wondered why the dolphin had died. There'd been rumours of oil spills, a leaking fishing boat had limped into harbour and there'd been more dead seals up the coast. I'd overheard Jinny and her colleagues discussing mutations in meiofaunae. People said the paint the fishermen used to protect the underside of their boats was toxic to marine life. I'd thought of this coast as a haven from

Belfast. But something was changing.

I didn't understand any of it. All I knew was that I wanted to be away from people. Everyone knew everybody here. They all had relatives in neighbouring villages, and news travelled fast. Going into a shop you exchanged stories as if they were tender.

So I walked, out of the village along the lough road, enjoying the quiet. The lough coast was more sheltered, there was little traffic this time of the day and the water was restful on the eyes. Deceptive. I knew how strong its tug was. Every year a child drowned underestimating the pull of the tides. For now, each ebb of the tide uncovered more rocks, more land. All along this coast there were small islands like Cullen Island that could only be reached at low tide. I'd sit in the hide. It was a good viewing point for birds, a refuge for anyone cut off by the tide, and the few who canoed down the lough. There would be no one about.

I turned down the wet pebbly path to the hide, and saw the outline of a man inside. No matter. I'd exchange polite greetings, make a show of looking at the lough's birdlife, turn back. I was fearless in those days.

It was the driver from the car. He hadn't struck me as the solitary type. Maybe his da had given him an earful and he was taking a moment. I relaxed, and we greeted each other as he stood at the hide entrance, friendly enough.

'Come in,' he said. 'Take a wee look at the seals.'

So we sat in companionable silence watching the mottled grey mournful faces of the seals, as they swam with grace, and lumbered onto rocks.

I stood up to go. I was ready for a bath, a cup of tea.

'Thanks,' I said.

There was a whiff of fresh salt from his direction, and I turned, drawn to him. We pulled each other's clothes off, and clawed each other where we stood, and coupled: quick, sticky and desperate. Afterwards he wrapped his arms around me, and stroked my face with roughened hands and then draped his jumper round my shoulders and patted his coat on the floor, and we lay down. His body was white and bony. All anger and hardness gone, there was

225

the look of a younger man on his face. He opened his mouth as if he wanted to tell me something, and then a great tenderness surged over me and we ran our hands up each other's legs and arms and kissed each other all over.

I must have dozed, for I came to chilled, and the smell of fresh salt had given way to the stench of rotting seaweed and the sickly sweet of the dolphin's corpse.

He had a bar of Cadbury's fruit and nut with him, so we devoured it, fully dressed by now, looking out through the hide windows. We spoke about the weather, and the possibility of a record high tide. He zipped up my coat for me, saying the tide was on the turn, that we needed to leave, and patted me on the back, and then we walked off separate, home.

In the pub that night Jinny and I drank whiskey chasers. I swallowed three before they made an impact on the cold. It was supposed to be summer, but I was chilled to the bone, and my neck still ached. A friend, Ben, was with us from Edinburgh. Ben had been schooled in England, and sounded posh, unScottish. After a while, the driver turned up, as I knew he would. There was nowhere else to go. He stayed in a corner with his mate, and then came over. I felt myself blushing. I still didn't know his name. It seemed too late to ask now. I made small talk, enquiring about his car. He shrugged.

'This here your fella?' He turned to Ben without acknowledging him.

'No, he's my friend.'

He gave me a look as if he didn't believe me, and then something hardened in his manner, and he went back to his mate.

'Probably thought he was in with a chance,' said Ben.

I turned my body so that Ben couldn't see my expression. My head was telling me that it was madness what had happened, the result of watching too many films: all those crashing waves, all that Celtic mist. I wasn't from here; we didn't have anything to say to each other. The village would close around us.

The lad returned, well tanked up this time. He kept one hand in his pocket, and I started. I knew nothing about this man, or his connections. If he thought I was playing with him, I had no idea what he'd do. Up in Belfast people were getting shot or abducted, bundled into cars. A body was laid out at the foot of Cave Hill. There were rumours of witchcraft and Satanism.

He smiled at my discomfort, and spoke softly so that Ben couldn't hear.

'Tell your wee friend here.'

I looked over at Ben, blinking in that mild mannered way he had.

'Tell him not to bring himself in this here pub again.'

'Aye?'

'Aye.' He drew himself up to his full height. His breath smelt of beer and smoke. I wanted to laugh, but I kept my face poker.

His hand pressed deeper into his pocket.

'I'll shoot him if he comes in here again, so I will. We don't want any of his sort. English, you know.'

I said nothing. I was from Liverpool, Jinny from Birmingham. Ben was Scottish as far back as he knew.

Ben left the next day as planned. I told him nothing of the threat, and travelled up to Belfast with him and stayed there for a fortnight, going the library each day, immersing myself in study, reading about Greek philosophers and the human need to create meaning. At night I dreamt of the dead dolphin. When I woke each morning, the room smelt of salt and rotting seaweed.

After ten days I decided to go back down to the village and speak to the lad. I owed him that. In my women's group, one girl had been talking about a man who had closed down on her after sex. I couldn't forget that look on the lad's face: open, hopeful, as if he might expect something different. I phoned Jinny and said I would be down the next day, Saturday.

'OK,' she said.

'I'm a bit busy though, you'll have to amuse yourself.'

Was there a touch of frost in her voice?

Then she softened. Jinny could never keep up a grudge.

'We'll go the pub. Oh, by the way, that lad who was driving came round the station asking for you. What would he want?'

'Dunno.'

'He's never called here before. Is something going on?'

She waited for me to speak. Down the wires, I could hear seagulls squawking. They'd be swooping into bins near the lough edge, carrying off bread crusts, hovering on the wind. If I told Jinny, she would go on about how it was OK for me just visiting, but she had to live in the village full-time, fit in.

'Of course not,' I said. 'I probably left something in his car. I'll speak to him tomorrow. If he calls again, tell him I'll be there after two.'

Late that afternoon, while I was in the library reading about the suppression of desire, those lads were killed as their car took a blind corner too fast on the lough road, and ploughed into the elderly couple's mini. Both cars ended up in the lough. The older couple were found, but bad weather meant the search was called off, and only resumed after a few days, when the tides would have carried the lads' bodies to the head of the lough and back out towards sea several times.

On Saturday I walked by the side of the lough with Jinny, watching the divers coming up empty.

'People think water is magic,' Jinny said out of nowhere, as we tightened our hoods against the wind.

'I read about an investigation once, when scientists found that the public believed that anything they dumped into water disappeared. That was the end of it, they thought.'

I peered at strands of seaweed bobbing on the water. Nothing disappeared, not even the things you couldn't see. They changed and mutated, were transformed.

The two lads were found four weeks later by a fishing boat, their bodies bloated and nibbled by fishes, and pitted with scars from being dashed against rocks.

I imagined them deep beneath the lough, with the glutinous dolphin, and the sightless seal, and the old couple, and all the people shot at their door as they put their bins out, or walked down the steps to McClure Street to buy cigarettes and cheese and onion crisps. You feel nothing, but there is unnatural quiet, and everything goes dark.

Light Waves

Her twenty – six Amstrad Pal 1 Nicam Digital
Stereo/Teletext TV finally packs up.
The only way to get the picture right

was jump up and down in front of the screen
until Phil took a soldering iron to the cables,
while I got the brush ready, for electrocution.

Fuzzy lines, slo-mo ghost images, faded sounds.
Little of her left. The tape from her answer phone:
'I'll get back to you later'; a photo of her and an elephant;

a violin shaped clock; a couple in clover turning:
When Irish eyes are smiling; 'Do not overwind!!!'
We wait until Christmas Day. Four years.

'Fire and Shock Hazard. Do not expose to moisture.'
Drag to the wet garden. 'To prevent electrical shock,
do not remove screws.' Remove screws. Wires and circuits;

'Dangerous High Voltage. No user serviceable parts.'
Hold tendrils. 'Refer servicing to qualified service personnel.'
Raise hammers. *In sure and certain hope*

we commend you, 105/00 2285. Commit you
to the ground. Spread a cloth to catch shiny bits.
Light perpetual. Let go.

Volume 52, Issue 8

Wednesday evening in Armstrong's printers, the junction
of English Scotch and Irish Street, Paddy laid out pages.
He held lino blocks, a scalpel. Wore a long leather apron.
Dark hair, blue eyes, pale, the one Catholic worker.
Every fortnight he set for us, in between gardening and army mags.
Behind us, rollers pressed out The Northern Ireland Builder.
Twelve pages done, Paddy moved onto Sports. *That there headline*
needs a wee cut, he said of the hockey story. *How's about*
'Defeat Blow', sure? At three a.m. we grinned.

Possibly we wouldn't make it. But Paddy sliced a leg
off the hockey team, fixed the photo in position, like a surgeon.
Right, that there's it. Photographed pages onto plates,
clipped them onto rollers, ready for the next shift.
Get yourselves away home, it's put to bed, so it is.
Heading out of English Street, we bombed down the motorway.
Past the lights of Long Kesh, into the Belfast dark.
Next morning, we'd be back, to pick up the five thousand.

Stella Maris

Mary's statue reaches arms across the harbour
where boys dive into clear water
flecked with diesel. The ferry cuts through
The Narrows, lets its front down as it nears shore.
Cars start up. Two men in caps at the Cuan Arms
discuss Sean, who hasn't been over
for twenty years, but is just after getting back.

Hot whiskey slides down easy in November
when the sea mist rolls in and the long call
of the lifeboat breaks into your sleep. Inspectors
from England say the boat paint is toxic
to fish. Fungicides root, bed deep. This north
we're not without consequence. On clear nights
the Milky Way is visible, and a galaxy of stars;
Calisto and Cassiopeia, The Dog Star, The Plough

and at St Brigit's Well, rags on a hawthorn bush, alders,
scribbled wishes. Please God cure her,
Jesus grant my plea. In the cairns, boulders
cover stalagmites. Nitrates leach into the water
table. Fossils on the beach. On the shore
uprooted stones, people mumbling a prayer
say he went quick at the end, how people ought to.

John O'Donoghue
A Mystery of Light

A Heroic Crown of Sonnets
On The Occasion of His Fiftieth Birthday

I

The rain has washed this summer all away.
From dale and field and out to sea the sun's
Been chased from England, banished from each bay,
Each inlet, blown like a puffball you once
Wished on as it drifted off with your hopes
Still clinging to the tiny afro of
Its soft head. Summer's gone, from upland slopes,
From valleys and from wealds, has taken off,
Absconded, disappeared. Now autumn falls
In the rain, a hawk poised to swoop and dive.
We can't go back, escape, can't stop or stall
The wheel we turn on, life's appetites, its drive.
    But if I shut my eyes another sun
    Dawns in my head, another day's begun.

2

Dawn's in my head: another day's begun.
A summer's day in Ireland, a huge blush
Of red covering the hills, sun-
Light glowing over all, so warm, so lush.
A night spent camping up in Jameson's field,
And the first dawn that I had ever seen,
A wonder that the world was slow to yield,
A mystery of light behind the screen
Night kept across the sky until the stars,
Exhausted, dissolved like dew into the dawn.
And then we found some sticks, a few old spars,
And lit a fire for breakfast. I should say *slean*
    To all that now, my childish things put away;
    Dreams haven't fed you, no matter what you say.

3

Dreams haven't fed you. No matter what you say
The past stays past, the dead forever there,
And memories won't bring back yesterday.
They may haunt this autumn, shimmer on the stair,
But better to look forward than look back.
And yet … That great red hill, the feeling that
We looked at the world through a secret crack
And saw deeper into Time, were all at
The dawning not just of a summer's day
But of a universe looming into view.
Are these childish things I should put away?
Are your memories illusion, or true?
    Perhaps you can't end what you've begun
    Because you'll never undo what you've done?

4

Because you'll never undo what you've done
The past takes on a different aspect,
A place where all that you might have become
Still exists. The past allows you to reflect
On who you are right now in ways the present
And the future never can. But the past
Is gone; Time will never pause nor relent.
If I've returned this summer, the last
Before my fiftieth birthday, to track
The boy I was in summers now long gone,
I know that nothing will ever bring him back.
Just what is left for me to reflect on?
    Dreams, and the dregs of dreams, mists and history.
    And that line of ancient Gaelic poetry.

5

And that line of ancient Gaelic poetry –
A dhruimfhionn donn dílis a shíoda na mBó –
Singing in my ear. It's her I can see,
Saying the words, familiar and strange, so
Musical they sound like drumbeats, like fifes
And the march of men coming to a tower.
The vision fades. It was so long ago … Life's
Twists and turns are in that line, its power
And its pity. For the chieftains that I saw
I saw in vain: the line is about a cow
Going slowly down the road. The Penal Laws,
So near, so distant from the Irish now,
    Made sure the Gaelic poets spoke in code:
    The cow is Ireland going down the road.

6

The cow is Ireland going down the road,
An image as homely and subversive
As her playing hurling round Ballinode,
And then writing in my book, her cursive
Script, as she taught me my letters, wrote lines
For me to copy before I ever
Went to school, the secret universe of signs,
The code the simple know before the clever –
Why should that too play out across the screen
Of memory? Past, present, future, loop
Inside my mind, so that what I have seen
I replay again and again, Betty Boop
    And JFK, signs floating away free…
    Kavanagh, and Behan, and O Rathaille.

7

Kavanagh and Behan and O Rathaille…
The doors open onto the distant past,
And these figures from my cracked history
Stand reflected in the tavern mirror, cast
Their shadows on the walls, and look at me
With due disdain. For have I paid my dues?
Am I summoned to this Court of Poetry?
Am I prepared to answer to the Muse?
They fade again, and I can't tell if they
Are shaking their heads or giving me the nod.
Every poet's fate: to live the way
The wild wind blows, aslant, eccentric, odd.
    For words alone don't constitute the code.
    Whisper it to me, speak of what you're owed.

8

Whisper it to me, speak of what you're owed…
Words fail, images fail, but in the context
Of the poem – the cow, the woman, the road –
All moves in a harmony that the text
Alone can't signify. Words must be said,
Their music makes the magic that won't work
Unless they're heard. What was our daily bread
Becomes art in heaven. A strange kind of quirk…
You chose between perfection of the life
And of the work, and knew that though your deeds
Might end in failure, that poverty, strife,
Were likely to be your lot, your heart bleeds
    More if a poem falters, doesn't sing.
    Your song is as fragile as a smoke ring.

9

Your song is as fragile as a smoke ring,
It fades as soon as breathed, and we who hear
Your words hear in them everything,
Life and Death, the great distance from there to here.
At the poem's turn, the year's turn, at the turn
Of my life from surplus to scarcity,
An old lesson now for me to learn:
What made me was the slow capacity
I had as a child to copy out her words,
To trace the slants and curves of her letters
And find in them my playthings. Like these birds
Singing because they must, I preen my feathers,
    Lift my voice with the poor and broken and mad,
    A melody at once happy and sad.

10

A melody at once happy and sad
Lilts through the house as the rain starts to lift
And though the news seems like a jeremiad,
Though loss and grief are harder now to sift
In the harsh sand falling through the hourglass
From the small particles of love and joy
That speckle Time, the days that pass
So fast, I make this as if I were a boy
Again copying her letters in my book.
She whispers to me now, as the sun breaks
Through its cloudy eclipse, and I see her look
At my blotted words, at what her prompting makes.
    O, to be always haunted, always searching!
    When I look forward, look back, it's you I sing.

11

When I look forward, look back, it's you I sing,
Your mischief, your laughter, and your snow white hair,
Young, old, you seem both at once, us walking
Down Clentoe Lane, you up ahead, and we're
All in a line, all in step, picking up sticks
For the range, and it's summer, and you're smiling
Through shadows and dapples, from the gloomy Styx,
Through a chequerwork of leaves, and we're filing
Behind to wherever you take us. The past
Is past, ashes burnt long ago in the fire.
Smoke lingers in the autumn air, fades fast
And all that lasts is growth, decay, desire.
    Summer ends, and I'm at once happy and sad.
    Did Sweeney sing sweeter because he went mad?

12

Did Sweeney sing sweeter because he went mad?
The song rises out of a different heart
When that heart has been broken, when you've had
To master strains beyond the bounds of art.
Hearts break, voices break, and from the broken
Rises up a deeper sound out of the depths.
Mad Sweeney cries out, high in his oaken
Canopy for what has been lost, laments
His fate. But all is changed, changed utterly.
The old myth speaks down the long centuries,
Of power and pity and poetry,
Of loss and pride and mysteries.
    I hear his song and like him I am astray.
    The red sun is rising on another day.

13

The red sun is rising on another day,
Rising on your memories, on your dreams,
Like suns that lit up childhood's enchanted way.
They light the road ahead, they are the themes
You sing like the birds in that red heaven
You heard first up in Jameson's field. Today
Take from the past what the past has given –
Before you lies a better, brighter way
And all your circlings shall lead not out of but
Into, not away from but towards. Down
Clentoe Lane, in dapples and shadows, foot-
Falls echo in the breeze. Don't turn around
    And don't look back, your childish things put away.
    Your memories, your dreams, begin to fray.

14

Your memories, your dreams, begin to fray.
The children all return to school, as leaves
Turn on the trees. As you watch them on their way
Your heart at once rejoices, at once grieves.
They know the secret signs, like you their playthings
Are words, are airs, by hand they've copied out
Your letters, by heart each pretty one sings
Your songs. O, go now with them! For without
You what are they, what shadows lie ahead?
They stretch their wings and sing new lilting songs
And soon forget every word you've said.
For they must fight new fights, and their wrongs,
 Their rights, are not over yesterday.
 The rain has washed this summer all away.

15

The rain has washed this summer all away.
Dawn's in my head: another day's begun.
Dreams haven't fed you, no matter what you say,
Because you'll never undo what you've done.
And that line of ancient Gaelic poetry -
(The cow is Ireland going down the road)
Kavanagh, and Behan, and O Rathaille
Whisper it to me, speak of what you're owed.
Your song is as fragile as a smoke ring,
A melody at once happy and sad.
When I look forward, look back, it's you I sing:
Did Sweeney sing sweeter because he went mad?
 The red sun is rising on another day.
 Your memories, your dreams begin to fray.

Biographies

Elizabeth Baines is the author of the novels *The Birth Machine* and *Too Many Magpies* and two collections of short stories, *Balancing on the Edge of the World* and *Used to Be*, all available from Salt Publishing. She has written prizewinning plays for BBC Radio 4 and written, produced and performed her own plays for fringe theatre. With Ailsa Cox, she co-founded and edited the short-story magazine Metropolitan. She has been a secondary-school teacher and has taught Creative Writing at Bolton Institute and the University of Manchester. http://www.elizabethbaines.com

Sean Campbell is Reader in Media and Culture in the School of Creative Industries at Anglia Ruskin in Cambridge. His book *'Irish Blood, English Heart': Second-Generation Irish Musicians in England* (Cork University Press, 2011) was named Music Book of the Year in the *Sunday Times* and in *Hot Press* magazine. Sean was series adviser on the television documentary series, *Guth: Musical Sons of the Irish Diaspora* (TG4, 2013), which explored the role of Irish ethnicity in the lives and work of musicians of Irish descent. He is currently writing a book on popular music and the Northern Ireland conflict.

Maude Casey was born in Luton to Irish parents and grew up in north London. She studied at the University of Sussex, the Universite d'Aix-Marseille and Goldsmiths' College, University of London. Her novel *Over the Water* (The Women's Press; London 1987) was shortlisted for the Whitbread Award, The Fawcett Book Prize and the Carnegie Medal. She works collaboratively with Brighton Migrant Solidarity, Migrant English Project, Brighton Against the Arms Trade and the Remaking Picasso's Guernica Collective https://remakingpicassosguernica.wordpress.com/ Her return to writing has seen her work shortlisted for the Bridport Short Story Prize.

Graham Caveney began his writing career at the New Musical Express in the 1980s before writing for a variety of papers and magazines including *The Face, City Limits, Q, The Guardian, The*

Independent, The Independent On Sunday, Arena and *GQ.* He is the author of four books: *Shopping In Space: Essays on Blank American Fiction* (Serpent's Tail, 1992, with Elizabeth Young); biographies of William Burroughs – *The Priest, They Called Him* (Bloomsbury, 1997) and Allen Ginsberg – *Screaming With Joy* (Bloomsbury, 1999). His most recent book, *The Boy With The Perpetual Nervousness* (Picador, 2017), is a memoir about growing up in the North of England during the 1970s and his experiences of Catholic clerical sexual abuse.He lives in Nottingham.

Ian Duhig became a full-time writer after working with homeless people for fifteen years and being made redundant. He has published since then, among other things, seven books of poetry, most recently *The Blind Roadmaker* (Picador 2016) shortlisted for the TS Eliot and Forward Prizes. He works with musicians, artists and socially excluded groups, recently editing *Any Change: Poetry in a Hostile Environment* (2018), a small poetry anthology from Leeds' immigrant communities chosen as a Poetry School Book of the Year. Duhig has won the Forward Best Poem Prize once and the National Poetry Competition twice

Ray French is the author of *The Red Jag & other stories* and the novels *All This Is Mine* and *Going Under* (both Vintage). He is also the co-author of *Four Fathers* and the co-editor with Kath Mckay of *End Notes: Ten stories about loss, mourning and commemoration.* His short stories have been broadcast on Radio 4 and appeared in a numerous magazines and compilations, including *Best European Fiction 2013.* He teaches Creative Writing at the University of Hull. Some of his essays and podcasts can be found on the Royal Literary Fund Website: https://www.rlf.org.uk/?s=Ray+French

Maria C. McCarthy is the author of a poetry collection, *strange fruits* (2011), and *As Long as it Takes* (2014), a collection of linked short stories about Irish women and their English-born daughters. Her poetry pamphlet, *There are Boats on the Orchard,* was published in 2017. All three are published by Cultured Llama. She has an MA with Distinction in Creative Writing from the University of Kent, and was the winner of the Society of Authors' Tom-Gallon Trust

Award 2015, for her story 'More Katharine than Audrey'. She lives in the Medway Towns. http://www.medwaymaria.co.uk

Moy McCrory is a writer and academic of Irish parentage who writes about identity and class. As a fiction writer she has had three collections of short stories and a novel published. Two of her books were serialized by the BBC and her work had been translated into fifteen languages. Her short fiction is widely anthologized and she was included in the seminal *Field Day Anthology of Irish Writing*. She was shortlisted for the Dylan Thomas Award, and was a Feminist Book Fortnight top ten author, two years running, and one of the authors chosen for the national Save our short story campaign top twenty recommended reads. She is a Hawthornden Fellow, a Senior Fellow of the HEA, has lectured in Bremen University, London University and is currently Senior Lecturer at the University of Derby and is a PhD examiner.

Kath Mckay has published two novels, three poetry collections, and short stories. Work includes *Hard Wired* (Moth, 2016), *Collision Forces* (Wrecking Ball, 2015) and *Telling the Bees* (Smiths Knoll 2014). Her short stories are anthologised and in magazines and have been broadcast on BBC Radio 4. She taught creative writing in London and now lectures at the University of Hull. Her most recent book (co-edited with Ray French) is *End Notes: Ten stories about loss, mourning and commemoration* (2017).

Tony Murray is Director of the Irish Writers in London Summer School and Curator of the Archive of the Irish in Britain. He joined the Irish Studies Centre at London Metropolitan University in 1995, eventually becoming its Director from 2012–2017. He has taught Irish Studies and English Literature for over twenty years, and has run the annual Irish Writers in London Summer School since its inception in 1996. Tony recently completed a major digitization project of the collections in the Archive of the Irish in Britain which was supported with a grant from the Irish Government's Emigrant Support Programme.

John O'Donoghue is the author of *Brunch Poems* (Waterloo Press, 2009); *Fools & Mad* (Waterloo Press, 2014); and *Sectioned: A Life In-*

terrupted (John Murray, 2009). *Sectioned* was awarded Mind Book of The Year 2010. His story 'The Irish Short Story That Never Ends' won The Irish Post Creative Writing Competition in 2016. He was awarded a Brookleaze Grant by the Royal Society of Literature, also in 2016, to work on a novel about John Clare and Robert Lowell, both patients in the same asylum over 100 years apart. He is a Lecturer in Creative Writing at the University of Brighton.

Marc Scully is a Lecturer in Psychology at Mary Immaculate College, Limerick. His main research interests lie in applying social psychology to questions of identification with place, predominantly in relation to migration, and local, national, transnational and diasporic identities. He has a particular interest in how 'authenticity' is constructed through discourse. His PhD work (completed at the Open University in 2010) looked at discourses of authenticity among the Irish in England: he has recently returned to this topic in the aftermath of Brexit. He is a former trustee of the London–Irish charity Mind Yourself, and is a semi-regular contributor to Irish media on diaspora issues.

Acknowledgements

Ahearne, Mary ed. (2014) 'Specimens' in *Incoming*, Hull, Humber Mouth. Copyright Kath Mckay, 2014.

Casey, Maude (1987) *Over the Water*, London, The Women's Press. Copyright Maude Casey 1987.

French, Ray (2017) 'The Two Funerals of Patrick Cullen' in *End Notes*, French, R. & Mckay, K. (eds) York, Edge Publishing. Copyright Ray French, 2017.

McCarthy, Maria C. (2014) *As Long as it Takes*, Cultured Llama. Copyright Maria C. McCarthy, 2014.

McCrory, Moy (2013) 'Combustible World', *The Warwick Review*, **7(4)** December 2013, ed. M. Hulse, Bristol, Oxford University Press. Copyright Moy McCrory, 2013.

Mckay, Kath (2015) *Collision Forces*, Hull, Wrecking Ball Press. Copyright Kath Mckay, 2015.

O'Donoghue, John (2009) *A Mystery Of Light*, The Echo Room, Brighton, The Echo Room 'in association with Pighog Press'. Copyright John O'Donoghue, 2013.